The Semi-Closed Openings in Action

ANATOLY KARPOV

Translated by Ian White

D1506415

Collier Books

Macmillan Publishing Company

New York

Collier Books
Macmillan Publishing Company
866 Third Avenue, New York, NY 10022
Collier Macmillan Canada, Inc.

Library of Congress Cataloging-in-Publication Data
Karpov, Anatoly, 1951–
    The semi-closed openings in action / Anatoly Karpov; translated
by Ian White.
        p.   cm.
    Translation from Russian.
    ISBN 0–02–021805–2
    1. Chess—Openings.   I. Title.
    GV1450.K364   1990   89–71176   CIP
794.1′22—dc20

Macmillan books are available at special discounts for bulk purchases for sales promotions, premiums, fund-raising, or educational use. For details contact:
                    Special Sales Director
            Macmillan Publishing Company
                    866 Third Avenue
                  New York, NY 10022

First Collier Books Edition 1990

10 9 8 7 6 5 4 3 2 1

Printed in Great Britain

Contents

Introduction to the four-volume series

This publication consists of four volumes: 'The Open Game in Action', 'The Semi-Open Game in Action', 'The Closed Openings in Action' and 'The Semi-Closed Openings in Action.'

What sort of books are they? It is difficult to define them exactly. Three aspects come to mind instantly.

1. These books contain games from the past few years, especially the period between 1984 and 1988, which have been the most interesting and valuable for opening theory. The games included are mainly by well known grandmasters, including the most important games between Kasparov and myself in our four world championship matches. Also included are games that developed further innovative and original opening ideas, first used in these matches.

So, first of all, these books are a selection of grandmaster games from the past few years with interesting opening ideas.

2. As we have already noticed these games are chosen according to the openings. But it is not only a matter of choice but of the form of presentation. Each of the main games concentrates on one particular opening, and within the notes to each game there are many references and even other complete games. So some of the main games look like an opening note and some even like a whole article. The notes to the main games often refer to earlier or later games, so the information on the opening idea can be presented in the context of its development, how it was perfected and refined. While commenting on the main games I am often "distracted" by my recollections of the examples of other grandmasters or of my own examples. I hope that these "lyrical deviations" will not confuse the reader.

Thus, secondly, the books are a selection of opening discussions that are devoted to the most critical openings, variations and plans played by grandmasters during the past few years.

3. The book includes many games played by the author. This is not surprising, as in less than ten years I have played six world championship matches—two with Korchnoi and four with Kasparov. As is well known, in any duel for the crown, the best developments of opening theory are used, and new ideas are born that attract huge attention and become very popular. As I have already mentioned, these books contain the most valuable theoretical games from my encounters with Kasparov. Apart from these, I have included games played by me

inbetween these world championship matches, none of which have been previously published with my notes in English.

Therefore, the third aim of these books is to be an addition to the selections of the games of the twelfth world champion during the years 1984–88.

Thus, the main idea of this series is to cover the modern state of opening theory, the most popular variations which occurred in the tournaments and matches of the mid-1980s using grandmaster games of recent years. Having become acquainted with the games in any one of the four volumes you will have sufficient knowledge of the most critical openings, variations and innovations which have attracted the close attention of theoreticians and players. You will be able to follow the development of the opening ideas and additionally their realisation at the highest grandmaster level. In this sense these four volumes are a true reflection of their titles. By going through the games you will acquire a lot of useful information on the openings in action and learn the latest developments. At the same time it is difficult to guarantee that you will be able to overpower any grandmaster in the chosen opening! Nobody has managed to write this sort of universal book and I doubt that it is possible at all. Playing successfully in the opening depends not only on the information you possess about the opening, or how many variations you remember, but more on your ability to find new opening ideas and exploit them over the board. You also need a mastery of playing the middlegame and the endgame.

Although the attention in these books is concentrated on the opening stage of the game all the main games are given from the beginning to the end. I think that going through the whole game is very beneficial because it allows the reader to trace the connection between the different stages of the game. The opening reference books consist of thousands and thousands of variations which usually come suddenly to an end in the most interesting place. I recall how sometimes I look through a game and it breaks off with an assessment of "unclear play", and regret that it is not possible to see how it ended. In this series this sort of disappointment is not going to befall the reader.

There is another consideration. Imagine that when the game is interrupted like this we are told that White has the better chances. But the question of the exploitation of this advantage is left open. At the same time, studying the connections between the middlegame and endgame is most important for an improving chess player. That is why the idea of this series seems good to me. On the one hand, the reader can enhance or broaden his opening repertoire and on the other hand the actual reading will not be a boring memorisation of a countless number of variations. The value of studying chess as a preparation for tournaments will increase considerably if you do not limit yourself by just getting acquainted with an opening but if you also analyse the grandmaster games to the end. The use of a small opening advantage, the art of transition from an opening to a middlegame, the technique of defending a difficult position—all these methods of play have great importance and much attention is devoted to them in these games. In the end I took into consideration that the actual acquaintance with exciting grandmaster games brings pleasure in itself!

The apparent difference between this series and specialised opening books is, firstly, that I have covered only fashionable openings and, secondly that even from them, I have picked out the most popular variations and systems. And this is understandable, because modern opening theory is so fully developed that detailed analysis of some individual variations would take as much space as any one of the four books. At the same time the games that I have annotated, as was mentioned before, were chosen with the aim of embracing the majority of the fashionable variations including many from the world championship matches.

I want to say some words about the structure of the four volume series. As is well known, chess openings are normally divided into three groups—open, semi-open and closed. This classification was formed as far back as the end of the last century and the beginning of this one. There was a time when 1 e4 was almost obligatory. If Black replied 1 . . . e5 it was called an open game, if 1 . . . e6 then semi-open, and all the rest (there were not many) were called closed. The situation has changed substantially in recent years and the popularity of closed openings has been continually growing. The number of games played with closed openings these days is probably higher than the number played with open openings and semi-open openings together. Thus it is possible to assume that there is a need to split closed openings into two classes—closed and semi-closed. Consequently, closed opening become the symmetrical systems—1 d4 d5 and 1 c4 c5, and semi-closed openings become the asymmetrical systems—1 d4 (1 c4) ♘f6. Although this classification hasn't been settled yet I believe that it will be official quite soon. Anyway, this classification is used for the four volume series.

Here are the statistics of the openings of the four matches between Kasparov and myself.

open games—12 games
semi-open games—14 games
closed openings—52 games
semi-closed openings—42 games

(120 games in all from the four matches). As you see, closed openings (mostly the Queen's Gambit) are played more frequently even in the new classification and, using the old classification, their predominance would be overwhelming.

I want to say a few words about my opening repertoire. It consists of the main open games (the Spanish, the Russian, the Italian), semi-open (the Sicilian, the French, the Caro-Kann, the Pirc), closed (the Queen's Gambit, the Slav, the English), semi-closed (the Nimzo-indian and the Queen's Indian). Among the popular openings, only the King's Indian quite seldom occurs in my games. I don't play it as Black and nobody plays it against me when I am White. All the other modern openings, as you see, are included in my repertoire and most of them I play as White and as Black. Therefore I am compelled to become an expert in opening theory. I hope that after all this is said the reader will not be surprised by the fact that there are so many games played by the author included in these books. It is understandable that when talking about the modern state of an opening it is always convenient to take your own game as a basis. But I want to point out that in the notes to my games it is possible that I refer to no less valuable games and in this case they are thoroughly discussed in the text of the main game.

Each book of the four volume series consists of about 30 main games and the notes cover about another 150 games. Thus in the whole series about 700 games are considered, most of them from the 1984–88 period.

Almost all grandmaster games and games from the world championship matches were annotated in dozens of publications and so in my notes I have tried to put different sources together. This series is not scientific but written in a light style with some lyrical reminiscences. Therefore, to sum up, that is why I decided not to name the authors of all the suggested variation, especially as quite often the same moves were suggested by different commentators.

In conclusion I would like to say that I haven't previously tried to write this kind of literary work which is based on the modern state of opening theory and practice. In the four volume series the period 1984–1988 is covered, including my four matches against Kasparov. If the reader finds my books interesting and useful, then I will probably write another series, on "The Openings in Action" on the material from the next "cycle", say 1988–1990.

A. Karpov

Preface to the Fourth Volume

When I conceived the idea of these four volumes, I of course planned to include in it the most interesting games from my own recent experiences, above all from my matches with Kasparov. But in general, I decided not to rely exclusively on my own works. However, you may have noticed, the number of the author's examples grows with each volume, and in this, the concluding volume, there are by now amongst the main games almost two thirds played by me. I hope these statistics don't provoke a rebuke from readers. The World Championship, as a rule, serves as a barometer of popularity and fashion of this or that opening by the frequency of its appearance. In this sense the Grünfeld Defence, from our battles in 1986 and 1987, would take first place: it was encountered nine times in each of these matches.

Of course, in the second half of the 1980s my games with Kasparov were not the only ones valuable as regards the theory of the Grünfeld Defence. However, it turned out that when I had finished the notes to all of my Grünfeld games, many valuable games by other chessplayers were in my notes. However, considering that 11 games were already dedicated to this current opening, the 'theme' had to be closed. That is how it came about that one of the foundations of the series (and only one!) turned out to be entirely represented by the author's games.

Second place amongst the semi-closed openings in my matches with Kasparov belongs to the Queen's Indian Defence. In a different way, perhaps, it is noticeably popular in modern practice, and 11 Queen's Indian games are also a fully appropriate number.

Quite a lot of attention is given to one of the sharpest openings, the King's Indian Defence, and, finally, the fourth semi-closed opening examined in this book, the Nimzo-Indian Defence. This list is restricted, but even so this last volume exceeds the length of its predecessors.

1 The Grünfeld Defence

Karpov–Kasparov
Game 5,
World Championship 3
London 1986

None of the nine games in the return match which featured the Grünfeld Defence turned out to have much in common. While one would flow calmly in a positional vein, another would lead to a sharp, combinational battle. I would remind you that the brilliancy prize in London was presented to both participants of a duel in which the Grünfeld Defence was played (game 11).

1	d4	♘f6
2	c4	g6
3	♘c3	d5
4	♗f4	♗g7
5	e3	c5

The system with this deployment of White's queen's bishop was also encountered in the first game of the return match. There Black also responded with the standard ... c7–c5 and equalized quickly. **Karpov–Kasparov, m (1), London/Leningrad 1986: 1 d4 ♘f6 2 c4 g6 3 ♘c3 d5 4 ♘f3 ♗g7 5 ♗f4 c5 6 dc ♕a5 7 ♖c1.** A novelty (7 cd had been played up till now), to which my opponent responded with utmost precision. **7 ... dc!** White doesn't rush into this central exchange so Black does. **8 e3 ♕xc5 9 ♕a4+ ♘c6 10 ♗xc4 0-0 11 0-0 ♗d7 12 ♕b5 ♕xb5 13 ♗xb5 ♖ac8 14 ♖fd1 ♖fd8 15 h3 h6 16 ♔f1 a6 17 ♗e2 ♗e6 18 ♖xd8+ ♖xd8 19 ♘e5 ♘xe5 20 ♗xe5 ♖d2 Draw agreed.**

6 dc

Grabbing the pawn—6 ♗xb8 ♖xb8 7 ♕a4+ ♗d7 8 ♕xa7—is too risky: 8 ... cd 9 ♕xd4 0-0 10 cd ♕a5 11 ♕d2 b5! 12 ♗d3 b4 13 ♘e2 ♕xd5.

| 6 | ... | ♕a5 |
| 7 | ♖c1 | |

Again, chasing material gain would lead to trouble: 7 cd ♘xd5 8 ♕xd5 ♗xc3+ 9 bc ♕xc3+ 10 ♔e2 ♕xa1 11 ♗e5 ♕b1 12 ♗xh8 ♗e6 13 ♕d3 ♕xa2+ with a strong Black initiative. And after 7 ♕a4+ ♕xa4 8 ♘xa4 ♘e4 9 ♗xb8 ♗d7 10 f3 ♗xa4, the game is level. However, Kasparov is able to find a new idea, even in such a quiet position, as in the following game.

Timman–Kasparov (Belfort 1988):

| 8 | ... | 0-0!? |
| 9 | ♘f3 | |

The encounter **Salov–Korchnoi (Brussels 1988)** concluded peacefully after 9 ♖c1 ♗d7 10 ♘c3 dc 11 ♗xc4 ♘a6 12 ♘f3 ♘xc5 13 ♔e2 ♖ac8 14 ♗e5 a6 15 a3 ♘a4 16 ♘xa4 ♗xa4 17 ♘d4 ♘e4 18 ♗xg7 ♔xg7 Draw agreed.

| 9 | ... | ♘e4 |
| 10 | ♗e5 | ♗d7 |

11	♘c3	♘xc3
12	bc	dc
13	♗xc4	♖c8
14	♗d4	

An improvement. In an earlier game between the same opponents, White unsuccessfully played 14 ♗d5. **Timman–Kasparov (Amsterdam 1988): 14 ♗d5?** ♗c6 15 ♗xc6 ♖xc6 (15 ... ♘xc6! 16 ♗xg7 ♔xg7 17 0-0-0 ♘d8 18 ♖d7 ♔f8 19 ♖hd1 ♔e8 20 ♖7d5 ♘e6 with advantage to Black, according to Kasparov) **16 ♗xg7 ♔xg7 17 ♖b1 ♖c7 18 ♘d4 ♘a6 19 c6 b6 20 f4 ♘b8 21 ♖b4 ♘xc6 22 ♖c4 ♖ac8 23 ♘b5 ♖d7 24 ♘d4 ♖dc7 Draw agreed.**

14	...	e5!
15	♗xe5	♖xc5
16	♗xg7	♔xg7
17	♗b3	♖xc3
18	0-0	

18 ♔d2 or 18 ♖d1 would obtain equal play, but now it is Black who seizes the initiative.

18	...	♘a6!
19	♘e5	♗e8
20	♗d5	♖c7
21	♖ab1	♘c5
22	e4	♖d8
23	♖fc1	♖dc8
24	g4	f6
25	♘f3	b6
26	♘d4	♗d7
27	f3	♘d3!
28	♖xc7	♖xc7
29	♖d1	♘f4
30	♔f2	♔f8
31	♗b3	♔e7
32	♘e2	♘xe2
33	♔xe2	♖c3

Black has an obviously superior endgame, which he quickly converts.

34	h4	h6
35	e5	♗b5+
36	♔f2	fe
37	♖d5	♖c5
38	♖xc5	bc
39	g5	hg
40	hg	♗d3
41	♗g8	♗f5
42	♗b3	♗e6
43	♗c2	♗xa2
44	♗xg6	a5
45	♔e3	a4

White resigned

Returning to the main game:

7	...	♘e4

Kasparov preferred 7 ... dc in the next two games in which the Grünfeld Defence was played, due to the unsatisfactory outcome of this continuation. Chances were level in the **ninth game** after **8 ♗xc4 0-0 9 ♘f3 ♘xc5 10 ♗b3 ♘c6 11 0-0 ♕a5 12 h3 ♗f5 13 ♘d4 ♗d7! 14 ♕e2 ♘xd4 15 ed e6.** A draw was agreed 5 moves later—**16 ♗d2 ♕b6 17 ♖fd1 ♗c6 18 ♗e3 ♕a5 19 ♗d2 ♕b6 20 ♗e3 ♕a5.** I played the immediate 13 ♕e2 in the 11th game, and an absorbing struggle ensued—this is discussed later.

8	cd	♘xc3
9	♕d2	♕xa2
10	bc*(1)*	

This variation was brought into practice after the famous game Petrosian–Fischer (match, 1971), which went **10 ... ♕a5 11 ♗c4 ♘d7** 12 ♘e2 ♘e5 13 ♗a2 ♗f5 14 ♗xe5! ♗xe5 15 ♘d4 ♕xc5 16 ♘xf5 gf 17 0-0 with a dangerous attack for White. Subsequently, a more effective variation for Black was suggested by Mikhalchishin: 12 ... ♘xc5 13 0-0 0-0 14 f3 e5! 15 ♗g3 b5 16 ♗a2 ♕b6! 17 ♔h1 a5 with sufficient counterplay. Later research came up with the move **12 ♘f3**, which has met variable success up till now. The game Agzamov–Gulko (Frunze 1985) developed interestingly: **12 ... ♘xc5** (12 ... 0-0 led to sharp play in the game Razuvayev–Mikhalchishin, Minsk 1985—13 0-0 ♘xc5 14 ♗e5 ♗xe5 15 ♘xe5 f6 16 ♖a1 ♘e4) **13 ♗e5 ♗xe5!** (a few months earlier in Sochi, an encounter between the same two contestants concluded swiftly **(Agzamov–Gulko, Sochi 1985)**: 13 ... 0-0 14 0-0 f6 15 ♖a1 ♕d8 16 ♗c7! ♕d7 17 d6+ e6 18 ♘d4 ♕f7 19 ♖a5 b6 20 ♖xc5! bc 21 ♘b3 ♕d7 22 ♕d3! ♖d8 23 ♕e4 **Black resigned**) 14 ♘xe5 f6 15 ♘f3 0-0 16 ♘d4 ♘e4 17 ♕b2 ♘d6 18 ♗a2 ♗d7 19 0-0 ♖ac8 20 e4! ♕c5 21 ♖fe1 with a White initiative.

10 ... ♕xd2+

Kasparov prefers to exchange queens. Up till now this move has dwelt in oblivion, and it is only recently that new ideas have been found for Black.

11	♔xd2	♘d7
12	♗b5	

White achieves nothing after 12 c6 bc 13 dc ♘b6 (or 13 ... ♘f6).

12	...	0-0
13	♗xd7	

And now on 13 c6 there follows 13 ... ♘c5. Black now has the advantage of the bishop pair, but, as soon becomes apparent, neither has much scope.

13	...	♗xd7
14	e4	f5

14 ... ♖ac8 is weaker: 15 ♗e3 f5 16 f3.

15 e5 e6!

An important moment. Why has Kasparov departed from his earlier try: 15 ... ♖ac8 16 c6 (16 e6 would be in Black's favour after 16 ... ♗a4 17 c4 ♖xc5 18 ♗e3 ♖c7 19 ♘f3 ♖fc8 20 ♔d3 b5!) 16 ... bc 17 d6 ed 18 ed ♖f6 with advantage to Black (Schmidt–Gross, Nalenchuv 1984)? The whole point is that on 15 ... ♖ac8 comes the stronger 16 c4! ♖xc5 17 ♗e3. In the game Seirawan–Adorjan (New York 1987) there followed 17 ... ♖c7 (17 ... ♖a5 18 f4 e6 19 d6) 18 ♘f3 b6 19 c5 bc 20 ♖xc5 ♖xc5 21 ♗xc5 ♖c8 22 ♗xa7, and White won.

16 c4 ♖fc8

After 16 ... g5 17 ♗xg5 ♗xe5 18 ♘f3 ♗g7 19 ♖b1, followed by ♖he1, White stops the exchanges, maintaining strong pressure.

17 c6!

White does not keep his extra pawn, but by returning it derives the maximum advantage—the creation of a passed pawn and the restriction of the mobility of Black's rook and light-squared bishop.

17 ... bc
18 d6 c5

Now the light-squared bishop finds some freedom, but the dark-squared bishop begins to suffocate. Maybe the destiny of the bishops could be 'reversed': 18 ... g5 19 ♗xg5 ♗xe5 20 c5 ♖cb8, and Black would have hope of counterplay.

19 h4! h6
20 ♘h3!(2)

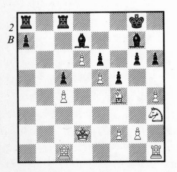

Probably Kasparov had examined the more natural 20 ♘f3, and then the reply 20 ... ♗c6! would lead to a sharp game with mutual chances. But I succeeded in finding an almost mathematical solution to the position. The white knight is directed on the only correct trajectory to its optimal square d3! Once it achieves its aim, the black bishop on g7 turns out to be forever locked in a cage constructed by the white pawns

on e5 and d6 and the bishop on f4. Incidentally, White also prevents the liberating advance ... g6–g5.

20 ... a5

The active passed a-pawn is not dangerous. It would however have followed to occupy immediately the open file—20 ... ♖cb8.

21 f3 a4
22 ♖he1!

An extra defence to the e5 pawn. On the hasty 22 ♘f2 then 22 ... g5! would now be possible: 23 hg hg 24 ♗h2 f4 25 ♘d3 ♗e8 26 ♗g1 and the situation is sufficiently complicated.

22 ... a3
23 ♘f2 a2

And on 23 ... ♗a4 then 24 ♘d3 is very strong.

24 ♘d3 ♖a3

Realizing that the c5 pawn is doomed anyway, Black seeks counterplay.

25 ♖a1 g5

25 ... ♖b8 is insufficient because of 26 ♖ec1 g5 27 hg hg 28 ♘xc5 (but not 28 ♗xg5—28 ... ♖bb3 29 ♘xc5 ♖b2+) 28 ... ♗a4 29 ♘xa4 ♖xa4 30 ♗xg5 ♗xe5 31 d7.

26 hg hg
27 ♗xg5(3)

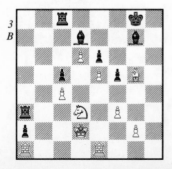

Now after 27 ... ♖b8 the contest could conclude in a study-like draw: 28 ♗f4 ♖bb3 29 ♘xc5 ♖b2+ 30 ♔c1 ♖xg2 31 ♗d2 ♗h6! 32 ♗xh6 ♖c3+ 33 ♔d1 ♖d3+! 34 ♘xd3 ♗a4+ 35 ♔c1 ♖c2+ with perpetual check. But there is a simple refutation to this study: 28 ♔e2! ♖bb3 29 ♘xc5 ♖b2+ 30 ♔f1, and White wins through.

27	...	♔f7
28	♗f4	♖b8
29	♖ec1	

The last stage of converting the advantage—rounding up the a-pawn.

29	...	♗c6
30	♖c3	♖a5
31	♖c2	♖ba8
32	♘c1	

Black resigned

Karpov–Kasparov
Game 11,
World Championship 3
London 1986

A brilliancy prize was awarded in the London half of the match for the finest game. It was given to us both for this fascinating draw in the 11th game. In terms of a spectacle, this encounter, it seems to me, looked even better after the Leningrad half.

1	d4	♘f6
2	c4	g6
3	♘c3	d5
4	♗f4	♗g7
5	e3	c5
6	dc	♕a5
7	♖c1	dc
8	♗xc4	0-0
9	♘f3	♕xc5
10	♗b3	♘c6
11	0-0	♕a5
12	h3	♗f5
13	♕e2	

In the ninth game I chose 13 ♘d4, but by continuing 13 ... ♗d7! 14 ♕e2 ♘xd4 15 ed e6 and 16 ... ♗c6, Black equalized easily.

| 13 | ... | ♘e4 |
| 14 | ♘d5 | e5(4) |

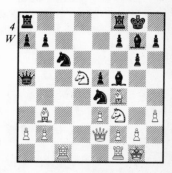

This is all well known up till now; the position arising after 15 ♗h2 ♗e6 is evaluated as level in the manuals.

15 ♖xc6!?

A surprising riposte, discovered by my trainer Igor Zaitsev during preparation for this game. This exchange sacrifice doesn't seriously challenge opening theory, but it looks highly interesting. Being convinced of the fact that White has nothing to lose, I made the decision to test this trick. It is worth mentioning though, that of late White has returned more often to the 'theoretical' 15 ♗h2.

Let's have a look at a very recent example on this theme.

Basin–Kozlov (USSR 1988): 15 ... ♗e6 16 ♖fd1 ♖fd8 17 ♕c4 (the exchanges after 17 ♕e1 ♖d7 18 ♕xa5 ♘xa5 19 ♘c7 ♘xb3 20 ♘xa8 ♘xc1 21 ♖xc1 f6 are in Black's favour)**17 ... ♘d4** (17 ... ♘f6 leads to a more complicated game after 18 e4 ♖ac8 19 ♘g5 ♘d4 20 ♘e7+ ♔f8 21 ♘xe6+ ♔xe7 22 ♘xd8 ♖xc4 23 ♗xc4 ♗h6 Huzman–Dorfman, Lvov 1988) **18 ed ♗xd5 19 ♕e2 ♗h6 20 ♖c2 ♗f4 21 ♗xd5 ♕xd5 22 ♘xe5 ♗xe5 23 ♗xe5 ♘g5 24 ♕g4 ♘e6 25 ♕h4 g5 26 ♕h6 ♕e4 27 ♕f6 ♔f8 28 ♖cd2 ♕g6 29 d5 ♘c5 30 d6 Black resigned**

15 ... ef

After a short period of meditation Kasparov declines the sacrifice. Many correspondents reported in their magazines that acceptance of it would hardly have led to defeat—15 ... bc 16 ♘e7+ ♔h8 17 ♘xe5 ♗xe5 18 ♘xc6, but here after 18 ... ♕d2! 19 ♗xe5+ f6 White incurs material loss. I was prepared to answer with 17 ♘xc6, and if 17 ... ♕b6 (17 ... ♕c5 18 ♘cxe5 ♕e7 19 ♘d4) then 18 ♘cxe5 ♗e6 19 Bxe6 ♕xe6 20 b3. White has two pawns for the exchange.

16 ♖c7 ♗e6

On 16 ... fe 17 ♕xe3 ♗xb2 then 18 ♘d4 is strong, if 17 ... ♘d6, then 18 ♖d1 is possible, with White increasing the pressure.

17 ♕e1!

The natural 17 ♖xb7 ♗xd5 18

♖b5 leads to a better game for Black after either 18 ... ♕a6 19 ♗xd5 ♖ae8 or 18 ... ♘c3 19 bc ♗xf3 20 gf ♕xc3. In a later game Szilagyi–Schmidt (Vengria 1986) Black played the even stronger 17 ... ♘d6! (depriving the rook of the b5 square) 18 ♘e7+ ♔h8 19 ♘c6 ♕c5 20 ♗xe6 ♕xc6!, and White was left a piece down.

The queen move was planned during preparation for the game. However, it later became apparent that stronger would have been 17 ♘e7+ ♔h8 18 ♖fc1 ♗xb3 19 ab with an initiative for White (19 ... fe 20 ♕xe3 ♘d6 21 ♕f4).

17 ... ♕b5!

Black would have few prospects in the endgame after 17 ... ♕xe1 18 ♖xe1 ♗xb2 19 ♘e7+ ♔h8 20 ♗xe6 fe 21 ef ♖xf4 22 ♖xb7 ♗c3 23 ♖e2.

18 ♘e7+ ♔h8

19 ♗xe6 fe

After 19 ... ♕b6 20 ♘d5 ♕xe6 21 ♘xf4 I would have remained a pawn up.

20 ♕b1

The White queen has made an unusual tour (♕d1-e2-e1-b1) and is suddenly aiming at the opponent's kingside.

20 ... ♘g5!

The only reply; on 20 ... ♕b6 would follow the simple 21 ♖fc1, and after any other deployment of the knight then 21 ♘xg6+ decides.

21 ♘h4! *(5)*

After 21 ♘xg5 (21 ♘d4 ♕e5) 21 ... ♕xg5 22 ef ♖xf4 23 ♖xb7 ♖e8 24 ♘c6 ♕c5 25 ♘xa7 ♗d4

Black is dangerously active.

21 ...   ♘xh3+!?

Each of us was hoping to outwit the other in this sharp position. Evidently, therefore, Kasparov refrained from playing 21 ... fe, for after 22 ♘hxg6+ hg 23 ♘xg6+ ♔g8 24 ♘e7+ I could have forced a draw.

22 ♔h2

Of course, not 22 gh ♛g5+ 23 ♘g2 f3.

22 ...   ♛h5?

A serious mistake. A draw was still there after 22 ... ♘xf2! 23 ♖xf2 fe 24 ♖xf8+ ♖xf8 25 ♔xh3 e2 26 ♛e4 ♛h5! 27 ♖c4 g5 28 ♛xe6 gh.

23 ♘exg6+

On 23 ♔xh3 there would follow 23 ... g5. Many considered that it would be stronger to take the other knight: 23 ♘hxg6+ hg 24 ♛xg6. This variation, as we shall now see, is actually unpleasant for Black, but the order of knight captures on g6 has no significance. The same position as in the game can be achieved after 23 ... hg 24 ♘xg6+ ♔g8 25 ♘e7+ ♔h8 26 ♛g6!

23 ...   hg

24 ♛xg6

An inaccuracy, which lets the victory slip! As previously mentioned 24 ♘xg6+ ♔g8 25 ♘e7+ ♔h8 26 ♛g6! (declining perpetual check with 26 ♘g6+) leads to an obvious advantage for White. Let's examine these interesting variations, given by International Master Khalifman: 26 ... ♛e5 (on 26 ... ♖f5 there follows 27 gh fe 28 ♛xh5+ ♖xh5 29 ♘g6+ ♔h7 30 fe!) 27 ♔xh3 fe (27 ... ♖f6 28 ♔g4!) 28 ♛g4! ♖f6 29 ♛h4+ ♗h6 30 f4! ♛xb2 31 ♖b1! ♛d4 32 ♖c4! 26 ... ♛h7 is more solid, but here also 27 gh ♖f6 (27 ... ♗e5 28 ♖c5!; 27 ... fe 28 ♛xe6 ♖f6 29 ♛xe3 with two extra pawns) 28 ♛g4 (good also would be 28 ♛xh7+ ♔xh7 29 ♖g1), and Black is in a critical position, as it would not serve to capture on e3—28 ... fe 29 fe! ♖xf1 30 ♘g6+ ♔g8 31 ♛xe6+ ♖f7 32 ♛xf7 mate.

24 ...   ♛e5!

A clever rejoinder, eliminating every danger. Now 25 ♔xh3 is impossible—the rook on c7 is hanging (with a knight on e7 the capture 25 ... ♛xc7 would not be possible due to 26 ♛h5+ ♗h6 27 ♛xh6 mate).

25 ♖f7

25 ♖xg7 would be bad: 25 ... fe+ 26 f4 ♛xg7 27 ♛h5+ ♔g8 28 gh ♛xb2+ 29 ♔h1 ♖f7! or 26 ♛g3 ♛xg7 27 ♘g6+ ♔g8 28 ♘xf8 ♘g5! 29 ♘d7 ♖d8 30 ♘e5 e2 31 ♖e1 ♖d1 32 ♘d3 ♛h7+ 33 ♔g1 ♛xd3 34 ♛xg5+ ♔f7 etc. However 25 ♛c2 forces a draw—25 ... fe+ 26 ♔xh3 ♔g8

27 f4 e2 28 fe ef (♛) 29 ♖xg7+
♚xg7 30 ♛g6+ etc.

   25 ...   **♖xf7**

Impossible would be both 25
... ♘g5 because of 26 ef, and 25
... ♚g8 because of 26 ♘f3 ♛xb2
27 ♖b1 with dangerous threats;
25 ... fe+ 26 ♚xh3 leads to
equality.

   26   **♛xf7**   **♘g5!**

After the game I learnt that a
computer suggested here 26 ...
♛b5, but then 27 ♘g6+ ♚h7 28
♘e7 ♛e8 29 ♛xe6 ♘g5 30 ♛f5+
♚h6 31 ♖h1! and despite his
extra pawn Black's position is
indefensible.

27	**♘g6+**	**♚h7**
28	**♘xe5**	**♘xf7**
29	**♘xf7**	**♚g6**
30	**♘d6**	**fe**

The position has been simpli-
fied, the sharpness dulled, with
Black even having a small advantage. However, it is only of a
symbolic nature.

31	**♘c4**	**ef**
32	**♖xf2**	**b5**
33	**♘e3**	**a5**
34	**♚g3**	**a4**
35	**♖c2**	**♖f8**
36	**♚g4**	**♗d4**
37	**♖e2**	**♗xe3**
38	**♖xe3**	**♖f2**
39	**b3**	**♖xg2+**
40	**♚f3**	**♖xa2**
41	**ba**	

Draw agreed.

A remarkable game!

Karpov–Kasparov
Game 17,
World Championship 3
Leningrad 1986

The present miniature establishes itself as a classic example of
a battle that is wholly determined
by the process of home preparation. One would not call it an
unusual novelty—it consists of
the simple advance of the h-pawn
by one square—though extensive
analysis shows Black's defence
after this move to be extremely
difficult.

1	**d4**	**♘f6**
2	**c4**	**g6**
3	**♘c3**	**d5**
4	**♘f3**	**♗g7**
5	**♛b3**	**dc**
6	**♛xc4**	**0-0**
7	**e4**	**♗g4**
8	**♗e3**	**♘fd7**
9	**♖d1**	**♘c6**
10	**♗e2**	**♘b6**
11	**♛c5**	**♛d6**(6)

The critical position of the
Smyslov Variation. What continuations are there left to be
tested? 12 ♛xd6, 12 ♘b5, 12 d5,
12 h3 and 12 0-0 have all been
tried. I remember how, in the well
known game Botvinnik–Fischer

(Varna 1962) after 12 h3 ♗xf3 13 gf ♖fd8 14 d5 ♘e5 15 ♘b5 ♕f6 16 f4 ♘ed7 17 e5 Fischer presented Botvinnik with an unpleasant surprise—17 ... ♕xf4! However, after mutual mistakes this fascinating encounter finally concluded in a draw. But it seems that White has yet one more interesting move at his disposal, which has not previously been tested in practice.

12   e5!

At first glance, a paradoxical choice. Not only does White hopelessly weaken his e5 pawn, but also allows the exchange of queens. But it is not all that straightforward.

12   ...   ♕xc5

13   dc   ♘c8

In reply to the more natural 13 ... ♘d7 there follows 14 h3! ♗xf3 15 gf!, and the doomed pawn on e5 is invulnerable, since on its capture by either knight, 16 f4! wins a piece. Otherwise White fortifies his e5 pawn with its neighbour, obtaining a clear advantage.

14   h3!

In the previous odd-numbered game (**game 15**), where the novelty 12 e5 was first employed, I played here **14 ♘b5** and after **14 ... ♖b8! 15 ♘xc7 e6!** Black succeeded in obtaining fully equal chances. Actually, the threat of trapping the knight by way of 16 ... a6 forces White to lose a tempo—**16 ♘b5**—and the black knight on c8 quickly comes to a comfortable position. The game concluded in the following manner: **16 ... ♘8e7 17 ♖d2 b6 18 cb ab 19 ♗g5 ♘f5 20 b3 h6 21 ♗f6 ♗xf3 22 ♗xf3 ♘xe5** (only now does Black regain the pawn) **23 ♗xe5 ♗xe5 24 0-0 ♖fd8 25 ♖fd1 ♖xd2 26 ♖xd2 ♖c8 27 g3 ♖c1+ 28 ♔g2 ♔f8 29 ♗e4 ♔e7 Draw agreed.**

The Grandmaster from Baku was evidently satisfied with the result of this encounter; he considered that Black had been in no danger, and, apparently, did not prepare thoroughly for the present game. Meanwhile, on re-setting up the position on the board, we discovered that the prospects of the knight on c8 may be significantly restricted.

14   ...   ♗xf3

In the event of 14 ... ♗e6 comes the unpleasant riposte 15 ♘g5 ♘xe5 16 ♘xe6 fe 17 f4.

15   ♗xf3   ♗xe5? *(7)*

Black is also faced with difficulties after the other pawn capture: 15 ... ♘xe5 16 ♗xb7 ♖b8 17 c6 ♘c4 18 ♖d7, and on 18 ... ♘xb2 White has a choice between two pleasant possibilities: 19 ♘d5 and 19 ♘b5. Nevertheless, it would still be better to capture the pawn with the knight.

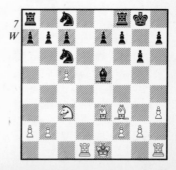

16	♗xc6!	bc
17	♗d4	

17 f4 is worthy of consideration—17 ... ♗f6 18 0-0 ♖b8 19 ♖f2 a5 20 ♖d7 ♖b7 21 ♖fd2 ♘a7 (21 ... e6 22 ♔f2 ♘e7 23 ♘e4) 22 a4!, and the black knight cannot get away.

17	...	♗f4

On the exchange of bishops—17 ... ♗xd4 18 ♖xd4 ♖b8 19 b3 a5—the white rook is able to penetrate to the seventh rank, but after 20 ♖d7 ♘a7 21 ♖xc7 ♘b5 22 ♘xb5 ♖xb5 23 ♖xc6 a4! counterplay emerges for Black. Stronger, however, would be 20 ♖a4 ♖a8 21 ♔e2 ♖d8 22 ♖d1 ♖xd1 23 ♘xd1 with a subsequent transfer of the knight to c4.

18	0-0	a5

Apparently the decisive mistake. It is necessary to move the e-pawn instead. While preparing for this game, it seemed to us that on **18 ... e5 19 ♗e3** (19 ♘e2 ed 20 ♘xf4 ♖b8, or 19 ... ♘e7!, directing the knight towards f5) **19 ... ♗xe3 20 fe** White has a definite advantage. However, soon after the match, this position was encountered in the game **Karpov–Timman (Tilburg 1986)**, and the Dutch Grandmaster demonstrated that Black has chances to hold this position. This is how our game continued: **20 ... ♘e7 21 ♖d7 ♘f5 22 ♖xc7** (22 ♔f2 also only leads to equality: 22 ... ♖ad8 23 ♖fd1 ♖xd7 24 ♖xd7 ♖c8 25 ♘e4 ♔f8 26 ♔f3 h5 27 ♘f6 ♔g7 28 ♘h7+ ♔e8 29 ♘f6+) **22 ... ♖fc8! 23 ♖d7 ♖d8**

24	♖fd1	♖xd7 25 ♖xd7 ♘xe3 26

♖c7 ♖b8 (26 ... ♘d5? 27 ♘xd5 cd 28 b4!) **27 b3 ♖d8 28 ♘e4 ♖d4 29 ♘f6+ ♔g7 30 ♖xc6 ♖d2 31 g4 ♘c2 32 ♔f1 ♘d4 33 ♖a6 ♘f3 Draw agreed**. A feeling remains that somewhere White should find an improvement, but where exactly? That is the question!

19	♖fe1	a4

No better either would be 19 ... f6 20 ♖e6 ♖a6 21 ♘d5.

20	♖e4	♗h6
21	♗e5	a3
22	b3	♘a7
23	♖d7	♗c1
24	♖xc7	♗b2
25	♘a4!	

Material balance is restored while White's threats grow.

25	...	♘b5
26	♖xc6	♖fd8
27	♖b6!	♖d5

Cunningly conceived: if 28 ♘xb2, then 28 ... ♖xe5! 29 ♖xe5 ab 30 ♖e1 ♘c3, and the b-pawn immediately carries victory to Black. But it is not difficult to avoid the trap.

28	♗g3	♘c3
29	♘xc3	♗xc3
30	c6	♗d4
31	♖b7	

Black resigned in view of the unstoppable c6–c7.

Karpov–Kasparov
Game 19,
World Championship 3
Leningrad 1986

Disillusioned with the Smyslov Variation (game 17), Kasparov all the same stayed with the Grünfeld Defence. This time he turns to a system brought into practice by Ragozin and subsequently developed by Najdorf. But here also an opening surprise is awaiting Black.

1	d4	♘f6
2	c4	g6
3	♘c3	d5
4	♘f3	♗g7
5	♕b3	dc
6	♕xc4	0-0
7	e4	♘a6

In the two previous odd-numbered games Black preferred 7 ... ♗g4.

| 8 | ♗e2 | c5 |
| 9 | d5 | |

9 dc is bad—9 ... ♗e6 10 ♕b5 ♖c8! 11 ♕xb7 ♘xc5 12 ♕xa7 ♖c7 13 ♕a3 (on 13 ♕a5 or 13 ♕b6 there follows 13 ... ♘cxe4 and 14 ♘xe4 is not possible due to 14 ... ♖xc1+!) 13 ... ♘d3+ 14 ♗xd3 ♕xd3 with a strong initiative for Black. Nothing is gained by 9 e5 ♘g4 10 h3 cd 11 hg dc 12 bc ♕a5.

| 9 | ... | e6 |
| 10 | 0-0 | |

10 ♗g5 is harmless for Black— 10 ... ed 11 ♘xd5 ♗e6 12 0-0-0 ♗xd5 13 ♖xd5 ♕b6 14 ♗xf6 ♕xf6 15 e5. In the game Flear—Korchnoi (Lugano 1988) there followed 15 ... ♕e7 16 ♖hd1 ♖ad8 17 ♖xd8 ♖xd8 18 ♖xd8 ♕xd8 19 e6 ♕b6 20 ef+ ♔f8 21 ♕c2 ♘b4 22 ♕b3 ♘c6 23 ♕xb6 ab 24 ♗c4 ♘e5 25 ♘xe5 ♗xe5, and 15 moves later the game concluded peaceably. But the follow-

ing duel ran quite a different course.

Belyavsky–Kasparov (Belfort 1988):

15	...	♕f5!
16	♗d3	♕c8
17	♖d1	

17 ♖d6 is correct, with a complex game.

17	...	b5!
18	♕h4	♘b4
19	♗xg6	fg
20	♖d7	♕e8!
21	♖e7(8)	

27	...	♗h6+!
22	♔b1	♖d8
23	♖d6	♕c6!
24	a3	♖xd6
25	ed	♕xd6
26	ab	cb
27	♕e4	b3

White resigned

Returning to the main game:

| 10 | ... | ed |
| 11 | ed | ♗f5 |

The continuation 11 ... ♖e8 and 12 ♗f4 ♗f5 leads to a transposition of moves. However, in the game Annageldiev–Arbakov (Uzgorod 1988) the Moscow Master, instead of the automatic move of the bishop to f5, unexpectedly played 12 ... b6!? By defending the c5 pawn in this way, the knight on a6 is immediately freed from a useless function. Incidentally, later Chiburdanidze against Tukmakov (Biel 1988) played 11 ... b6 a move earlier, and after 12 ♖d1 ♘b4 13 a3 ♗a6 14 ♕b3 ♗xe2 15 ♘xe2 ♘bxd5!? 16 ♘f4 c4! 17 ♕xc4 ♕c7! reached a balanced position. In the stem-game, after 13 d6 ♘b4 14 ♘g5 ♕d7 15 ♕b3, Arbakov, in view of his unpleasant position, found the vigorous 15 ... ♖xe2!, giving up material, but giving life to his bishops. There followed 16 ♘e2 ♗a6, and now 17 ♖fe1 is dangerous for White: 17 ... ♘d3 18 ♖ed1 h6! 19 ♘f3 (19 ♖xd3 c4) 19 ... ♘h5! with a fine game. White decided to return the material, and after 17 ♘c3 a complicated position arises with level chances.

12   ♗f4(9)

Unclear play arises after 12 ♗g5 h6 13 ♗xf6 ♕xf6 14 ♖ad1 ♖ad8 15 ♗d3 ♗d7. In the game Ree–De Boer (Amsterdam 1983) the bishop was placed on the neighbouring square, 12 ♗e3!?, and 12 ... ♖e8 13 ♖ad1 ♘e4 14 ♘xe4 ♖xe4 15 ♕c1 ♘b4 16 a3 ♘c2 17 ♗g5 f6 18 ♕xc2 fg 19 ♗d3 ♖f4 20 ♕xc5 g4 21 ♕e3 led to a clear advantage for White.

In Seville I twice played 12 ♖d1 with the further 12 ... ♖e8 13 d6 h6 14 h3 (game 15) or 14 ♗f4 (game 21). Both encounters ended in a draw. After the match such a sequence of moves gained great popularity.

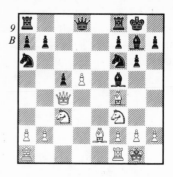

12   ...   ♖e8

In the 54th USSR Championship (Minsk 1987) Grandmaster Gavrikov used the move 12 ... ♕b6 three times. Let's examine these examples.

Belyavsky–Gavrikov: 13 h3? A new, though unsuccessful move. After 13 ... ♕xb2 14 g4 ♗c2! 15 ♖ac1 ♘d7 16 ♘b5 ♗a4! Black obtained an overwhelming advantage.

Gurevich–Gavrikov: 13 ♗e5. This move was first encountered in the game Ivanchuk–Lputyan (Irkutsk 1986). The game continued 13 ... ♕xb2 14 ♘e4 ♕b6 15 ♖ab1 ♘b4 16 ♗xf6, and now, by playing 16 ... ♗xe4!, Black obtained serious counterplay. Possibly, somewhere White could have played more accurately; in any case Gavrikov chose a different path.

13 ... ♖ad8 14 ♖fd1 (14 ♖ad1 is better) 14 ... ♖fe8. Against Lputyan, Gavrikov continued with the less successful 14 ... ♘e8

15 ♘a4! ♕a5 16 ♗xg7 ♔xg7
17 ♖ac1, and White has strong
pressure on the c-file.

15 ♕h4 ♘d7 16 ♗xg7 ♔xg7 17
b3 ♕a5 16 ♖ac1 ♘f6. Black has
only the slightest of problems,
and his opponent soon conceded
a draw.

13　♖ad1　♘e4

13 ... ♕b6 is also encountered
here, with a further 14 ♕b5 or
♘h4 with mutual chances. 13 ...
♘d7 is apparently weaker. In the
game Ivanchuk–Kotronias (Lvov
1988) after 14 ♕b3 ♘b4 15 ♖d2
♘b6 16 ♗b5 ♗d7 17 ♗g5 ♕c8
18 ♖c1 a5 19 ♘a4 c4 20 ♕d1
♘xa4 21 ♕xa4 ♗xb5 22 ♕xb5
♕f5 23 h4 c3 24 bc ♖ec8 25 c4
Black is no better than before.

14　♘b5!

This leap of the knight stems
from home preparation. Up till
now only 14 ♗e3 or 14 ♗d3 have
been tested, with White achieving
nothing, for example: **14 ♗d3
♗xc3! 15 bc b5 16 ♕xb5 ♘xc3 17
♕xa6 ♗xd3 18 ♕xd3** (18 ♖xd3
♘e2+ 19 ♔h1 ♘xf4) **18 ...
♘e2+ 19 ♔h1 ♘xf4 20 ♕c4 ♕f6**
with equality (Iten–Lay,
corr.1975). It is strange that such
an experienced Grandmaster as
Gurevich, trainer of the World
Champion, should reach this
position again, 13 years later, in
an encounter with his ward. Gurevich–Kasparov (Moscow 1988)
deviates from the last example
only on the 20th move. After **20
... ♕d6**(*10*) (instead of 20 ...
♕f6) a position arises which can

already be evaluated as favourable for Black.

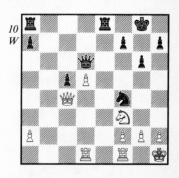

21 ♖fe1. The first original
move by White, in Kasparov's
opinion, wrecks his position. 21
♘d2 ♘xd5 22 ♘e4 ♕f4 23 ♕xc5
♖xe4 24 ♕xd5 ♖ae8 leads to
equality. **21 ... ♖xe1+ 22 ♘xe1
♖b8 23 a3 ♖b2 24 f3 ♕e5 25 ♕e4
♕g5 26 g3 ♕h5 27 h4 ♘e2 28
♕e8+ ♔g7 29 d6 ♘xg3+ 30
♔g1 ♘e2+ 31 ♔f1 ♕f5 32 ♕xe2
♕h3+ White resigned.** The correct game plan involves material
sacrifice, as Gurevich demonstrated in another game: 17 ♕c4!?
♘xd1 18 ♖xd1 ♗xd3 19 ♖xd3
♕b6 20 ♖b3 ♕f6 21 g3! ♖ad8 22
♗g5 ♕d6 23 ♗f4 ♕f6 24 a3!
(Gurevich–Kotronias, Reykjavik
1988). The black knight is not
positioned well, and White's active piece play provides him with
more than sufficient compensation for the exchange.

Let's return to my game. The
basic strategic middlegame con-
flict revolves around the d-pawn.
If White can succeed in using its
potential energy, the initiative will

belong to him, and if Black is able to set up a solid blockade his position will be the more prospective. Having despatched the knight to b5, I was prepared to part with my b-pawn, so that after 14 ... ♗xb2 15 d6 ♗f6 16 ♗d3! and 17 ♖fe1 I could develop an offensive in the centre. Kasparov refuses to accept the gift.

14 ...   ♕f6!?

Grandmaster Taimanov recommended 14 ... g5, but after 15 ♗c1 g4 16 ♘e1 White has a clear positional advantage.

15   ♗d3

From the way the game subsequently developed, many felt that Black's opening formation was flatly refuted. But this happens quite rarely in chess, and soon after the match it was Kasparov himself who returned to the present variation. So in the game **Belyavsky–Kasparov (Moscow 1987)** White diverged from the well-trodden path, immediately advancing his d-pawn. The resulting stormy skirmish led to a speedy destruction of the forces: **15 d6 ♗d7 16 g3 g5 17 ♗e3 h6 18 ♘c7 ♘xc7 19 dc ♗c6 20 ♘d2 ♖ac8 21 ♘xe4 ♖xe4 22 ♕xc5 ♖xc7 23 ♖d6 b6 24 ♖xf6 bc 25 ♖xc6 ♖xc6 26 ♗f3 ♖xe3 Draw agreed.**

15 ...   ♘b4(11)

Not wishing to be doomed to passive defence, Black goes for broke. However, the material sacrifice is not justified. Perhaps it would be possible to grab the pawn—15 ... ♕xb2—although this also involves a certain risk.

However, Black himself can sacrifice a pawn. This improvement was dreamt up by Kasparov, using it in a Dvortz pioneers tournament during a simultaneous game with clocks. His opponent was the only Master in the competition.

Dzhandzhava–Kasparov (Baku 1987): 15 ... ♖ad8! Possibly it was this move that decided Belyavsky to decline 15 ♗d3 in favour of 15 d6. Now 16 ♖fe1 deserves White's attention: 16 ... ♕xb2 17 ♗xe4 (or 17 ♖b1 ♕xf2+ 18 ♔h1 with the threats 19 ♗e3 and 19 ♗xe4) 17 ... ♖xe4 18 ♖xe4 ♗xe4 19 ♕xe4 ♕xb5 20 d6. Also worth checking would be 16 ♘xa7 ♕xb2 17 ♘b5 ♘b4 18 ♗b1, and 18 ... ♘xd5 19 ♖xd5 ♖xd5 20 ♕xd5 ♕xb5 would be unsuitable because of 21 ♘e5!

The young player replied **16 ♖de1**, and after **16 ... ♕xb2 17 ♘c7 ♘xc7 18 ♗xc7** Kasparov used a fine trick— **18 ... ♘d2!**, ridding himself of all difficulties. In a sharp endgame he easily outplayed his youthful opponent. Here is how the game concluded: **19 ♖xe8+ ♖xe8 20 ♘xd2 ♕xd2 21 ♗xf5 gf 22 g3 ♗d4 23 d6 ♖e1**

24 ♔g2 ♖xf1 25 ♕xf1 ♕xa2 26 ♕b5 ♔g7 27 ♔h3 ♕d5 28 ♕e8 ♕c4! 29 ♔g2 ♕c2 30 ♕e1 ♕a4! 31 ♕d2 ♕c6+ 32 f3 ♗f6 **White resigned**.

Instead of 15 ... ♖ad8, also interesting is 15 ... ♗d7, as employed in the game Ivanchuk–Dorfman (Lvov 1988) by one of Kasparov's trainers. Fascinating events were to develop: 16 ♗e5 ♗xb5 17 ♕xb5 ♖xe5 18 ♘xe5 ♘d6! 19 ♘g4 ♕f4 20 ♕d7 c4 21 g3 ♘c5 22 ♕c7 ♕xg4 23 ♕xc5 ♕d7 24 ♗e2 ♖xb2 25 ♕b4 c3 26 ♗d3 a5 27 ♕f4 ♗a3 28 ♖fe1 ♗c5 29 ♔g2 b5 30 h4 h5 31 ♕f6 ♕d8 32 ♕xc3 ♗b4 33 ♕e5 ♗xe1 34 ♖xe1. A tense tactical melée is finally resolved peacefully, with the contestants agreeing a draw a few moves later.

16	♘c7	♘xd3
17	♘xe8	♖xe8
18	♕xd3!	

The trouble for Black is that neither 18 ... ♘xf2 nor 18 ... ♘g3 are any use because of the counterstroke 19 ♕b5.

18	...	♕xb2

Black has a pawn and active piece-play for the exchange, but the passed d-pawn has yet to show its full merit.

19	♖de1	

The straightforward 19 d6 ♖d8! (19 ... ♘c3 20 d7 ♖d8 21 ♕e3 or 21 ♖e1) 20 ♕e3 h5 (21 g4 was threatened) 21 ♖b1 ♕xa2 22 ♖xb7 ♕d5 23 ♖xa7 ♘xd6 24 ♗xd6 ♕xd6 25 ♘g5 is unpleasant for Black, and it would probably have been good to play it. However, I decided to pin the

knight, restricting the activity of the hostile pieces, incidentally threatening 20 g4. It goes without saying not to continue with 19 ♖fe1 in view of 19 ... ♕xf2+ 20 ♔h1 ♕xe1+! 21 ♖xe1 ♘f2+ 22 ♔g1 ♖xe1+ and 23 ... ♘xd3.

19	...	♕b4

The decisive mistake. After 19 ... ♘f6 20 ♖xe8+ ♘xe8 21 ♕e3 it would not be difficult to convert the material advantage, but in the event of 19 ... ♕xa2 20 ♕b5 (20 g4 c4!) 20 ... ♖d8 21 ♕xb7 ♕xd5 Black holds on. In the variation 22 ♕xd5 ♖xd5 23 g4 Kasparov, while commenting on the game, pointed out the witty manoeuvre 23 ... ♘f6!

20	♘d2!	

Play on the pin—the main motif of White's strategy.

20	...	♕a4
21	♕c4	

Forcing the exchange of queens. 21 ♘xe4 ♖xe4 22 ♖xe4 ♗xe4 23 ♕d2 c4 with counterplay is not so clear.

21	...	♕xc4
22	♘xc4	♗c3

22 ... b5 loses immediately (22 ... ♖d8 23 g4): 23 ♘d2 ♘f6 24 ♖xe8+ ♘xe8 25 ♖e1 etc.

23	♘d2	♗xd2
24	♗xd2	♗d7 *(12)*

During the game, it appeared to some spectators that Black had wriggled out of it more than successfully: the bishop on d2 is under attack and ... ♗b5 is threatened. However, the exchange may be returned.

25 ♗f4!   ♗b5
26 f3!   g5

After 26 ... ♗xf1 27 ♔xf1 ♘f6 28 ♖xe8+ ♘xe8 29 ♗e5! The d-pawn finally shows its true potential: 29 ... f6 30 d6! and a piece must be given up.

27 ♗xg5   ♗xf1

No better either would be 27 ... ♘xg5 28 ♖xe8+ ♗xe8 29 h4!, winning the knight.

28 ♔xf1   ♘d6
29 ♗e7

29 ♖xe8+ is not so convincing: 29 ... ♘xe8 30 ♗e7 f5 31 ♗xc5 b6 32 ♗d4 (32 d6 ♘f6) 32 ... ♔f7

29 ...   ♘c8

29 ... ♘c4 is also bad: 30 d6 ♘b6 31 ♖b1 ♘d7 (♖xb6 was threatened) 32 ♖xb7.

30 ♗xc5   ♖d8
31 ♖e5   f6
32 ♖f5   b6
33 ♗d4   ♘e7
34 ♗xf6   ♖xd5
35 ♖g5+   ♖xg5
36 ♗xg5   ♘c6
37 ♔e2   ♔f7
38 ♔d3   ♔e6

After 38 ... ♘b4+ 39 ♔c4 ♘xa2 40 ♔b3 the black knight finds itself trapped.

39 ♔c4   ♘e5+
40 ♔d4   ♘c6+
41 ♔c4

The game was adjourned here, and **Black resigned** without further play. After 41 ... ♘e5+ either 42 ♔b5 or 42 ♔d4 leads to the goal: 42 ♔d4 ♘c6+ 43 ♔e4, and the White pawns are irrepressible.

Karpov–Kasparov
Game 21,
World Championship 4
Seville 1987

This is our most recent discussion of the Grünfeld Defence in the matches for the Crown (although the argument was to continue soon after Seville) and it makes certain inroads into the development of the ♕b3 variation, a stormy battle in the opening leading to a quick truce. We shall examine different problematic positions below.

1 d4   ♘f6
2 c4   g6
3 ♘c3   d5
4 ♘f3   ♗g7
5 ♕b3

A comparatively rare variation was played in the **13th game** of this very match: **5 cd ♘xd5 6 e4 ♘xc3 7 bc c5 8 ♖b1.** However, it is beginning to acquire a second youth thanks to the endeavours of International Masters Khalifman and Gelfand. **8 ... 0-0 9 ♗e2 cd 10 cd ♕a5+ 11 ♕d2 ♕xd2+ 12 ♗xd2 e6 13 0-0 b6 14 ♖fd1 ♗b7 15 d5 ed 16 ed ♘d7 17 ♗b4 ♖fc8 18 ♗e7 ♗f6.** A novelty, which, combined with the next move,

allows Black to solve his opening problems successfully. **19 d6 ♗g7!
20 ♖e1 ♖c5 21 ♗b5 ♗c6 22 ♗xc6 ♖xc6 23 ♖bd1 ♗c3! 24 ♖e3 f6 25 g4 g5 26 h4 h6 27 hg hg***(13)*.

Some commentators suggested here **28 ♖d5**, considering that after the knight sacrifice on g5, White has at least a draw. But there is risk attached to this route, for example: **28 ... ♖c4 29 ♘xg5 fg 30 ♖xg5+ ♔f7 31 ♖f5+ (31 ♖f3+ ♔e6 32 ♖e3+ ♗e5) 31 ... ♔g8 32 ♖g5+ ♗g7**, or **29 ... ♖xg4+ 30 ♔f1 ♗e5! 31 ♘e6+ ♔f7 32 ♘d8+ ♔g6 33 ♘c6 ♖h8**. In Kasparov's opinion **28 ♖c1** leads to immediate equality: **28 ... ♖ac8 29 ♗d8!**

28 ♘d4 ♗xd4 29 ♖xd4 ♖h8 30 ♖e1 ♖c2 31 a4 a5. Black could display a certain amount of activity by continuing immediately with **31 ... ♔g6**, but now peace draws nigh. **32 f4 ♔g6 33 fg ♔xg5 34 ♖f1 ♔g6 35 ♖f2 ♖hc8 36 ♖df4 ♖xf2 Draw agreed.**

5	...	dc
6	♕xc4	0-0
7	e4	♘a6
8	♗e2	

Apart from this move, in the

current position, if I am not mistaken, there have been encountered 8(!) different continuations: 8 ♕b3, ♗g5, ♗f4, ♕a4, ♗e3, h3 e5 and even b4!? Practice has shown that Black obtains fully equal chances in all of these, and now the most popular idea is the quiet development of the light-squared bishop to e2. However, we can look now at a fresh example of a different type.

Petrosian–Mikhalchishin (Lvov 1986):

8	♕b3	c5
9	d5	e6
10	♗xa6	ba
11	0-0	ed
12	ed	♖e8
13	♗f4	♕b6
14	♖ad1	♗b7
15	♘d2	♖ad8
16	♕xb6	ab
17	♗c7	♖xd5!
18	♘xd5	♘xd5
19	♘c4!	♘xc7
20	♖d7	♗e4!
21	♘d6?!	♖e6
22	♘xf7	♘b5
23	♘g5	♖e5!
24	f4	♖e8

A sharp fight in the opening has led to an advantage to Black with complications, although it is true that after **25 ♖e1 ♗d4+ 26 ♖xd4 ♘xd4 27 ♘xe4** his advantage would be minimal.

25	a4?	♗d4+
26	♔h1	♗c6
27	♖xh7	♖e2
28	♖g1	♗xg2+!
29	♖xg2	♖e1+

White resigned

8	...	c5
9	d5	e6
10	0-0	ed
11	ed	♗f5

And here Black now has a wide choice of continuations—11 ... b5, ... b6, ... ♘e8, ... ♕b6 and ... ♖e8. However, similar to the move 8 ♗e2 the thrust of the light-squared bishop to f5 has also become canon law.

| 12 | ♖d1 | |

In game 19 of the third match, as you will remember, there was encountered 12 ♗f4 ♖e8 13 ♖ad1 ♘e4 14 ♘b5 etc. The idea of the move 12 ♖d1 is to prepare the advance of the d-pawn, and to bring out the bishop later. Exactly where depends on the circumstances.

| 12 | ... | ♖e8 |

In the old game Gufeld–Savon (USSR 1965) Black replied 12 ... ♕b6, and a sharp, intense game ensured. However, the move 12 ... ♖e8 looks more natural.

| 13 | d6 | |

This move was first used in game 15. In the event of 13 ♗g5 h6 14 ♗xf6 ♗xf6 15 a3 ♕b6 16 ♖d2 ♖ad8 Black has the better changes (Adamski–Timoshchenko, Slupsk 1979).

| 13 | ... | h6 |
| 14 | ♗f4 *(14)* | |

I played 14 h3 in **game 15** and after 14 ... ♘b4! Black obtained a fine position. The struggle subsequently became very nervy: the initiative swinging back and forth, and, as you will now see, everything ended in peace. The game went:

14
B

15	♗f4	♘d7
16	♖d2	a6
17	♕b3	b5
18	♕d1	c4
19	a4	♘c5
20	ab	♘bd3
21	♗xd3	♘xd3
22	♖xd3!	cd

During the game, I considered that the exchange sacrifice would give White abundant chances. Many commentators were of the same opinion. However, as Kasparov later established, the situation is not quite thus. 22 ♘d5! would lead to double-edged play: 22 ... ♘xf4 23 ♘xf4 c3! (23 ... ab 24 d7!) 24 bc ♗xc3, but here 22 ♖xd3 would just allow Black to obtain the advantage after 22 ... ♗xd3! 23 ♘d5 g5!

23	♘d5	ab
24	♘e7+	♔h7
25	♖xa8	♕xa8
26	♘xf5	gf
27	♕xd3	♕e4
28	♕xb5	♖a8
29	♗d2	♖d8
30	♕c5	♕e6
31	♗f4	♗xb2
32	♘h4	♗f6
33	♕xf5+	♕xf5

34	♘xf5	h5!
35	g4	hg
36	hg	♔g6
37	♔g2	♗b2
38	♘e7+	♔f6
39	♘c6	♖d7
40	♘b8	♖d8
41	d7	♔e6
42	♔f3	♗a3

Draw agreed.

Instead of 14 ♗f4, 14 ♗e3 would be worse, for example: 14 ... ♘g4!? 15 ♗f4 (15 d7 ♖xe3) 15 ... ♗xc3 16 bc ♖e4 17 ♕b3 ♖xf4 18 ♕xb7 ♖a4 19 ♗xa6 ♖b8 20 ♕c6 ♗d7, and Black wins.

14 ... ♘d7

More accurate than 14 ... ♘h5 15 ♗e3, when the white bishop entices the hostile knight to the edge of the board, and is most conveniently placed on e3.

15 ♖d2

15♕b3 ♘b4 leads to a transposition of moves (15 ... ♗xc3 16 ♗xa6!) 16 ♗c4 ♕f6! 17 ♖d2.

15 ... ♘b4

16 ♕b3 ♗e6

Better than 16 ... a6 17 a3 ♘c6 18 ♘d5!

17 ♗c4 ♘b6

18 ♗xe6 ♖xe6(15)

19 a3?

Not a successful move. Also bad would be 19 ♘b5 ♖e4! 20 ♗e3 ♘c4 21 ♗xc5 ♘a6!, and Black wins the exchange. 19 ♗g3 ♘d3 leads to double-edged play: 20 ♘b5 (or 20 ♘d5 c4 21 ♕b5 ♘xd5 22 ♕xd5 ♘xb2 23 ♕xb7 c3 24 ♖c2) 20 ... c4 21 ♕a3. While giving a simultaneous display with clocks against six strong American juniors (New York 1988), the World Champion went into this position again, but in response to 19 ♗g3 in the game Rao–Kasparov, instead of hopping his knight to d3 chose the modest 19 ... ♕d7. There followed 20 a3 ♘c6 21 ♕b5?! ♖c8! 22 ♖ad1? ♗xc3 23 bc ♘e5! 24 ♕xd7 ♘xf3+ 25 gf ♘xd7, and Black obtained a winning endgame.

I think that here all is not yet clear, and the diagram position hasn't occurred in practice since. Moreover, apart from 19 ♗g3, a recommendation of Tal deserves attention: 19 ♘a4!?

19 ... ♘d3!

The appearance of the knight carries some turmoil into White's camp. Evidently the capture would fail to the fork 20 ... c4!

20 ♗g3 c4

21 ♕c2 ♖c8

22 ♖ad1 ♕d7

22 ... ♘xb2 wouldn't pass muster: 23 ♕xb2 ♘a4 24 ♘xa4! ♗xb2 25 ♖xb2 ♕a5 26 ♖b4.

23 h4 f5

Perhaps 23 ... ♖c6 or 23 ... ♖c5 would be more precise, and the exchange sacrifice on d3 would not achieve its aim; White would have to play 24 ♕b1 and thereupon 25 ♘e1 or ♘e2.

24	♖xd3	cd
25	♕xd3	♘c4
26	♕d5	♘b6

Seemingly, the weakness of black's king is not to Kasparov's taste, and he decides not to take risks. Nevertheless, after 26 ... ♔h7! Black has created the better chances. It would seem that there is little difference in where to retreat the king: h8 or h7. However, it is highly important. In the event of 26 ... ♔h8 (26 ... ♘xb2 27 ♖e1 ♖e8 28 ♖xe6 ♖xe6—28 ... ♕xe6? 29 d7!—29 ♘b5 ♔h7 30 ♘e5! ♗xe5 31 ♗xe5 ♘c4 32 f4! a6 33 ♘d4 with advantage to White) 27 ♘b5 ♘xb2 28 ♖b1 ♘a4 (28 ... ♘c4 29 ♘xa7) 29 ♘c7 ♖xc7 30 dc ♕xd5 31 c8(♕)+ ♔h7 32 ♖xb7 with winning chances for White. With the king on h7 the c-pawn would not promote with check, making the whole of this variation unsuitable.

27 ♕d3

More accurate than 27 ♕b3 ♕f7! 28 ♘d5 (28 ♔h2 f4) 28 ... ♖d8 with better chances for Black.

27	...	♘c4
28	♕d5	♘b6

Draw agreed.

Thus, in a tense struggle both players blundered in turn, and matters were concluded by three-fold repetition. But it's too early to form a final opinion on the opening variation: White's resources, it seems to me, are not yet exhausted to the full.

Karpov–Timman
Amsterdam 1987

The system with the flank development of White's bishop was played in both my return match with Kasparov and also in Seville (and there twice) and therefore warrants attention. In recent years I have come across the central exchange c4xd5 c6xd5 four times against Kasparov, and, more interesting than those, in other encounters: one with Chiburdanidze and two with Timman. Six of these seven ended in draws, but to all intents and purposes White can count on more. It goes without saying that this variation is far from being unused by me. I have selected the current game with Timman, in as far as it is distinguished by its fascinating plot from beginning to end, as the main game, though the opening stage will be examined in fair detail drawing on all available material.

1	d4	♘f6
2	c4	g6
3	♘f3	♗g7
4	g3	c6

Although the move ... d7–d5 is the proper definition of the Grünfeld Defence, Black still has the option of delaying it. After 4 ... d5 5 cd ♘xd5 6 ♗g2 a theoretical position arises which has been known since time immemorial. It is interesting that, in the World Title match, Kasparov preferred the symmetrical system with ... c7–c6 followed by ... d7–d5, and in a later encounter with me returned to the basic variation. I have difficulty in working out what this means: the desire to present me with a surprise or concern over the symmetrical structure. Let's also examine this significant game.

Karpov–Kasparov (Amsterdam 1988)

| 6 | ... | ♘b6 |

A popular reply. Another route is associated with the advance of the c-pawn by one or two squares.

| 7 | ♘c3 | ♘c6 |
| 8 | e3 | |

This seems to be more precise than the immediate d5. 8 ♗f4 is also met in practice, and either move can also be made after mutual castling.

| 8 | ... | 0-0 |
| 9 | 0-0 | ♖e8 |

The most flexible response.

10	♖e1	e5
11	d5	♘a5
12	e4	c6
13	♗g5	f6
14	♗e3	

Curiously for the past twenty years this position has arisen on the board time and again, but always with rooks on f1 and f8. The actual position in this game is new.

| 14 | ... | ♘ac4! *(16)* |

In the old game Portisch–Schmidt (Bath 1973) after 13 ... cd (the rooks are standing on f1 and f8, therefore the game is a move behind) 14 ♗xb6 (also possible would be 14 ed ♘ac4 15 ♗c5 ♖f7 16 ♘d2 ♗f8 17 ♗xf8

♕xf8 18 b3 ♘d6 19 a4 Gligoric–Savon, Yugoslavia 1968) 14 ... ♕xb6 15 ♘xd5 ♕d8 16 ♖c1 ♘c6 17 ♕b3 ♖f7 18 ♖fd1 White obtained a definite advantage.

| 15 | dc | |

No other method seems apparent in the fight for the advantage.

| 15 | ... | ♘xe3 |

Black is content to shed a little material as long as he doesn't have any flaws in his pawn structure. This way he activates his forces.

| 16 | ♕xd8 | ♖xd8 |
| 17 | cb | ♗xb7 |

Possibly considering the variation 17 ... ♘xg2 18 ba(♕) ♘xe1, but 19 ♕xa7 bursts the balloon.

18	♖xe3	♗h6
19	♖ee1	♘c4
20	♖ad1	♔f8
21	h4	♖ac8
22	♗h3	

It seems as though this allows White to seize the initiative, but it soon becomes clear that it bears a temporary character and Black finds a reliable way of neutralizing it.

| 22 | ... | ♖xd1 |
| 23 | ♖xd1 | ♘xb2 |

24	♖d7	♖xc3
25	♖xb7	

White could play the preliminary 25 ♖d8+ ♔e7 26 ♖d7+ ♔f8, testing Black—26 ... ♔e8 is risky. The king must control the g7 square for the retreat of the bishop.

25	...	♘c4!

The opposite-coloured bishop ending would be unpleasant for Black after 25 ... ♖xf3 26 ♖xb2.

26	♘h2	

26 ♖c7? would be bad in view of 26 ... ♖c1+ 27 ♗f1 ♘d2 28 ♖xc1 ♘xf3+ 29 ♔g2 ♘xh4+ 30 gh ♗xc1, and White must now save an opposite-coloured bishop ending a pawn down.

26	...	♘d6
27	♖xh7	

27 ♖xa7 ♖xg3+! 28 fg ♗e3+.

27	...	♗g7
28	h5	gh
29	♖xh5	♖c1+
30	♔g2	♖c2
31	♗e6	♘xe4
32	♘g4	♖d2
33	♗b3	a5
34	♖f5	♘d6

35 ... ♔e7 35 ♘xe5!

35	h5	♘e4
36	♖f5	♘d6
37	♖h5	♘e4

Draw agreed.

5	♗g2	0-0
6	♘c3	d5
7	cd	

The drawing sequence after the exchange on d5 (although it doesn't quite reflect the state of affairs in the opening) gave me the mind to deviate. I then finally succeeded in winning the game!

Karpov–Georgiev (Wijk aan Zee 1988):

7	♕b3	e6
8	0-0	♘bd7
9	♗f4	♘b6?!

9 ... b6 is a more proven continuation.

10	c5	♘c4
11	♕c2	♘h5
12	b3	♘xf4
13	gf	♘a3
14	♕d2	b5

On 14 ... b6 then 15 ♕b2 bc 16 ♕xa3 cd 17 ♘a4 d3 18 ♖ac1 de 19 ♖fe1 is possible.

15	♖fe1	♖b8
16	♔h1	a5
17	e3	f5?

17 ... b4 18 ♘a4 ♘b5 or 17 ... ♕c7 with a further f6 and e5 would be more solid.

18	♗f1	♗d7

18 ... b4 19 ♘a4 ♘b5 20 ♘b6 ♘c7 21 a3.

19	♗e2	♗f6
20	♖g1	♔h8
21	♖g3	♕e7
22	♖ag1	♖g8
23	♕c1!	b4
24	♘a4	♖g7
25	♕f1	♖bg8
26	♕h3	♗e8
27	♘b6	♕d8
28	♕h6	♖c7
29	♘e5	♖cg7
30	♗d3	♘b5
31	♗xb5	cb
32	f3	♗h4

There is no salvation in 32 ... ♗e7 33 ♘bd7! ♗xd7 34 ♖xg6 ♗f6 35 ♖xg7 ♖xg7 36 ♖xg7 ♗xg7 37 ♘f7+ ♔g8 38 ♕xg7+ ♔xg7 39 ♘xd8.

33	♖h3	♗f2

34	♖xg6	♗xe3
35	♖xg7	♖xg7
36	♖g3	♕e7
37	♖xg7	♕xg7
38	♕xg7+	♔xg7
39	c6	♗xc6
40	♘xc6	♗xf4
41	♘d7	

Black resigned

Despite the success in that game I nevertheless consider the immediate exchange on d5 to promise White a serious initiative.

7	...	cd
8	♘e5	e6
9	0-0	

I gave preference to the move 9 ♗g5 in a different encounter with the same opponent.

Karpov–Timman (Bugojno 1986): 9 ... ♕b6 10 ♕d2 ♘fd7 11 ♘f3 ♘c6 12 ♖d1 ♘f6 13 0-0 ♗d7 14 ♗xf6 ♗xf6 15 e4 ♕a5 16 ♕f4 ♗g7 17 ♖fe1 ♖ad8 18 ed ed 19 ♘e5 ♗e6. Chances are balanced. We both subsequently went on to make many mistakes. At first I found myself in a difficult position, whereupon Timman provided me with the chance to equalize the game, and soon to obtain the advantage also. Finally, on the 71st move, I won. From the opening we can learn that instead of 16 ♕f4, better would be 16 ed ed 17 ♘e5! ♘xe5 18 ♘xd5 ♕xd2 19 ♘xf6+ ♔g7 20 ♖xd2 ♘c4 21 ♘xd7 ♘xd2 22 ♖d1 ♖fd8 23 ♗xb7 with advantage to White. On the other hand, after 12 ... ♕b4, Black would hardly have cause for concern over his position.

9	...	♘fd7

We return once more to the World Championship match, though amongst women. In the contest **Akhmilovskaya–Chiburdanidze (Sofija–Borzomi 1986)** the current variation of the Grünfeld Defence, strange as it may seem, was one of the most prominent. In ten of the games there followed the risky **9 ... ♘c6** and after **10 ♘xc6 bc 11 ♘a4 ♘d7 12 ♗f4** the World Champion had to seek a path to equality. However, she managed this successfully. **12 ... ♕a5 13 a3 ♗a6 14 b4 ♕d8 15 ♖e1 ♗c4 16 ♘c5 ♖e8 17 ♖c1 ♘xc5 18 bc ♕a5!** (18 ... e5 19 de ♗xe5 20 ♗xe5 ♖xe5 21 ♕d4) **19 e4 ♕xa3 20 ♗d6 ♕d3 21 ♕xd3 ♗xd3 22 e5 a5 23 ♖c3 ♗b5 24 ♗f1 ♗xf1 Draw agreed.**

| 10 | f4*(17)* | |

The symmetrical variation was tested for the first time in single combat with Kasparov in game 3 of the return match. White then replied differently: **10 ♘f3** (nothing is gained by the exchange **10 ♘xd7 ♗xd7—11 e3 ♘c6 12 b3 ♕e7 13 ♗b2 ♖fc8 Draw agreed; Portisch–Nunn,**

Budapest 1987) with the further **10 ... ♘c6 11 ♗f4 ♘f6 12 ♘e5.**

Let's make a 'double digression', in order to bring the 'tragic' epilogue of the eighth game of the previously mentioned match **Akhmilovskaya–Chiburdanidze: 12 ♖c1 h6 13 ♗e5 ♗d7 14 ♗d6 ♖e8 15 ♘e5 ♘xe5 16 de** (16 ♗xe5 ♖c8 leads to equality) **16 ... ♘g4 17 ♕d4 h5 18 h3 ♘h6 19 e4 ♗c6 20 ed ed 21 ♗xd5?? ♕xd6**, and **White resigned**. Chiburdanidze proposes that 21 ♘xd5 ♘f5 22 ♕c5 ♗xe5 23 ♗xe5 ♖xe5 24 ♖fd1 leads to unclear play.

Let's return to the game **Karpov–Kasparov, m(3) London 1986:**

12	**...**	**♗d7**

After 12 ... ♘xe5 13 ♗xe5 White's chances are preferable.

13	**♕d2**	**♘xe5**
14	**♗xe5**	**♗c6**
15	**♖fd1**	

15 ♖ac1 would have maintained the initiative with the prospect of f2–f3 and e3–e4.

15	**...**	**♘d7**
16	**♗xg7**	**♚xg7**
17	**♖ac1**	**♘f6**
18	**♕f4**	**♕b8**

Chances are probably equal.

19	**♕xb8**	**♖axb8**
20	**f3**	**♖fd8**
21	**♚f2**	**♖bc8**
22	**e3**	**♘e8**
23	**♖d2**	**♘d6**
24	**♖dc2**	**♚f8**
25	**♗f1**	**♚e7**
26	**♗d3**	**f5**
27	**h4**	**h6**
28	**b3**	

Kasparov, commenting on the game, pointed out that after 28 g4 Black's position is in some danger. However, it seems to me, that the reply 28 ... ♖f8 29 g5 ♘e4+ 30 ♗xe4 (30 fe fe+ 31 ♚e2 ed+ 32 ♚xd3 hg 33 hg ♖f5!) 30 ... fe 31 f4 h5 promises White nothing.

28	**...**	**g5**
29	**♘e2**	**♗d7**
30	**♖c5**	**b6**
31	**♖c7**	**♖xc7**
32	**♖xc7**	**♖a8**
33	**♘g1**	**♘e8**
34	**♖c1**	**♖c8**
35	**♖xc8**	

Draw agreed

10	**...**	**♘c6**

In the game Karpov–Kasparov, m(13), Leningrad 1976, Black temporarily drove the knight away—10 ... f6—and after 11 ♘f3 ♘c6 12 ♗e3 ♘b6 13 ♗f2 f5 14 ♘e5 ♗d7 15 ♕d2 ♘c8 16 ♕e3 White created a certain pressure, although the game finally ended in a draw after mutual errors. White maintains the initiative by a different knight retreat: 11 ♘d3 ♘c6 12 e3 (12 ♗e3 ♘b6 13 b3 ♗d7 14 ♘c5 ♖b8 15 ♕d2 f5 16 ♖fc1 ♘c8 17 ♗f2 ♘d6 with a level game, Nikolic–Nunn, Linares 1988) 12 ... f5 13 ♗d2 ♘f6 14 ♖c1 ♗d7 15 ♘e5 ♖e8 16 h3 ♘xe5 17 de ♘e4 18 ♘xe4 de 19 ♕b3 (Hulak–H. Olafsson, Wijk aan Zee 1987).

Soon after the return match the World Champion himself chose the variation as White, and in the game Kasparov–Nunn (Brussels 1986) the exchange on e5 10 ...

♘xe5 11 fe ♘c6 unexpectedly led to a quick defeat: **12 e4! de 13 ♗e3***(18)*.

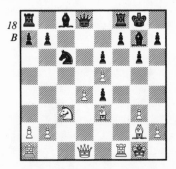

18
B

It is difficult to conceive that Black, not having made a single mistake, and currently having an extra pawn, surrenders only 6(!) moves later. **13 ... f5 14 ef ♖xf6**. This is still a well known position: for example, by a transposition of moves, it arose in the game Sveshnikov–Mikhalchishin (Lvov 1983); after 15 ♖xf6 ♗xf6 16 ♘e2 White's advantage has evaporated. Kasparov doesn't lose time exchanging Rooks, and after **15 ♘xe4 ♖xf1+ 16 ♕xf1 ♘xd4? 17 ♖d1 e5 18 ♘g5** Black stopped the clock.

The question arises, why did Nunn give up the struggle here, seeing as there was apparently nothing forcing for White? A couple of days after this game one of the amateurs handed to Kasparov and his trainer Nikitin a fresh edition of a special bulletin, issued from Sweden. And in it was shown the continuation of the game Kasparov–Nunn, which occurred, in fact, in a correspondence duel **Hjorth–M. Andersson:**

18 ... ♕e7 19 ♗d5+ ♗e6 20 ♖xd4 ed 21 ♗xe6+ ♔h8 22 ♘f7+ ♔g8 23 ♘d8+ ♔h8 24 ♗g5! ♕b4 25 ♘f7+ ♔g8 26 ♘e5+ ♔h8 27 ♘xg6+ hg 28 ♕h3+ Black resigned.

An elegant finale, and for confirmation of Kasparov's authority as an openings connoisseur, it could be noted that he knew exactly how to operate with the White pieces in this game. However, one must compliment the World Champion: without any knowledge whatsoever of the above game, he demonstrated the whole variation, up to and including the 28th move, to the aggrieved Nunn immediately after the game!

The following sequence of moves is used in many games: 10 ... ♘dxe5 11 fe ♘c6 12 ♗e3. In this event the position arising is the one now reached in our main game.

11 ♗e3 ♘dxe5

Here we should digress and examine a less committal move for Black **11 ... ♘b6,** encountered twice in Seville. Here is the peaceful game: **Karpov–Kasparov, m (1) Seville 1987.**

12 ♗f2 ♗d7
13 e4 ♘e7
14 ♘xd7

In the game **Drashko–Nikolic (Vrnjacka Banja 1987),** where apparently this position first arose, White chose **14 ed ♘bxd5 15 ♘xd5 ♘xd5 16 ♕b3 ♗c6 17 ♖ac1 ♕a5 18 ♖c5 ♕a6,** and the opponents agreed a **draw.** The exchange on d7 can be considered a novelty, though not dangerous for Black.

14	...	♛xd7
15	e5	♖fc8
16	♖c1	♝f8
17	♝f3	

Here many commentators recommended 17 g4 ♖c4 18 f5! with a dangerous initiative. However, Black has the reply 17 ... ♝h6, after which the f-pawn is brought to a halt and Black has sufficient counterplay.

17	...	♖c7
18	b3	♖ac8
19	♛d2	♞c6
20	♛b2	a6
21	♝e2	♛e7!
22	♞b1	♞b4
23	♞c3	♞c6
24	♞b1	♞b4
25	♖c5	♞d7
26	♖xc7	♖xc7
27	♞c3	♞c6
28	♞b1	♞b4
29	♞c3	♞c6
30	♞b1	

Draw agreed

Karpov–Kasparov, m (3) Seville 1987. On the 12th move, instead of 12 ... ♝d7, there followed the more accurate **12 ... ♞e7!**, which led to immediate equality.

13	a4	a5
14	♛b3	♝d7
15	♖fc1	♝c6
16	♞b5	♞bc8
17	e3	

Some commentators recommended here the doubling of rooks on the c-file. I don't think

that this could have an essential influence on the situation; Black's position is impregnable.

17	...	♞d6
18	♞xd6	♛xd6
19	♝e1	♖fb8
20	♝f1	f6
21	♞f3	♛d7
22	♛c2	♞f5
23	♝d2	♞d6
24	b3	♖c8
25	♛d1	h6
26	♝e1	g5
27	♖a2	♛e8
28	♖ac2	♝f8
29	♝d3	g4

Draw agreed

Here is one more example on the theme 12 ... ♞b6: **Portisch–Korchnoi (Reggio-Emilia 1987/8). 12 b3** (instead of 12 ♝f2) **12 ... ♝d7 13 ♛d2 ♖e8 14 ♖fc1 f6 15 ♞d3 ♖e7 16 ♚h1 ♝e8 Draw agreed.**

Thus, thanks to the move 11 ... ♞b6, Kasparov, in Seville, succeeded in rendering harmless the symmetrical variation of the Grünfeld Defence. Does this solve all of Black's problems? I recall that right after the match Kasparov refrained from 4 ... c6 in favour of the immediate 4 ... d5. Of course, this is not being discussed here, but, I confess that I have some considerations for the cause of the move 4 ... c6, and I will possibly demonstrate them in my next tournament, possibly before this volume is released to the world.

12 fe

Now the plans of both sides are clear: White must try to attack in the centre, preparing e2–e4, and Black must take care of freeing his game and the development of his queen's bishop, which is hindered by his own pawns.

12	...	f6
13	ef	♖xf6
14	♛d2	♗d7
15	♔h1	♖xf1+
16	♖xf1	♛e7 *(19)*

19
W

This position has arisen time and again in Grandmaster practice. The placing of the queen on e7 is more solid than on a5: 16 ... ♛a5 17 a3 ♖f8 18 ♖xf8+ ♗xf8 19 ♗g1.

17 ♖d1

This move involves the over-protection of both the d4 pawn and the queen, while preparing ♗e3–g1 and e2–e4. The immediate retreat of the bishop to g1 is also possible; here is a very recent example.

Ribli–Nunn (Dortmund 1987): 17 ♗g1 ♖d8 18 a3 ♔h8? (18 ... ♗c8 19 ♗e3 ♖f8 would be safer for Black) 19 e4! The fiasco in his game with Kasparov did not frighten Nunn away from this variation, but again, this central pawn advance puts him in a difficult position. 19 ... de 20 ♘xe4 ♗c8 21 ♗e3 (21 ♘g5 ♗f6) 21 ... ♖f8 22 ♖xf8+ ♛xf8 23 b4 and White has a clear advantage.

17 ... ♖c8

A month later, in the game Karpov–Chiburdanidze (Bilbao 1987) the Women's World Champion replied 17 ... ♔h8 and only on 18 a3 did she play 18 ... ♖c8. After 19 ♗g5 ♛f8 20 ♖f1 ♛g8 21 e3 h6 22 ♗f6 ♗xf6 23 ♖xf6 ♖f8 24 ♖f2 ♛g7 25 ♖xf8+ ♛xf8 26 e4 de 27 ♘xe4 b6 28 ♔g1 ♛g7 29 d5 ed 30 ♛xd5 ♛d4+ 31 ♛xd4 ♘xd4 the players had made the transition from the opening to the endgame, with White retaining a minimal advantage. However, Maya defended accurately, and, despite my efforts, guided the game to a draw.

In the present game I carried out the idea ♗e3–g1, subsequently conquering the centre. However, in the event of the immediate 18 ♗g1 Timman had prepared the thrust 18 ... ♛b4!, after which 19 e4 would be disadvantageous in view of 19 ... de; now on 20 ♗xe4 there follows 20 ... ♗e8, and Black succeeds in fortifying his position by the means of ... ♗e8–f7, for the immediate break 21 d5? wouldn't do because of 21 ... ♗xc3! If instead 20 ♘xe4, then firstly after the exchange of queens 20 ... ♛xd2 21 ♖xd2 b6 White's attacking potential loses its force, and secondly Black has the tactical operation: 21 ... ♘xd4 22 ♖xd4 ♗xd4 23 ♗xd4 ♖c1+ 24 ♗g1 ♗c6 with counterplay in a complex ending. But why such storms in fine weather?

18 a3!

The manoeuvre 18 ... ♘a5 had to be considered here, though it is refuted by 19 ♘xd5 ed 20 ♗g5 ♘c4 21 ♗xe7 (this is more accurate than 21 ♗xd5+ ♗e6) 21 ... ♘xd2 22 ♗xd5+ ♔h8 23 ♖xd2.

18 ... ♗f6
19 ♗g1 ♗g5

19 ... ♕g7 is more precise, still preventing 20 e4 because 20 ... de 21 ♘xe4 (21 ♗xe4 ♖d8) 21 ... ♗xd4 22 ♗xd4 ♘xd4 23 ♕xd4 ♕xd4 24 ♖xd4 ♖c1+ 25 ♗f1 ♗b5!

20 ♕e1

All is ready for the break in the centre, and it cannot be prevented. Black now goes into deep defence.

20 ... ♘d8
21 e4 de
22 ♕xe4 b6

23 d5 is very strong after 22 ... ♗c6.

23 d5 ♗f6
24 ♗d4 ♗xd4
25 ♕xd4 ♕g7
26 ♕h4!

After the exchange of the dark-squared bishops a gaping hole has been generated in the enemy camp, to which all of White's pieces are directed. The manoeuvre ♘c3–e4–f6+ is particularly threatened.

26 ... ♘f7

Preparing to meet the thrust 27 ♘e4 with the counterblow 27 ...

g5. Here White has many ways of developing an initiative, for example 27 d6, with the intention of exploiting his well advanced passed pawn. I preferred a more forcing move.

27 de ♗xe6
28 ♕e7 ♗b3
29 ♖d7 *(20)*

29 ♖e1 doesn't look bad either.

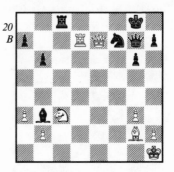

The White pieces are positioned very menacingly, and I considered 29 ... ♕h6 to be Black's solitary chance of counterplay, after which I would have the choice between 30 h4 ♕c1+ 31 ♔h2 ♕xb2 32 ♘e4 with the attack (though this is not quite clear) and the quiet reply 30 ♕e1, maintaining all the advantages of the position. However, Timman, afraid of White's activity, tries to simplify and, forcing the exchange of queens, goes for salvation in a dismal endgame.

29 ... ♕e5
30 ♖xa7 ♖e8
31 ♕xe5 ♖xe5
32 h3

The first in a series of imprecise moves; 32 h4 is better. But even simpler would be 32 ♔g1 ♖e1+ 33 ♔f2 ♖c1 34 ♗e4 ♘d6 35

♖d7, retaining a single, though healthy, extra pawn: 35 ... ♖xc3 36 ♖xd6; 35 ... ♘xe4+ 36 ♘xe4 or 35 ... ♘c4 ♗d5+.

32	...	♖e1+
33	♔h2	♖c1
34	♖b7	♖c2
35	♔g1	♖c1+
36	♔h2	♖c2
37	♖xb6	♗c4

Black is not liberated in the event of 37 ... ♖xb2? 38 a4.

38	♔g1	♖c1+
39	♔h2	♖c2
40	♔g1	

I found myself in time-trouble and repeated moves to gain time.

40	...	♖c1+
41	♔f2	♖c2+
42	♔f3	

Otherwise there is no way out of this 'box'.

42	...	♘g5+
43	♔g4	♖xg2
44	♔xg5	♖xg3+
45	♔f6	♖f3+
46	♔e5	♖xh3 *(21)*

Black has succeeded in redressing the material balance, but the advantage is, as before, on the side of White: the pawns quickly begin to advance.

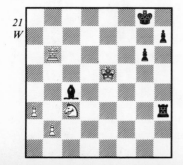

47	a4	♗f1
48	♘d5	♖h5+
49	♔d6	♖h2
50	b4	

50 a5 is significantly stronger.

| 50 | ... | ♖d2 |
| 51 | ♔e5 | |

It would also follow to play 51 a5 here, ignoring the pin, in as far as the continuation 51 ... ♗c4 (51 ... h5 52 ♔e5) 52 ♔c5 ♗xd5 53 ♖d6 leads to a pin in return. I discovered the possibility of this omission on my next move, and my opponent, seemingly, did so too, for he prudently refrained from repeating the position.

51	...	♖e2+
52	♔d4	♖d2+
53	♔c5	♖c2+
54	♔d6	h5

In comparison with the position after 51 moves White has lost a tempo.

| 55 | ♘e3 | ♖c1 |
| 56 | b5 | |

The rook ending is drawn.

| 56 | ... | ♗e2 |
| 57 | a5? | |

Does it make sense, having declined this move three times, to play it now at the most inappropriate moment? Despite all these errors, White could still fight for the win after 57 ♖c6 ♖b1 58 b6, and if 58 ... h4, then 59 ♔c7 h3 60 ♖xg6+ ♔h7 61 ♖g3 or 60 ... ♔f7 61 ♖h6. 58 ... ♗a6 would be more stubborn, though in this event also White has sufficiently high chances. Now it all ends trivially.

| 57 | ... | ♖a1 |

Draw agreed

After 58 a6 Black gives up his bishop for two pawns.

There is an interesting epilogue to this game. The draw meant that Timman and myself shared first and second place in the Amsterdam tournament, though I was adjudged the winner on tie-break. In the closing speech there were congratulations, and, of course, flowers. They all seemed most pleasant and unusually rewarding. Over the last eight years, Dutch gardeners have attempted to provide pink chrysanthemums, which, I am told, don't exist in nature. And here, at the beginning of 1987, their endeavours had been crowned with glory. It was decided beforehand that the new flower would be named after the tournament winner. And if you, the readers of this book, hear somewhere about the 'Karpov Chrysanthemum', then please don't think that its name was my choice. This delicate pink flower was brought by Mr Breding from the Dutch town of Scravensand. Seeing that the g2–g3 system and the symmetrical centre variation hasn't yet been given a name, its popularity is sufficient, perhaps, to call it the 'Chrysanthemum Opening'!

Karpov–Kasparov
Game 5,
World Championship 4
Seville 1987

The continuation associated with the move 12 ♗xf7+ is employed in this game. After the match Kasparov said that White's chosen plan is seemingly prospectless. I cannot agree with this point of view: the pawn structure which arises gives White the basis on which to count on an advantage, and, moreover, he still wins a pawn. Another possibility is that the position is highly dynamic and may fit in to the spirit of the player of the Black pieces. The four contests in which this variation was played produced the level scoreline 2–2, which, in principle, suits Black. But let's look at the position from White's standpoint. I won the current game, and I was also close to victory in the 11th game, where I suffered defeat due to a gross oversight. I coud also have won the seventh encounter, and had a definite advantage in the ninth. Now judge for yourselves, if this very topical variation is so harmless for Black.

1	d4	♘f6
2	c4	g6
3	♘c3	d5
4	cd	♘xd5
5	e4	♘xc3
6	bc	♗g7
7	♗c4	c5
8	♘e2	♘c6
9	♗e3	0-0
10	0-0	♗g4
11	f3	♘a5 (22)

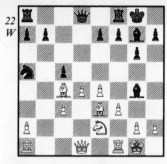

22
W

12   ♗xf7+!?

This is still rarely played in this position—the more popular continuation 12 ♗d3 is discussed in the notes to game 9 of the same match. It is true that a similar variation has occurred more than once: 10 ... cd 11 cd ♗g4 12 f3 ♘a5 13 ♗xf7+ ♖xf7 14 fg ♖xf1+ 15 ♔xf1 (15 ♕xf1 is worse, 15 ... ♘c4 16 ♕f3 ♕b6 17 ♗f2 ♕b2 18 ♖c1 ♕xa2). In the older game Pantaleev–Prakhov (Bulgaria 1970) after 15 ... ♕d7 16 h3 ♕e6 17 ♕d3 ♕c4 18 ♕xc4 ♘xc4 19 ♗g5 e6 a sharp, though probably equal, endgame has arisen. The immediate strike on f7 was suggested by Igor Zaitsev.

12   ...   ♖xf7
13   fg   ♖xf1+
14   ♔xf1   ♕d6

In game 9, after the preliminary exchange on d4, the black queen went to b6, but we shall discuss this later. The immediate 14 ... ♕b6 is also possible. In the game Chernin–Gavrikov (Lvov 1987), Black came up with the new 14 ... ♕d7. This is how the situation developed.

15   dc   ♖f8+
15 ... ♕xg4 16 ♘f4!

16   ♔g1   ♕xg4
17   ♘f4   ♕xd1
17 ... ♖xf4 is bad: 18 ♗xf4 ♕xf4 19 ♕d8+.

18   ♖xd1   ♗xc3
19   ♘d5

The initiative is on White's side, but Black is standing his ground. Nothing is given by 19 ♘e6 ♖c8 20 ♖d7 ♔f7 21 ♗g5? ♗f6! 22 ♗xf6 ♔xe6 (21 ♘g5+ ♔e8 22 ♖d3 ♗b4).

19   ...   ♗f6
20   ♗h6   ♖e8

But not 20 ... ♖f7 21 ♘xf6+ ♖xf6 22 e5 ♖f5 23 g4 and White wins.

21   ♘xf6+   ef
22   ♖d7   ♖xe4
23   ♖g7+   ♔h8
24   ♖c7   ♔g8
25   ♖g7+
25 ♗d2 ♘c6 26 ♖xb7 ♖e7
25   ...   ♔h8
26   ♖c7   ♔g8
27   ♖g7+   ♔h8
Draw agreed

In reply to 14 ... ♕d7, instead of 15 dc the more logical looking 15 g5 was encountered in the game **Karpov–Gavrikov, European Quickplay Championship (Spain 1988)**. Taking into account the 'lightness' of the competition, let's look at this interesting game with short notes.

Thus, **14 ... ♕d7 15 g5** (15 h3 is not bad either) **15 ... ♕e6 16 e5! ♕c4! 17 ♔g1 ♖d8 18 ♕e1 ♘c6 19 ♗f2 a6** (is 19 ... b5!? not better?) **20 a4 ♘a5 21 h4 ♗f8 22 dc! ♘b3 23 ♖b1!** (more precise than 23 ♖d1 ♖xd1 24 ♕xd1

♘xc5) **23 ... e6** (and here 23 ... ♘xc5 loses to 24 ♖b4 ♕d5 25 ♖d4) **24 c6! bc 25 ♘d4 ♘xd4 26 cd ♕xa4 27 ♕c3.** White has an evident advantage in the endgame. **27 ... ♖c8 28 h5! gh 29 ♕h3 ♖e8 30 ♕xh5 ♖e7** (30 ... ♕c2 31 ♖b7) **31 g6 ♕c2 32 gh+ ♖xh7 33 ♕g4+ ♔h8 34 ♖f1 ♕f5** (34 ... ♕d3 35 ♗h4!) **35 ♕xf5 ef 36 ♗e3 ♖h5 37 g4! ♖h3 38 ♖xf5 ♖xe3 39 ♖xf8+ ♔g7 40 ♖f4!** The subsequent ending is won for White. **40 ... a5 41 ♔f2 ♖b3 42 ♖f6 ♖d3** (42 ... ♖c3 43 ♔e2 a4 44 ♔d2 etc.) **43 ♖d6 a4 44 ♔e2 ♖g3 46 ♖xc6 ♖xg4 46 ♔d3 a3 47 ♖a6 ♔f7 46 ♔c4 ♖g3 47 d5 Black resigned.**

15 e5

15 ♔g1 is another possibility. I turned to this move in the 11th game. Subsequently, as we shall see below, it has been repeatedly encountered in practice.

15 ... ♕d5

After 15 ... ♕e6 16 g5 (16 h3 is not bad either) 16 ... ♕c4 17 ♔g1 a position arises that has already been examined in the game Karpov–Gavrikov. In the event of 16 ... ♘c4 it would follow simply to retreat the bishop to f2, chiefly to avoid the trap 17 ♕d3 ♕f5+!, when Black gains the upper hand.

16 ♗f2 ♖f8

Black preferred the d8 square for his rook in the seventh game, which is quite reasonable in that the white queen must abandon the central file.

17 ♔g1 ♗h6

18	h4		♕f7
19	♗g3		♗e3+
20	♔h2		♕c4
21	♖b1	*(23)*	

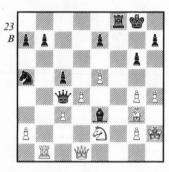

A minimal advantage would be retained after 21 dc ♕xg4, though I wouldn't like to break up the pawn chain before time. Incidentally, 21 d5 ♕xg4 22 d6 ♗f2 23 de ♗xg3+ 24 ♘xg3 ♕xh4+ 25 ♔g1 ♕xe7 is in Black's favour.

21 ... b6

It is dangerous to take the a2 pawn: 21 ... ♕xa2 22 ♖a1 ♕b3 23 ♕d3 ♘c4 24 ♖b1 ♕a2 25 ♖xb7.

22 ♖b2

Perhaps it would now be good to release the tension in the centre and exchange on c5. The possible following variations: 22 dc bc (22 ... ♕xc5 23 ♕d7, or 22 ... ♗xc5 23 ♘d4 ♕xa2 24 h5 are worse) 23 ♘g1 ♗f2! (otherwise White obtains a big advantage after either 23 ... ♕xc3 24 ♕d5+ ♔h8 25 ♘f3 or 23 ... ♕xa2 24 ♖a1 ♕b3 25 ♕xb3 ♘xb3 26 ♖xa7 ♘d2 27 ♘f3!) 24 ♘f3 ♗xg3+ 25 ♔xg3 ♕f4+ 26 ♔h3 ♘c4 27 ♕d5+ ♔h8 28 ♕xc5 h5 (or 28 ... ♘e3 29 ♕d4 ♘xg2, going into the ending a pawn down, though probably drawing) 29 gh ♕f5+ (29 ... ♘e3 30 ♕d4 ♕f5+ 31 ♔h2 is unclear) 30 ♔h2 ♕xb1 31 ♕xc4 gh 32 ♕e6. White has the advantage, although the win is not simple. Now Black seizes the initiative.

22 ...   ♕d5!
23 ♕d3   ♘c4
24 ♖b1 *(24)*

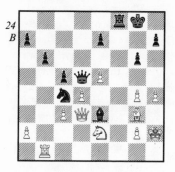

24
B

A critical position. After Black's chosen ... b6–b5 the sharp struggle should have ended in a draw. Soon after the match Kasparov demonstrated how, by moving the other pawn ... g6–g5, he could have gained the victory. This possibility was deeply analysed by Zaitsev, who found that everything is not quite so clear. Let's look at the main variations which arise after 24 ... g5.

25 hg is uninviting for White: 25 ... ♗xg5 26 ♘g1 ♘e3 27 ♖b2 (27 ♕e2 ♖f2! or 27 ♘f3 ♖xf3!) 27 ... c4! 28 ♕b1 ♖f1 etc.

If 25 h5, then 25 ... ♗f2! 26 ♗xf2 ♖xf2 27 ♖g1 ♘xe5 28 ♕g3 ♖xe2 29 de ♕xe5.

On 25 ♘g1, both 25 ... ♘xe5 and 25 ... gh 26 ♗xh4 ♘xe5 are

very strong, and on 25 ♔h3 there comes 25 ... ♗f2 26 ♗xf2 ♖xf2 27 ♖g1 gh! with dangerous threats.

The best answer to the advance of the g-pawn is 25 ♖d1, with the further 25 ... gh 26 ♗xh4 ♗f2 27 ♕h3! ♕e4! (in the event of 27 ... ♘e3 28 ♖d3 ♕e4 29 ♗xf2 ♘xg4+ 30 ♕xg4+ ♕xg4 31 ♖g3 White gains the upper hand, but after 28 ... ♘f1+ 29 ♔h1 ♕xa2 30 ♗xf2 ♕xe2 31 ♖f3 ♖xf3 32 ♕xf3 ♕xf3 33 gf c4 34 d5 ♘d2 35 ♔g2 chances are level) 28 ♗xe7 ♖f7 (a showy drawing variation is obtained by 28 ... ♕xe2 29 ♕h6! ♖f7 30 ♕g5+ ♖g7 31 ♕f4! ♖xe7 32 ♕g5+ ♔f8 33 ♕f6+ ♔e8 34 ♕c6+ ♖d7 35 e6 ♘e5! 36 ed+ ♘xd7 37 ♕f3 ♕xf3 38 gf) 29 ♗f6 ♘e3! 30 g5! ♘g4+! (30 ... ♘xd1 31 ♕c8+ with perpetual check) 31 ♔h1 ♗xd4! (31 ... ♕xe2 32 ♕f3 ♕xf3 33 gf ♘xf6 34 gf cd 35 cd is not quite so clear) 32 ♘g3 ♕f4 33 ♕h5 (33 ♖f1 ♕xf1+ 34 ♘xf1 ♘f2+ 35 ♔h2 ♗xe5+) 33 ... ♕xg3 34 cd ♘f2+ 35 ♔g1 ♘xd1 36 ♕xd1 ♕e3+ 37 ♔h1 ♕xd4 38 ♕e1. White maintains chances of a draw, for example: 38 ... ♖d7 39 e6! ♕d1 40 ed! ♕xe1+ 41 ♔h2, and Black is forced to settle for perpetual check.

Along with the move 24 ... g5 is the interesting 24 ... ♖f2. At first it looks dangerous for White: 25 ♗xf2 ♘xe5! 26 ♕xe3 ♘xg4+ 27 ♔g1 ♘xe3 28 ♗xe3 ♕e4, and Black prevails, or 26 ♕c2 ♘xg4+ 27 ♔g3 ♗xf2+ 28 ♔xg4

♕e6+ 29 ♔f3 ♕e3+ 30 ♔g4 h5
mate. More careful examination
of the position shows that the
transference of the rook to f2 is
erroneous: 26 c4! ♘xg4+ 27
♔g3! ♗xf2+ 28 ♔xg4, or 26 ...
♕d6 27 ♔g3! ♘xg4 28 ♔h3 ♕d7
29 ♕b3 with an extra rook.

However, even closer investiga-
tion of the position helps to re-
establish the status quo: a dynamic equilibrium arising after the
retreat of the queen to d7 (but not
d6): 26 ... ♕d7! 27 ♕xe3 (27 ♕e4
♘xg4+ 28 ♔f3 ♗xf2+ 29 ♔f3
♘f6! 30 ♕a8+ ♔f7 31 ♔xf2
♕f5+) 27 ... ♘xg4+ 28 ♔g1
♘xe3 29 ♗xe3 ♕e6 30 ♖b3! (30
♗h6 g5! 31 hg ♕e3+ 32 ♔f1 cd)
30 ... ♕xc4 31 ♔f2 cd (not 31 ...
e5? straightaway, in view of 32
♗h6 cd 33 ♖f3 ♕c5 34 ♖f8+
♕xf8 25 ♗xf8 ♔xf8 36 ♔f3 with
a won ending) 32 ♘xd4 e5! with
equality.

24	...	b5
25	♔h3!	

The situation is extremely sharp
and fascinating, in that both contestants are playing to win. If I so
wished, I could now have immediately forced the draw: 25
♖xb5 ♘xe5 26 ♖xc5 ♘xg4+ (26
... ♕xc5 27 ♗xe5!) 27 ♔h3 ♕d7
28 ♕c4+ ♔g7 29 ♕d5 ♘f2+ 30
♔h2 ♘g4+ with perpetual
check.

Instead of 27 ... ♕d7, 27 ...
♘f2+ would be risky because of
28 ♗xf2 ♕e6+ 29 g4! ♗xf2 (29
... h5 30 ♕xe3 ♕xg4+ 31 ♔h2
♖f3 32 ♖e5!) 30 ♖e5 ♕f7 31
♕e4! ♗xh4! 32 g5! ♗e1 33 ♖xe7

♕f3+ (33 ... ♕f1+ 34 ♔g4!) 34
♕xf3 ♖xf3+ 35 ♔g4 with an
endgame advantage for White.

25	...	a6

On 25 ... ♘d2 there follows 26
♖d1!, but not 26 ♖xb5 ♖f1! 27
♕xe3 ♖h1+ 28 ♗h2 ♖xh2+.

26	♘g1	cd
27	♘f3	♖d8

27 ... ♖xf3 loses to 28 gf ♘d2
29 ♖d1!

28	a4	dc
29	♕xc3	♕e6
30	♔h2	ba

A probably equal position is
reached after 30 ... ♕xg4 31 ab
ab 32 ♖xb5 ♘d2 33 ♖xd2 ♗xd2.

31	♖b4	♘d2
32	♖xa4	♘f1+
33	♔h3	♖d1

33 ... h5 34 ♕c4 is more solid.

34	♕c2 (25)

The queen move is inaccurate,
and it would follow to take the
pawn: 34 ♖xa6 ♕xa6 35 ♕b3+
♔g7 36 ♕xd1 ♘xg3 37 ♔xg3
with better chances.

34	...	♖c1
35	♕e2	h5
36	♗e1	♕d7?

Neither side is functioning well
in severe time trouble, but it is

Black who makes the decisive mistake. 36 ... ♖a1! would have been the quickest way to a draw: 37 ♘g5 (37 ♕c4 gives nothing) 37 ... hg+ (37 ... ♖xa4 38 ♘xe6 hg+ 39 ♕xg4 ♖xg4 40 ♔xg4 with the better endgame for White) 38 ♖xg4 ♗xg5 39 hg ♖a4 40 ♔h4.

| 37 | ♕xa6 | ♖a1?? |
| 38 | ♕xg6+ | |

Black resigned.

Karpov–Kasparov
Game 7,
World Championship 4
Seville 1987

The discourse started in the fifth game is continued in this encounter. Kasparov again obtains counterplay in return for the pawn, but the course of this duel turns out in my favour. I let slip several times the opportunity to obtain a decisive endgame advantage, and further attempts were all in vain.

This game was significant to the outcome of the whole contest. If I had won it (and the win was close), I would have gone two points clear. Taking into account that Kasparov was not in his best form, such a lapse might have been the decisive factor. It turned out quite to the contrary. Having been upset that I hadn't made the most of a propitious chance to go ahead, I lost the next game and essentially began the match all over again.

1	d4	♘f6
2	c4	g6
3	♘c3	d5
4	cd	♘xd5
5	e4	♘xc3
6	bc	♗g7
7	♗c4	c5
8	♘e2	♘c6
9	♗e3	0-0
10	0-0	♗g4
11	f3	♘a5
12	♗xf7+	♖xf7
13	fg	♖xf1+
14	♔xf1	♕d6
15	e5	

The 11th game of the match, as previously mentioned, is devoted to the move 15 ♔g1.

| 15 | ... | ♕d5 |
| 16 | ♗f2 | ♖d8 |

In the previous odd-numbered game Kasparov went along the well-trodden path, when he preferred 16 ... ♖f8. The queen was well-positioned on d1, but now the threat 17 ... ♗xe5 compels it to abandon its post.

17 ♕e1

The move 17 ♕c2 and the particularly significant improvement 17 ♕a4! is covered in the notes to my game in Belfort. In the event of 17 ♘f4 ♕f7! 18 ♕f3 ♘c4 19 ♔g1 (19 ♖d1 ♗h6) 19 ... cd 20 cd ♘xe5 21 de ♗xe5 22 ♖f1 ♕xf4 23 ♕xf4 ♗xf4 24 ♗xa7 a draw is not far off. Zaitsev found the flashy variation (for future study): 24 ... g5 25 g3 ♗d2 26 ♔g2 ♖a8 27 ♗c5 ♖xa2 28 ♗xe7 ♗b4+ 29 ♔h3 ♗xe7 30 ♖f8+ ♔xf8 stalemate! *(26)*

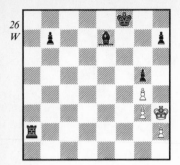

An unexpected and paradoxical conclusion to a sharp opening duel!

| 17 | ... | ♛e4 |
| 18 | g5 | ♛f5 |

The immediate 18 ... ♛g4 looks to be more natural, and after 19 h4 ♞c4 20 ♞g1 (with the aim of transferring the knight to f3) 20 ... ♝xe5! 21 de is imposs- ible due to 21 ... ♞d2+ winning the queen. However, I hadn't intended to defend the pawn. After 19 ♞g3 ♛xg5 20 ♞e4 ♛f4 21 ♞xc5! ♛xh2 22 ♞e6 White has a strong initiative.

19	h4	♞c4
20	♚g1	♛g4
21	a4!	h6!

White is hurrying to add his rook to the defence, and Black hastens to obtain counterplay.

22 ♜a2

22 gh won't do—22 ... ♝xh6 23 ♞g3 cd 24 cd ♜xd4!

| 22 | ... | hg |
| 23 | ♛b1!? *(27)* |

In this way White succeeds in utilizing the weakness of the a2– g8 diagonal, presenting bewilder- ing complications.

23 ... gh

The attempt to bring all of his forces to the defence of the knight on c4 hardly deserves considera- tion: 23 ... cd 24 cd gh 25 ♛b3 ♜c8 26 ♜c2 h3 27 ♝g3! ♛e6 28 gh with advantage to White. White also has the better chances in the event of 23 ... ♚h7 24 hg ♛xg5 25 ♛d3 ♞a5 (25 ... ♞xe5 26 ♛h3+; 25 ... ♞b6 26 ♜b2 ♛xe5 27 a5 ♞c8 28 ♜xb7 cd 29 ♜b5 with the initiative) 26 ♛h3+ ♝h6 27 ♛e6 ♜f8 28 ♜b2.

24	♛b3	♛e6
25	♞f4	♛f7
26	♞xg6	♛xg6

Many commentators recom- mended the continuations 26 ... h3 or 26 ... ♞xe5, but these are connected with a certain degree of risk, for example:

26 ... h3 27 ♞xe7+ ♚h8 28 ♝h4! cd 29 ♜f2 ♛e6 30 ♜f5 d3 31 ♜h5+ ♝h6 32 ♝f6+ ♚h7 33 ♛xb7 ♛b6+ (bad also is 33 ... ♛g4 34 ♞f5+ ♚g6 35 ♜xh6+ ♚xf5 36 ♛h7+ ♚f4 37 ♜h4 d2 38 ♜xg4+ ♚xg4 39 ♛xh3+ ♚f4 40 ♛f3 mate) 34 ♛xb6 ab 35 ♝g5 d2 36 ♜xh6+ ♚g7 37 ♞f5+ ♚g8 38 ♝xd2 ♜xd2 39

♖xh3 with a winning position for White;

26 ... ♘xe5 27 ♕xf7+ ♘xf7 28 ♘xe7+ ♔h7 29 ♘f5 ♗f6 (29 ... cd 30 ♘xg7 d3 31 ♗d4; 30 ... ♔xg7 31 ♗d4+ ♔g6 32 ♗xa7) 30 dc ♖d1+ 31 ♔h2 ♗e5+ 32 ♔h3 ♘g5+ 33 ♔xh4 ♘e4 34 ♖e2 ♖h1+ 35 ♔g4 ♘xf2+ 36 ♖xf2 ♗xc3 37 ♔g5, and Black loses ground in the ending.

27 ♕xc4+ ♔h8

The forces of both sides are exhausted and now the most solid would be 27 ... ♔h7 28 ♕e2 h3 29 ♕c2. Who would have thought that the game would last for yet another 50 moves!?

28 ♖b2

Nothing is promised by 28 ♗xh4 ♕b1+ 29 ♔h2 cd 30 cd ♖xd4, but 28 ♕e2 deserves attention.

28 ... cd

29 cd ♕g4

... h4–h3 was possible on this or the preceding move, but then also the game would turn out to White's advantage: 29 ... h3 30 g3 ♕f5 31 ♔h2 b6 32 ♕e2 ♗h6 33 ♖b3 ♖f8 34 ♗g1. In any event, this would have been more accurate than the text move.

30 ♕f7!*(28)*

30 ... ♖xd4

Black's king is in danger, but by continuing 30 ... ♗h6 (30 ... h3 31 ♕f3! ♖xd4 32 ♗xd4 ♕xd4+ 33 ♖f2 with the better chances for White; 30 ... ♖f8 is also insufficient—31 ♕xe7) he would retain a solid position; on 31 ♕f3 the thrust 31 ... ♖xd4! is now fully appropriate—32 ♗xd4 ♕xd4+ 33 ♖f2 ♗e3, and matters end in perpetual check. Serious risk is attached to the immediate exchange sacrifice.

31 ♗xd4 ♕xd4+

The correct order of moves is 31 ... ♕d1+ 32 ♔h2 ♕xd4 33 ♕h5+ ♔g8 34 ♖e2 ♕f4+ 35 ♔g1 ♕c1+ 36 ♔f2 ♕f4+ 37 ♕f3 ♕d4+ 38 ♔f1 ♗xe5, with an imminent draw.

32 ♖f2 ♕xe5

33 ♖f5 ♕e1+

34 ♖f1 ♕e5*(29)*

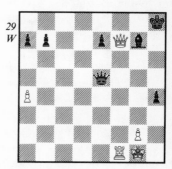

35 ♔h1?

In reply to this precautionary king move, Black advances his b-pawn one square, and upon the appearance of the white queen on f4, defends the h4 pawn with his own queen to h5. In the event of the immediate 35 ♕f4! this deviation would not now be possible in view of ♕b8+, ♕xb7, and the white queen successfully returns to the kingside. The exchange on f4 now would lead to a lost endgame for Black: 35 ... ♕xf4 36 ♖xf4 ♗f6 37 ♖c4 ♔g7 38 ♖c7 b6 39 ♔f1 etc. However, White hasn't yet lost the chance of victory.

| 35 | ... | b6 |
| 36 | ♕f4 | ♕h5 |

Capturing the pawn now leads to nothing: 37 ♕b8+ ♔h7 38 ♕xa7, and the white queen has moved away from the centre of things. Then, after 38 ... ♕e2 Black has the initiative, sufficient for a draw. But can White otherwise exploit the clumsy placing of Black's queen on the outside file?

| 37 | ♕f5? | |

It looks as though 37 ♖f3! here would have decided the issue. It's a pity that, over the course of the last three moves I could have twice prevailed.

37	...	♕e2
38	♖c1	♗f6
39	♕g6	♕e6
40	♖d1	♕c8
41	♖f1	

41 ♖d5? doesn't work: 41 ... ♕c1+ 42 ♔h2 ♗e5+! 43 ♖xe5 ♕f4+ and 44 ... ♕xe5.

| 41 | ... | ♕d7 |
| 42 | ♕h5+ | |

Again, the text move is worthy of reproach. It isn't good to release the king from his incarceration before time. However, after 42 ♖f4 ♕d5 43 ♔h2 e5 44 ♕f5 ♔g7 45 ♔h3 ♕d3+ 46 ♔g4 (46

♖f3 ♕e1 47 ♔g4 h3! 48 ♖xh3 ♕d1+) 46 ... ♕e2+, or 42 ♖f5 ♕d1+ 43 ♔h2 ♕d6+ 44 ♔h3 ♕d3+ 45 ♔f4 ♕e2+ a drawn result is imminent (46 ♔f4?? e5+).

42	...	♔g7
43	♖f4	♕d2
44	♖g4+	♔f8
45	♕f5	♕c1+
46	♔h2	♕c7+
47	♕f4	

47 ♔h3 is also harmless for Black: 47 ... ♕c1 48 ♖f4 ♔g7 (48 ... ♕h1+ is bad because of 49 ♔g4 ♕xg2+ 50 ♔h5 ♕g8 51 ♕c8+ ♔f7 52 ♕xg8+ ♔xg8 53 ♔g6) 49 ♔g4 ♕d1+ 50 ♖f3 h3! 51 gh ♕xa4 with a draw.

| 47 | ... | ♕xf4 |
| 48 | ♖xf4 | ♔e8 |

The probability of a peaceful result grows after the exchange of queens, but, as before, accurate play is demanded from Black.

49	♔g1	a6
50	♔f2	♔d7
51	♔e2	♔d6
52	♔d3	♔c5
53	♖c4+	♔d5
54	♖c7	

White's plan to fortify his position is lacking in as far as after 54 ... ♔d6 55 ♖a7 ♔c6, 56 ♖xa6?? is not possible because of 56 ... ♔b7 trapping the rook. The only possibility would have been to play for zugzwang: 56 ♔e4 ♗g5 57 ♔e5 ♗f6+ 58 ♔f5 a5 59 ♔e4 ♔c5 60 ♖a6. But in this case Black could revert to the variation played in the game, or implement the exchange of the a4 and b6 pawns.

54	...	a5
55	Rc4	e5
56	Rg4	Be7
57	Rg7	e4+
58	Ke3	Bc5+
59	Ke2	Bd4
60	Rg5+	Kc4
61	Rf5	

Or 61 Rg4 b5 62 ab a4 with a draw.

| 61 | ... | Kc3! |

61 ... Kb3 is highly dangerous for Black—62 Rf4 Bc5 63 Rxe4 Bb4 64 Rxh4.

| 62 | Rh5 | |

Or 62 Rf4 b5 63 ab a4 64 Rf8 Kb4!

62	...	Kc4
63	Rf5	Kc3
64	Rg5	Kc4
65	Rh5	Bf6!

One inaccurate move, 65 ... Kc3?, and White achieves his aim: 66 Rxh4 b5 67 ab a4 68 Rxe4 a3 69 Re6 a2 70 Ra6—the two passed pawns will 'break' the bishop.

| 66 | Rh6 | |

A draw results also after 66 Ke3 Kb3 67 Rb5+ Kxa4 68 Rxb6 Bc3 69 Ke4 Bb4 threatening ... Kb3.

66	...	Bd4
67	Rh5	Bf6
68	Rh6	Bd4
69	Rxh4	b5
70	ab	a4
71	Rxe4	a3
72	b6	a2
73	Rxd4+	

After 73 b7 a1(Q) 74 b8(Q) Qa2+ 75 Kf3 Qf2+ the last white pawn goes with check.

73	...	Kxd4
74	b7	a1(Q)
75	b8(Q)	

A queen ending arises with an extra pawn for White. Possibly with a different configuration of pieces he would retain winning chances, but in the present situation Black succeeds in forcing the draw.

75	...	Qa6+
76	Kf2	Qf6+
77	Kg1	Ke4
78	Qb4+	

Or 78 Qb7+ Kf4 79 Qf3+ Kg5 80 Qxf6+ Kxf6 81 Kh2 Kg6!

78	...	Kf5
79	Qe1	Qd4+

Draw agreed.

Karpov–Kasparov
Game 9,
World Championship 4
Seville 1987

The preceding two games continued the discourse on the manoeuvre of Black's queen to d6, provoking the advance e4–e5. Now Kasparov places his queen differently, but it doesn't solve the problems of this harmless position.

1	d4	Nf6
2	c4	g6
3	Nc3	d5
4	cd	Nxd5
5	e4	Nxc3
6	bc	Bg7
7	Bc4	c5
8	Ne2	

The development of the bishop on c4 and the knight on e2 determines the so-called main variation of the Grünfeld Defence. The appearance of the knight on f3 does not, in so many words, promise White any special achievements. However, one interesting opening coup springs to mind.

McCambridge–Hjartarson (Grindavik 1984): 7 ♘f3 c5 8 ♖b1 0-0 9 ♗e2 ♘c6. Correct is 9 ... cd 10 cd ♕a5+. The appearance of the knight on c6 has since been cast into doubt. 10 d5 ♘e5 11 ♘xe5 ♗xe5 12 ♕d2 e6 13 f4 ♗h8 14 c4 ♖e8 15 e5 f6 16 f5!! *(30)* A pretty position! 16 ... gf. The other capture is not better either: 16 ... ed 17 e6! d4 18 g4 b6 19 ♗f3 ♖b8 20 ♕g2! ♕c7 21 0-0 g5 22 ♗d5 ♕e7 23 h4! h6 24 hg hg 25 ♖b3 ♗b7 26 ♖h3 ♗g7 27 ♖h2! ♖ed8 28 ♕h3 etc. (Vaiser–Pribyl, Sochi 1984). 17 ♖b3 ♖e7 18 d6 ♖g7 19 ef ♕xf6 20 ♗b2 e5 21 ♗xe5! ♕xe5 22 ♖e3 ♕e6. On 22 ... ♕a1+ 23 ♔f2 ♕xh1 then 24 ♖e8+ decides: 24 ... ♔f7 25 ♗h5+ ♖g6 26 ♖e7+ ♔f6 27 ♕c3+ ♔g5 28 ♕g3+ ♔f6 29 ♗xg6 ♕c1 30 ♕h4+ ♕g5 31

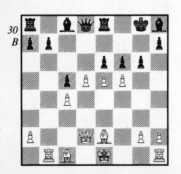

♖f7+ ♔xg6 32 ♕xh7 mate. 23 ♖xe6 ♗xe6 24 ♕e3! ♖e8 25 ♕xc5 ♖xg2 26 d7 ♖xe2+ 27 ♔xe2 ♗xd7+ 28 ♔d2 ♗e6 29 ♕c7, and White won.

8	...	♘c6
9	♗e3	0-0
10	0-0	♗g4
11	f3	♘a5
12	♗xf7+	

The traditional continuation here is 12 ♗d3 (the moves 12 ♖c1 and 12 ♗d5 were sent to the archives by theory long ago). Let's look at a few modern examples, which go to show that the retreat of the bishop is no more dangerous for Black than exchanging it.

Events turn out well in this variation for Balashov. Balashov–Sibarevic (Lugano 1988): 12 ♗d3 cd 13 cd ♗e6 14 ♖c1. The once fashionable attack of Sokolsky— 14 d5 ♗xa1 15 ♕xa1 f6—is not now met in practice. Having the extra material, Black defends easily. 14 ... ♗xa2 15 ♕a4. More accurate than the immediate 15 d5. 15 ... ♗e6 16 d5 ♗d7 17 ♕b4 b5 18 ♖fd1 ♗e5 19 ♘c5 ♘b7 20 ♗xe7 ♕b6+ 21 ♔h1 a5 22 ♕d2 ♖fc8 23 f4 ♗g7? It would follow to place the bishop on d6. 24 e5 b4 25 ♗c4 b3 26 ♗a3! with a winning position.

Balashov–Hansen (Malmo 1987/8). This time the black b-pawn advances one square. 17 ... b6 18 f4 e6. The immediate 18 ... e5 is interesting: 19 f5 (19 ♗a6 straight away is better) 19 ... ♖e8 20 ♗a6 ♗f8 21 ♕c3 b5! 22 ♖b1

♘c4 23 ♗xb5 ♗xb5 24 ♖xb5 ♖c8, and Black seizes the initiative (Vaiser–Gavrikov, USSR 1988). 19 d6 e5 20 f5 ♖c8 21 ♘c3 ♗c6 22 ♘b5 ♕d7 23 f6! with advantage to White.

Two significant games were played by Kasparov in the 55th USSR Championship (Moscow 1988). The first 16½ moves are the same as those in Balashov's game, when Black played here **17 ... e6***(31)*.

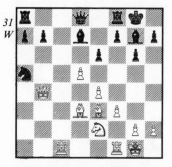

This position arose 35 years ago in the game Geller–Lilienthal (21st USSR Championship 1954): 18 de ♗xe6 19 ♖fd1 b6 20 ♗a6 ♕h4 21 ♘d4 and now, by continuing 21 ... ♗c8 22 ♗b5 ♗e5 23 g3 ♕f6 24 f4 ♗d6 25 ♕a4 ♗g4, Black retains the extra pawn in a solid position. 18 d6 gives White nothing, for example 18 ... ♘c6 ♕xb7 ♖b8 20 ♕c7 ♖b3! 21 ♖fd1 ♘e5 with an initiative for Black (Razuvayev–Lputyan, Sochi 1987).

Subsequently **18 ♘c3** became the usual continuation. In the game **Belyavsky–Kasparov** there followed **18 ... ed** (also interesting is 18 ... b6 19 f4 ed 20 ♘xd5 ♗e6

21 ♖fd1 ♗xd5 22 ♗b5 ♕f6 23 ♖xd5 ♖ac8 24 ♖xc8 ♖xc8 25 e5 ♕e6 26 ♕e4 ♗f8 27 ♗d7 ♖c4 28 ♕d3 ♕e7 29 e6 Naumkin–Krasenkov, Vilnius 1988) **19 ed ♖e8 20 ♗f2 ♗f8.**

The game Yusupov–Smejkal (Munich 1988) concluded quickly: **20 ... b5 21 ♖fd1 ♘c4 22 ♗xc4 a5 23 ♕b3 bc 24 ♕xc4 ♖c8 25 ♕d3 Draw agreed.**

Returning to Belyavsky–Kasparov: **21 ♕b2 ♗g7 22 ♕b4 ♗f8 23 ♕b2 Draw agreed.**

And now the other game, **Yusupov–Kasparov: 18 ♖fd1** (an attempt to improve play in comparison with 18 ♘c3) **18 ... ed 19 ed ♖e8 20 ♗f2 b5!** This looks to be seriously weakening, but Black ensures the quickest route to the centre for his knight (via c4), where it returns to the main action.

21 ♘d4 ♘c4 22 ♘c6!? Exchanging the annoying knight on c4 re-establishes the material balance, but White could hardly count on the advantage. Yusupov tries to elicit the maximum from the position.

22 ... ♗xc6 23 dc ♘b2! *(32)*

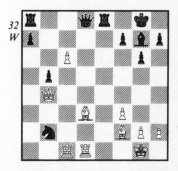

24 ♗xb5 ♘xd1 25 c7 ♕d5! 26 ♗xe8 ♘xf2 27 c8(♕) ♖xc8 28 ♖xc8 ♘h3+ 29 gh. In the event of 29 ♔f1 Black delivers mate with a small part of his forces: 29 ... ♕d3+ 30 ♔e1 ♕e3+ 31 ♔d1 ♘f2+ 32 ♔c2 ♕d3+ 33 ♔c1 ♕d1 mate.

29 ... ♕d1+ 30 ♔g2 ♕e2+ 31 ♔g1 Draw agreed. The stormy skirmish ends in perpetual check.

12	**...**	**♖xf7**
13	**fg**	**♖xf1+**
14	**♔xf1**	**cd**

This move may be considered part of theory; it had also been encountered before our match.

15	**cd**	**♕b6**
16	**♔g1**	**♕e6**
17	**♕d3!**	

An idea of Zaitsev: White returns the pawn, retaining all of his positional plus. In the game Alfayevsky–Verner (corr. 1984) after 17 ♘g3 ♖d8 18 ♖c1 ♕b6 19 ♘e2 ♘c6 20 ♖b1 ♘xd4! 21 ♖xb6 ♘f3+ 22 ♔f2 ♖xd1 23 ♖xb7 ♘xh2 24 g5 ♘g4+ the players were reconciled to perpetual check.

17	**...**	**♕xg4**

White now obtains a significant advantage. The correct way comprises the transfer of the queen to c4 with the aim of exchanging the strongest piece (game 11).

18	**♖f1**	**♖c8**

18 ... ♖f8 is worse due to 19 ♖xf8+ ♗xf8 20 d5 b6 21 ♘d4!

19	**h3**	**♕d7**
20	**d5**	**♘c4**
21	**♗d4**	

More accurate than 21 ♘d4

♘xe3 22 ♕xe3 ♖c4 23 ♘e6 ♕xe6 24 de ♗xd4 25 ♕xd4 ♖xd4 26 ♖f7 ♖xe4 27 ♖xe7 b5 with equality, but 21 ♗xa7 b6 22 ♗xb8!? is worthy of consideration.

21	**...**	**e5**

On 21 ... ♘e5 22 ♕b3 or 22 ♗xe5 ♗xe5 23 ♘d4 ♗xd4 24 ♕xd4 b6 25 e5 ♕c7 26 ♕g4!

22	**de**	**♕xe6**
23	**♗xg7**	**♔xg7**
24	**♘f4**	**♕d6**
25	**♕c3+**	**♔h6** *(33)*

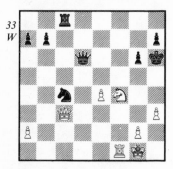

33
W

The only move. The game would effectively be over after 25 ... ♕e5: 26 ♘e6+ ♔g8 27 ♕xc4! ♖xc4 28 ♖f8 mate. 25 ... ♔g8 isn't good enough either: 26 ♘d5 ♘b6 27 ♘f6+ ♔h8 28 ♕b2 ♕c5+ 29 ♔h2 ♕c3 30 ♘e8 ♘d7 (30 ... ♔g8 31 ♕b5 ♖c5 32 ♘f6+!) 31 ♕xc3 ♖xc3 32 ♖f7 ♖d3 (32 ... ♖c8 33 ♘d6) 33 e5 ♔g8 34 e6, and White wins.

26	**♘d5**	

The position of Black's king is unenviable and it would follow to try to get to it in a different way— 26 ♘d3!—and the threat ♘d3–f2–g4+ is quite dangerous.

26	**...**	**♕e5**

27 ♕d3

27 ♕e1 would maintain the tension. Many commentators recommended 27 ♕b4 here, but, as Zaitzev pointed out, it isn't exactly dangerous for Black: 27 ... ♕xe4! 28 ♘f6 a5! 29 ♕b5 (29 ♕c3 ♕e3+ or 29 ♕a4 ♕d4+ 30 ♔h1 ♖f8 31 ♘g4+ ♔g7 with advantage to Black) 29 ... ♕d4+ 30 ♖f2 (in the event of 30 ♔h1 ♘e3 31 ♕xb7 ♘xf1 32 ♘g4+ the black king goes intrepidly forward: 32 ... ♔g5 33 ♕e7+ ♔f4 34 ♕f7+ ♔g3 35 ♕xf1 h5 36 ♕f3+ ♔h4 37 g3+ ♔xh3 38 ♘f2+ ♕xf2! 39 ♕xf2 ♖c1+ winning) 30 ... ♕a1+ 31 ♖f1 ♕d4+ 32 ♖f2 ♕a1+ 33 ♔h2 ♕e5+, and the struggle may end with perpetual check.

27	...	♔g7
28	♘f6	♕d6
29	♕c3	♕e5
30	♕d3	♕d6
31	♕c3	♕e5
32	♕b3	♖c7
33	♕d3	♖f7
34	♕xc4	♖xf6
35	♖d1	b5

The position is drawn, but Black is playing aggressively. Simplest would be 35 ... ♖e6 36 ♖d7+ ♖e7 37 ♖xe7+ ♕xe7 38 ♕d4+ ♔f7 39 ♕xa7 ♕xe4.

36	♖d7+	♔h6
37	♕e2	♕c5+
38	♔h2	♕e5+
39	g3	♕c3
40	♔g2	♕c4
41	♕e3+	g5
42	♖d2	♕f1+
43	♔h2	♕f3

The sealed move. Again, as also in the seventh game, I persistently find chances of a victory, going into the endgame a pawn to the good, but, alas, a drawn result is unavoidable.

44	♕d4	♖e6
45	e5	♕f5
46	♖e2	a5

As the following variation shows, the position is still far from simple: 46 ... ♕f7 47 ♖c2 ♕f5 48 ♖c5 ♕f3 (48 ... ♕b1 49 ♕f2 ♔g6 50 ♖c7) 49 ♕d2 ♕e4 50 ♕f2 ♔g6 51 ♖c7, and White has good chances of a win.

47	♕d5	b4
48	♕xa5	♕d3
49	♖g2	♕d4
50	♕a8	♕xe5
51	♕f8+	♔g6
52	♕xb4	h5
53	h4	gh
54	♕xh4	♖d6
55	♕c4	♖d4
56	♕c6+	♔g7
57	♕b7+	♔h6
58	♕c6+	♔g7
59	♖c2	♖h4+
60	♔g2	♕e4+
61	♕xe4	♖xe4
62	♖c7+	♔g6
63	♖a7	♖e3
64	♔h3	♖c3
65	♖a8	♖c4
66	a4	♔g5
67	a5	♖a4
68	a6	♔h6
69	♔g2	♖a3
70	♔f2	♔g7

Draw agreed.

Karpov–Kasparov
Game 11,
World Championship 4
Seville 1987

If at the first try and, possibly, the second, Kasparov was surprised by my choice of variation with ♗xf7+, then now, encountering it for the fourth time, he could be prepared in the best manner. As White succeeds in obtaining a tangible advantage, a lot is said about the merit of his choice. What a pity that the fate of the game is decided by a gross blunder.

1	d4	♘f6
2	c4	g6
3	♘c3	d5
4	cd	♘xd5
5	e4	♘xc3
6	bc	♗g7
7	♗c4	c5
8	♘e2	♘c6
9	♗e3	0-0
10	0-0	♗g4
11	f3	♘a5
12	♗xf7+	♖xf7
13	fg	♖xf1+
14	♔xf1	♕d6
15	♔g1	

In the fifth and seventh games, as you will remember, I continued 15 e5, and the king retreated to g1 later. Now, as in the ninth game, White is prepared to return the pawn in order to obtain a strong centre.

15	...	♕e6
16	♕d3	♕c4

This time Kasparov refrains from capturing on g4, and leads the game into the ending. In the game Chernin–Malishauskas, which was being played at the same time as my match (Lvov 1987), Black was in no hurry to exchange queens and chose 16 ... cd 17 cd ♖d8. After 18 g5 ♘c4 19 ♗f2 b5 20 a4 ba 21 ♘f4 ♕f7 22 ♘d5 ♖f8 23 ♗g3 ♘b6 (but not 23 ... ♘b2 24 ♕c3 a3 25 h3 and the further ♗e5 with advantage) 24 h4 (24 ♘xb6 ♕b3!) 24 ... ♘xd5 25 ed ♕xd5 the chances are on the side of equality.

Gurevich pointed out that instead of 18 g5, 18 h3 is better, and now in the event of the exchange of queens by 18 ... ♕c4 19 ♕xc4 ♘xc4 20 ♗f2 e5 21 d5 ♗h6 22 a4 b6 23 h4 ♗d2 24 ♖a2 ♗a5 25 ♖c2 White maintains the advantage. Interestingly, such a configuration of pieces also arose in the text game.

17	♕xc4	

White can hardly avoid the exchange of queens: 17 ♕d2 cd 18 cd ♕a6!

17	...	♘xc4
18	♗f2	

Grandmaster Seirawan, who took the present variation into his armoury, here twice chose 18 ♗g5. Both games are worthy of examination.

Seirawan–Lputyan (St John 1988): 18 ... h6 19 ♗xe7 cd (an inaccuracy; 19 ... ♖e8 leads to unclear play in Lputyan's opinion: 20 ♗xc5 b6 21 ♗xb6 ab 22 e5) 20 cd ♖e8 21 ♖c1 ♘a5 22 ♖c7 ♘c6 23 ♗c5 ♖xe4 24 ♔f2 ♗xd4+ 25 ♘xd4 ♘xd4 26 ♖xb7

♘c6 27 h3 ♖a4 28 a3. White has a healthy extra pawn, which he eventually promoted.

Seirawan–Hort (Lugano 1988): 18 ... cd (this is a novelty in the current position) 19 cd e5 20 ♖c1 b5 21 de ♗xe5 22 ♖d1 ♖c8 23 ♗f4 ♗g7 24 ♖d5 a6 25 ♔f2 ♖e8 26 ♔f3 ♔f7 27 h4, and White again has an extra pawn, although this time Black succeeded in holding his own.

The defeat by Seirawan made such a strong impression on Lputyan that, at his earliest opportunity he chose the variation as White. In the game Lputyan–Hansen (Dortmund 1988) all the moves are repeated right up to 18 ♗g5. Here Black played the immediate 18 ... e5. There subsequently followed 19 d5 b5 20 ♖b1 ♖b8 21 ♔f2 (21 a4! is more accurate) 21 ... a5 22 ♘c1 h6 (22 ... ♘a3 23 ♖b3 b4 24 cb cb 25 d6) 23 ♗e3 ♘xe3. According to Lputyan, 23 ... ♘d6 would lead to a level game (23 ... ♖f8+ 24 ♔e2 ♘xe3 25 ♔xe3 ♖f1 26 ♖a1! preparing 27 ♘b3!): 24 ♔f3 ♖f8+ 25 ♔e2 c4 26 ♔e1 ♘xe4 27 ♖xb5 ♘xc3 28 ♖xa5 ♖d8. 24 ♔xe3 c4 25 ♘e2 ♗f8 26 ♘g1 ♗c5+ 27 ♔e2 ♗xg1 28 ♖xg1 ♔f7 29 a3 ♔e7 (29 ... b4 would have retained saving chances) 30 ♖b1, and White wins this rook ending.

| 18 | ... | cd |
| 19 | cd | e5 |

After 19 ... b5 20 ♖b1 White's chances are greater.

20	d5	♗h6
21	h4	♗d2
22	♖d1	♗a5 *(34)*

34
W

The majority of commentators condemned this move, giving their preference to 22 ... b5. But in this case also after 23 ♘c1 (or 23 ♘g3 with the further ♘f1–e3), by directing the knight via b3 to c5 White has the more pleasant position.

| 23 | ♖c1 | b5 |

23 ... ♘d6 is bad: 24 ♘g3 ♗b6 25 ♗xb6 ab 26 ♖c7 ♖a4 27 ♖e7 ♘xe4 28 ♘xe4 ♖xe4 29 d6 ♔f8 30 ♖xh7 ♔e8 31 h5, and Black perishes.

24	♖c2	♘d6
25	♘g3	♘c4
26	♘f1	♘d6
27	♘g3	♘c4
28	g5!	♔f7

White's advantage is stabilized. On 28 ... a6 there follows 29 ♘f1 ♘d6 30 ♖c6 ♘xe4 31 ♘g3!

29	♘f1	♘d6
30	♘g3	♘c4
31	♔f1	♔e7
32	♗c5+	

32 ♔e2 ♗b6 33 ♗e1 is not bad either.

| 32 | ... | ♔f7 *(35)* |

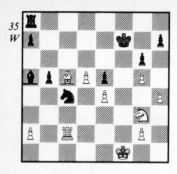

33   ♖f2 + ?

The critical moment of the game, yes possibly also of the whole contest for the Crown. Evidently after 33 ♔e2 Black would hardly succeed in surviving: 33 . . . ♗b6 34 a4 ♗xc5 35 ab ♖b8 36 ♔d3! ♖xb5 (36 . . . a6 37 ♔xc4 ab + 38 ♔b3 ♗d6 39 ♖c6 ♔e7 40 ♘e2 ♖a8 41 ♘c3 ♖a3 + 42 ♔b2, or 40 . . . b4 41 ♘c1 with a winning position) 37 ♔xc4 ♖b7 38 ♘f1 ♗d6 (38 . . . a5 39 ♘d2, 38 . . . ♗b4 39 ♘e3) 39 ♘d2 etc. White has a clear advantage and after 34 . . . a6 35 ♖xc4 ♖c8 36 ♗xb6 ♖xc4 37 ab ab 38 ♔d3.

33   . . .   ♔g7
34   ♖f6   ♗b6 *(36)*

35   ♖c6??

White would maintain better chances by retreating his bishop to f2. But instead of this I made a fatal error. It is sad, but true, that it slipped my attention that the black knight may leap to the edge of the board. Of course, annoying mistakes and miscalculations are found even in matches for the World Championship. There were also quite a lot in Seville; take Kasparov's 37th move in the fifth game or his 50th move in the 23rd. But it's one thing when a miscalculation is made in severe time-trouble, and you make it solving complicated problems set by your opponent, and quite different when a dreadful oversight is made when under no pressure. Seeing that at this moment I had approximately half an hour in reserve, the rook move to c6 may be fully considered as a generous gift to my opponent.

35   . . .   ♘a5

Winning the exchange, and with it the game. The final part contains some subtlety, but it has no influence on the result.

36   ♗xb6   ♘xc6
37   ♗c7   ♖f8 +

37 . . . ♖c8 leads to the goal more quickly: 38 ♗d6 ♖d8.

38   ♔e2

38 ♘f5 + doesn't help: 38 . . . gf 39 dc fe + 40 ♔e2 ♖c8 41 ♗xe5 + ♔g6 42 c7 a5.

38   . . .   ♖f7
39   ♗d6   ♖d7
40   ♗c5   ♘a5
41   ♘f1   ♖c7!

41 . . . ♘c4 would also win, but by more complex means: 42 ♘e3 ♘xe3 43 ♔xe3 ♔f7 44 ♔d3 a5 45

♗b6 ♔e8 46 ♗f2 ♖c7 47 ♗g3
♖c4 48 ♗xe5 ♖a4 49 ♗f6
♖a3+ 50 ♔d4 ♖xa2 51 e5
♖d2+ 52 ♔c5 b4 53 e6 a4 54
♔xb4 ♖xd5 55 ♔xa4 ♖d6 56 e7
♖e6.

42	♗d6	♖c2+	
43	♔d3	♖xa2	
44	♘e3	♔f7	
45	♘g4	♘c4	
46	♘xe5+	♘xe5	
47	♗xe5	b4	
48	♗f6	b3	
49	e5	♖xg2	
50	e6+	♔f8!	

White resigned

Karpov–Kasparov
Belfort 1988

1	d4	♘f6
2	c4	g6
3	♘c3	d5
4	cd	♘xd5
5	e4	♘xc3
6	bc	♗g7
7	♗c4	c5
8	♘e2	♘c6
9	♗e3	0-0
10	0-0	♗g4
11	f3	♘a5
12	♗xf7+	♖xf7
13	fg	♖xf1+
14	♔xf1	♕d6
15	e5	♕d5
16	♗f2	♖d8

As I have already noted, this is more logical than 16 ... ♖f8, as was played in the fifth game of the Seville match. The present position arose in the seventh game, in which I played 17 ♕e1. Then the idea to develop the queen on the d1–a4 diagonal already hung in the air, but the discourse was not continued.

17   ♕a4! *(37)*

A month earlier, in an Amsterdam tournament where this variation was also encountered, I played the new, but not too successful, move 17 ♕c2. It seems that during my preparation for the game with Kasparov the subtle point had escaped me that after 17 ♕a4 b6 18 ♕c2 ♕c4 19 ♕e4! the black knight remains without support. So that this idea would take proper shape I also played it in the Amsterdam encounter (without the inclusion of the moves ♕d1–a4 b7–b6) in order that the position would becom clearer. So now I shall digress a little, in order to show the text of the previous 'argument' of our dispute.

Karpov–Kasparov (Amsterdam 1988):

17	♕c2	♕c4
18	♕b2	♗h6
19	h4	♕f7
20	♔g1	♖f8

21 ♘g3

On 21 ♗g3 then 21 ... ♗e3+ is not bad: 22 ♔h2 ♕e6 23 g5 ♕g4.

21 ... ♘c4

22 ♕e2 ♗xf2+!

Other continuations lead to a White advantage: 22 ... ♗d2 23 ♘e4, 22 ... cd 23 cd ♕xf2+ 24 ♕xf2 ♗e3 25 ♕xe3 ♘xe3 26 ♖c1.

23	♕xf2	♗e3
24	♕xe3	♘xe3
25	dc	♖c8
26	♖b1	♖xc5
27	♖xb7	♘xg4
28	♖b4	

Maybe also 28 ♖xe7 ♖xc3 29 ♘f1 ♖a3 30 e6 ♖xa2 with equality.

28	...	h5
29	♘e4	♖xe5
30	g3	

And here 30 ♔f1 ♘e3+ 31 ♔e2 ♘d5 32 ♖b8+ leads to a level game.

30	...	♔f7
31	♔g2	♔e6
32	♔f3	♔f5!

Black now obtains the better endgame. However, it is sufficiently harmless for me.

33	a4	♖d5
34	♘f2!	

But not 34 ♖b5? ♘e5+ 35 ♔e3 ♖d3+ 36 ♔e2 ♔xe4 37 ♖xe5+ ♔xe5 38 ♔xd3 ♔d5 etc.

34	...	♘xf2
35	♔xf2	♖d3
36	♖c4	e5
37	a5	♖d5
38	a6	♖d6
39	♖a4	♖c6
40	♖a3	♔e4

41	♔e2	♖c4
42	♔f2	♔d3
43	♖a5	♖c6
44	♖xe5	♖f6+
45	♔g2	♔xc3
46	♖e7	♖xa6
47	♖g7	♔d4
48	♔h3	♔e5
49	♔g2	♖a2+
50	♔f3	♖a3+
51	♔g2	♔f6
52	♖c7	a5
53	♖c6+	♔f5
54	♖c5+	♔e4
55	♖g5	♖a2+
56	♔h3	a4
57	♖xg6	a3
58	♖a6	

Draw agreed

Let's return to the Belfort game.

17 ... b6

18 ♕c2! ♖f8

Thus on 18 ... ♕c4 there would follow 19 ♕e4 with an advantageous consolidation of forces. But there is also another feature arising as a consequence of the move 17 ... b6: Black must now constantly be aware of the exchange d4xc5.

19 ♔g1

The pin on the f-file should be broken quickly. In the game **Lputyan–Dzhandzhava (Simferopol 1988)**, which took place later, after **18 ... ♖c8 19 ♕d1 ♖d8 20 ♕c1 ♖f8** a position arose in which, in contrast to my game with Kasparov, the white queen finds itself on c1. This is not the only difference as the move played now, **21 h3** (instead of the correct 21 ♔g1), is a serious inaccuracy.

After **21 ... ♕f7 22 ♕e1 ♗h6 23
♘g3 ♘c4 24 e6 ♕g7 25 ♘e4 ♗e3
26 ♕e2 b5 27 ♔g1 ♗xf2+ 28
♘xf2 cd** Black regains the pawn
and seizes the initiative. The game
did not last very long. **29 cd ♕xd4
30 ♖c1 g5 31 ♖c2 ♘e3 32 ♖d2
♕a1+ 33 ♘d1 ♖f1+ 34 ♔h2
♕e5+ 35 g3 ♕e4 36 ♖d8+ ♔g7
37 ♕b2+ ♔h6 White resigned.**

19 ...   ♕c4

20 ♕d2

White continues to play on the
restricted mobility of the bishop.
In the event of 20 ♕e4 the replies
20 ... ♗h6 and particularly 20 ...
♘c6!? should be considered, after
which the capture on e5 is threatened, and 21 ♕xc6 ♕xe2 naturally gives no cause for enthusiasm
on White's part.

20 ...   ♕e6

It would not be advantageous
to play 20 ... ♕f7. After 21 ♘g3
everything turns out well for
White: the knight is transferred to
e4 and the queen to e2. 20 ...
♗h6 21 ♕xh6 ♕xe2 doesn't ease
Black's difficulties either, in view
of 22 ♕e3.

21 h3   ♘c4

22 ♕g5! *(38)*

One of the main motifs of the
game. Now, besides ♘e2–f4.
♗f2–h4 is also a threat.

22 ...   h6

22 ... ♗f6 doesn't work, if only
because of 23 ef (23 ♘f4 is also
strong) 23 ... ef 24 ♘f4.

23 ♕c1   ♕f7

With the object of creating
counterplay. It would possibly
also be good to play 23 ... b5 with
the idea of, say, 24 ♘f4 ♕f7 25
♘d3 b4!?, although 25 ♗g3
would retain White's advantage.
23 ... ♕d5 wouldn't achieve its
aim due to 24 ♕c2!, though 23 ...
h5!? is interesting.

24 ♗g3   g5

This move was severely criti-
cized by many commentators.
But, as far as I remember, no
serious alternative was suggested
in return. For example, 24 ♕d5
was recommended, but then 25
♘f4 ♕e4 26 ♘e6 leads to a highly
dangerous position for Black.
Three variations arise here; let's
examine them:

(a) 26 ... ♖c8 27 ♕b1! ♕e3+
28 ♗f2 ♕xc3 29 ♕xg6 ♕xa1+
30 ♔h2 with mate unavoidable.

(b) 26 ... ♘e3 27 ♕d2 cd 28 cd
(28 ♘xf8 dc 29 ♕e2 is less clear)
28 ... ♖c8 29 ♖e1 ♖c2 30 ♖xe3
♕c6 31 d5 is also bad for Black.
One could try to drive the queen
to e2 by playing 27 ... ♘c4 28
♕e1 ♘e3 29 ♕e2 cd. Now 30 cd
♖c8 gives Black strong counterplay, but 30 ♘xf8 ♗xf8 (30 ... d3
31 ♕f2) 31 ♕f3! ♕d3 32 cd ♕xd4
33 ♖e1 fully clarifies the situation
on the board, since 33 ... ♘c2+
34 ♗f2 ♘xe1 doesn't hold

because of the intermediate 35 ♕b3+.

(c) 26 ... cd 27 ♘xf8 ♘e3 28 ♕d2 dc 29 ♕e2 ♗xf8 30 ♕f3 with a big advantage to White.

25	♕c2	♕d5
26	♗f2	b5
27	♘g3	♖f7

A necessary defensive move. On 27 ... b4, 28 ♘f5 is unpleasant, and if 28 ... ♖f7, then 29 e6 ♕xe6 30 ♖e1 ♕d7 31 cb.

28 ♖e1

One might choose to halt queenside counterplay with the help of 28 ♖c1.

28	...	b4
29	♕g6	♔f8

29 ... bc would lose immediately—30 ♘f5 ♔f8 31 e6 ♖xf5 32 gf ♘d6 33 dc.

30 ♘e4

30 ♘f5 e6 31 ♘xh6 ♖f4 32 ♕xg5 or 32 ♕h7 is also strong.

30	...	♖xf2

The exchange sacrifice does nothing to rectify the situation. Subsequently, only elementary accuracy is demanded of White.

31	♔xf2	bc
32	♕f5+	♔g8
33	♕c8+	♔h7
34	♕xc5	♕f7+
35	♔g1	c2
36	♘g3	♗f8
37	♘f5	♔g8
38	♖c1	

Black resigned

His kingside pieces cannot break free.

The reader may be surprised that so much attention has been devoted to the move ♗xf7+, as though the destiny of the whole Grünfeld Defence depends on this bishop move. But that may be the case if this variation continues to be as fashionable as in my World Championship battles with Kasparov, and in subsequent games. Moreover, I have no doubt that the opening dual will be continued.

2 The Nimzo–Indian Defence

Kasparov–Karpov
Game 7,
World Championship 2
Moscow 1985

The Nimzo–Indian · Defence was encountered eight times in my four matches with Kasparov (six times in the second and twice in the third), much less often than the Queen's Indian and the Grünfeld. I don't have the most pleasant memories of the 'Nimzowitsch'. However, my chagrin, which is pursued through a number of games, wasn't always connected with the opening (it wasn't by chance that Kasparov preferred the English Opening as White in the fourth match). A feature of our matches is comprised not so much of the logic of a contest, but of most unusual blunders by the players. This aspect of the matter will also be given fundamental consideration.

1	d4	♘f6
2	c4	e6
3	♘c3	♗b4

This bishop move defines the Nimzo–Indian Defence, while the move ... b7–b6 is the Queen's Indian Defence, which is looked at later. What name do you give to the opening which arises from some hybrid of the two defences? It really is a difficult problem, but I go by established tradition: as soon as the move ... ♗f8–b4 is played then this signifies the Nimzo–Indian Defence.

| 4 | ♘f3 | 0-0 |
| 5 | ♗g5 | d6 |

As the opening didn't turn out too well for me in the current game, I gave preference to the move 5 ... c5 in game 11, immediately challenging White's centre. This game is discussed later.

| 6 | e3 | ♘bd7 |
| 7 | ♕c2 | b6 |

The above-mentioned blend of two openings now arises. 7 ... e5 is the more well-known move, while 7 ... ♕e8 also deserves attention.

| 8 | ♗d3 | ♗xc3+ |

This exchange is unavoidable with Black's chosen pawn structure.

| 9 | bc | |

White creates a powerful pawn centre. The continuation 9 ♕xc3 ♗b7 10 0-0 h6 11 ♗h4 c5 allows Black to obtain fully equal chances.

| 9 | ... | h6 |
| 10 | ♗h4 | ♗b7 *(39)* |

While studying the Queen's Indian Defence below, you will surely recall this position, the difference being that in the games in which the Queen's Indian Defence is played, the moves ... d7–d6 and ... ♘b8–d7 are played slightly later. Instead of these Black immediately operates in the centre: ... g7–g5, ... ♘f6–e4 (or ... ♘h5). The relevant material will be given in the narrative to the Queen's Indian games. In such a way, although the name of the opening is different, we return to the Nimzo–Indian Defence. A somewhat different order of moves in the text game allows White to seize the initiative.

11 ♘d2!

In the event of 11 0-0 g5 12 ♗g3 ♘h5 Black realizes his intention, achieving a satisfactory game. Therefore White doesn't hurry to castle: the circumstance of the rook remaining on h1 is to White's advantage. It's true that the retreat of the knight to d2 offers a pawn, but it would be dangerous to take it: 11 ... ♗xg2 12 ♖g1 ♗b7, and now White has two possibilities: 13 ♘e4 ♗xe4 14 ♗xe4 c5 (14 ... ♖c8 15 ♗c6 ♘b8 16 ♗b7) 15 f4 ♔h8 16 ♕g2 ♖g8 17 ♗xa8 ♕xa8 18 ♕xa8 ♖xa8; or 13 0-0-0 b5!? 14 f4 (14 cb a6) 14 ... bc 15 ♘xc4, threatening e4, ♕g2, in which case ♘e5 is also highly unpleasant. There is yet one more effective variation: 13 f4 e5 14 de de 15 0-0-0 ef 16 ♗f5 ♕e7 17 ♗xd7 ♕a3+ 18 ♔b1

♘xd7 19 ♘b3 ♘c5? 20 ♖xg7+! with mate.

11 ... g5

11 ... e5 may be more solid.

12 ♗g3 ♘h5

But here the pawn capture should be given more serious consideration. 12 ... ♗xg2 13 ♖g1 ♗b7 14 f4 ♔h8, followed by:

(a) 15 h4 gf (15 ... g4) 16 ♗xf4 ♘h5;

(b) 15 e4 gf 16 ♗xf4 ♖g8 (16 ... ♘g8 loses after 17 0-0-0 e5 18 ♗e3 f6 19 ♘f3 ♖f7 20 ♘h4 ♘f8 21 ♕g2) 17 0-0-0 ♘h5 18 ♗xh6 (or 18 ♖xg8+ ♕xg8 19 ♗xh6 ♕g2) 18 ... ♕f6 with sharp play;

(c) 15 fg hg 16 h4 ♘g4 (16 ... ♘h5? 17 ♕d1) 17 ♗e4 ♗xe4 18 ♘xe4 f5 19 ♘xg5 ♕f6 with mutual chances.

13 ♕d1

An original move: the queen doesn't stand badly on the b1–h7 diagonal, but it can afford this tempo to strengthen its position. In the case of 13 0-0-0 ♗xg2 14 ♖hg1 ♗h3 15 f4 the situation is not so clear, but apparently unpleasant for Black would be 13 f3 ♘xg3 14 hg ♔g7 15 g4 c5 16 ♘f1 and ♘g3.

13 ... ♘g7

I decided to keep the knight in order to keep the hostile queen away from h5. However, after 13 ... ♘xg3 14 hg ♔g7 15 ♕h5 (15 f3 f5!) 15 ... ♖h8 16 e4 ♘f6 17 ♕e2 e5 is double-edged, according to Kasparov. So it would have followed to deprive White of the advantage of the two bishops.

14	h4	f5
15	hg	hg
16	f3	♕e7
17	♕b3	

As nothing much is promised on the kingside, the queen alters course. But best of all, to my mind, would be to return the queen to c2.

17	...	♔f7
18	0-0-0	♖h8 *(40)*

40
W

It was necessary here to prevent the break c4–c5. After 18 ... c5 19 ♕c2 ♖h8 and ... ♖ag8 Black's position is sufficiently solid.

19	c5!	dc
20	♘c4	

White gives up a pawn without the immediate intention of regaining it. Moreover, after 20 · ♗xc7 ♖ac8 or 20 ... cd 21 ed ♘c5! 22 dc ♕xc7 23 cb ab 24 ♘c4 ♖xh1 25 ♖xh1 ♗d5 26 ♕xb6 ♕f4+ 27 ♘d2 ♖xa2 Black has the advantage.

20 e4 looks stronger: 20 ... f4 21 ♗f2 ♖ad8 (preparing to meet 22 e5 with 22 ... ♘xe5 23 de ♖xh1 24 ♖xh1 ♖xd3; 23 ♗b1 c4) 22 ♕c2 cd (22 ... e5 23 ♕b3+ ♔f6 24 g3) 23 cd c5 24 e5 cd 25 ♘c4 with a strong attack.

20	...	cd
21	cd	

21 ♗xc7 ♘c5! or 21 ed ♗d5 are in Black's favour.

21	...	f4

This move gains in strength in the variation 21 ... ♗d5 22 e4 ♗xc4 23 ♗xc4 f4 with a blockade, but it is not so successful in the present situation. However, White answers Black's mistake with a mistake.

22	♗f2	

It was necessary to play 22 ef ♘h5 23 ♖xh5! ♖xh5 24 f5 ♗d5 25 ♖e1 with a strong attack. I considered that 22 ... ♗d5 (instead of ♘h5) 23 ♕c2 b5 leads to a sharp game, although, commenting on the game, Kasparov continued the variation, showing the vulnerability of Black's position: 24 ♗g6+ ♔g8 25 ♖xh8+ ♔xh8 26 ♖h1+ ♔g8 27 ♗h7+ ♔f7 (27 ... ♔f8 28 ♗e4!) 28 ♕g6+ ♔f8 29 ♘b2! gf 30 ♗xf4 ♕f6 31 ♕g3 ♕xd4 32 ♗c2, and White should win.

22	...	♘h5
23	♗c2	

A complex game arises after 23 e4 ♘g3 24 ♖he1. Black now seizes the initiative.

23	...	fe
24	♗xe3	

24 ♘xe3 is more precise, although after 24 ... ♘f4 25 g3 (25 d5 ♘c5!) 25 ... ♘d5 26 ♕d3 ♖ag8 Black stands very well.

24	...	♗d5
25	♕d3	♖ag8!
26	♘e5+	♘xe5

Here I declined the draw offered by my opponent, but on my very next move I permit an inaccuracy.

27 de*(41)*

41
B

27 ... ♘f4?

As time-trouble looms it is my turn to err, and I let slip a probable victory. The black king has not been subjected to any discomfort through the entire game, and now after 27 ... c5! with the threat c5–c4, the white king appears to be in a defenceless position, for example: 28 ♔b2 (28 ♕c3 ♘g3) 28 ... c4 29 ♕c3 ♘f4 30 ♗xf4 gf 31 ♖xh8 ♖xh8 32 ♖xd5 (32 ♖d4 ♕g5) 32 ... ed 33 e6+ ♔g8.

28 ♗xf4 gf
29 ♖xh8

This is the whole point. After the suggested 29 ♖h7+ ♖xh7 30 ♕xh7+ ♔f8 31 ♕h6+ ♔e8 32 ♖xd5 ed 33 ♕c6+ ♔f8 34 ♕h6+ ♖g7 35 ♕xf4+ ♔g8 the black king escapes his pursuer.

29 ... ♖xh8
30 ♕g6+ ♔f8
31 ♖xd5!

Draw agreed

A tactical blow allows White to get out of a ticklish situation. After 31 ... ed 32 ♕f5+ he declares perpetual check.

Here now is the promised game 11 of the second match.

1	**d4**	**♘f6**
2	**c4**	**e6**
3	**♘c3**	**♗b4**
4	**♘f3**	**0-0**
5	**♗g5**	**c5**

Thus, in this instance, I refrained from 5 ... d6 and played more energetically.

6	**e3**	**cd**
7	**ed**	**h6**
8	**♗h4**	**d5**

A new move. Now the game takes the form of a Queen's Gambit.

9	**♖c1**	**dc**
10	**♗xc4**	**♘c6**
11	**0-0**	**♗e7**
12	**♖e1**	**b6**
13	**a3**	**♗b7**
14	**♗g3**	**♖c8**
15	**♗a2**	**♗d6**
16	**d5**	

White is afraid of the manoeuvre ... ♘e7 with a firm blockade of d5. However, this thematic break in the centre leads to a string of simplifications with drawing tendencies.

16	**...**	**♘xd5**
17	**♘xd5**	**♗xg3**
18	**hg**	**ed**
19	**♗xd5**	**♕f6**
20	**♕a4**	**♖fd8**
21	**♖cd1**	**♖d7**
22	**♕g4**	**♖cd8??***(42)*

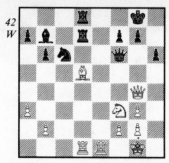

After 21 ... ♖c7 on the preceding move, or now 22 ... ♖d6 (mainly to withdraw the rook from the fatal d7 square), chances would be perfectly level. Instead of which, I make a rare blunder.

23 ♕xd7!!

Interestingly, this blow was discovered by every chess computer (even the not very strong ones), to which this position was fed.

23	...	♖xd7
24	♖e8 +	♚h7
25	♗e4 +	

Black resigned

Many commentators awarded Black's 22nd move the various epithets 'Blunder of the Century', 'a unique event in the battles for the chess Crown' etc. In his book *Dva Matcha*, Kasparov, discussing the current game, doubted the justification of the epithets and in the context of a 'refutation' gave six examples from other World Championship matches in which gross blunders were also committed. I suggest that, nevertheless, my blunder was one of the most dramatic in the entire history of chess. The last time such a mistake occurred was exactly a hundred years ago *(43)*.

This position is from the 23rd game of the World Championship match Chigorin–Steinitz (1889!). Chigorin has an extra piece and, by capturing a pawn—32 ♖xb7—he would have won this key game, retaining good chances of becoming the chess king. However, there followed the inconceivable 31 ♗b4??, and after 31 ... ♖xh2 + the match concluded 33 ♚g1 ♖dg2 mate.

The examples given by Kasparov are not quite convincing—they are either gross mistakes made in time trouble, or have no great sporting significance, as regards the games. Finally, the reaction to my lapse is notable not so much for its aesthetic strength, but for the move ♕g4xd7. I confine myself to one example from Kasparov *(44)*.

This position is from the first game of the Spassky–Fischer match (Reykjavik 1972). The position is drawn, but after 29 ... ♗xh2? 30 g3 h5 31 ♚e2 h4 32 ♚f3 hg 33 fg ♚e7 34 ♚g2 Spassky won.

Can one really compare that event with ours? Fischer presented Spassky with the point, and in the next game, as is well known, failed to turn up. The score stood at 2–0 in Spassky's favour, but none of this had much significance: the match concluded in a victory for Fischer by a large margin. In my battles with Kasparov every half-point was worth its weight in gold. I remember how, before the 11th game of the 1985 match, I was in the lead (and in the 10th game I was close to widening the gap), and such an annoying defeat (with no hint of time-trouble) completely unsettled me. The score was suddenly levelled, and I completely lost my form, which I didn't find until the end of the contest. Fischer (returning again to that former episode) declined the call of the draw and made some kind of miscalculation; possibly in the event of 32 ... h3 33 ♚g4 ♗g1 34 ♚xh3 ♗xf2 he had overlooked the quiet move 35 ♗d2, when the black bishop is incarcerated. It may be said that the American champion was punished for his aggression, that is to say that this analogy with our situation is also absent. Finally, the realization of White's advantage is sufficiently elemen-

tary, and doesn't leave such an impression, as does Kasparov's blow ♕xd7.

I have somewhat digressed from a pure chess narrative, though, I think, such a unique lapse in a match for the Crown is quite worthy of a few lines.

Kasparov–Karpov
Game 17,
World Championship 2
Moscow 1985

This game, in my opinion, did not receive sufficient illumination from the commentators, and, as you know, it could have played a major role in the process of our second contest. My opponent played well in the preceding 16th game, employing as Black a surprising innovation in the Sicilian Defence (the 'Kasparov Gambit' is discussed in *The Semi-Open Game in Action*), and went ahead. And here, a day later, I also employed a novelty, again as Black, in an opening which Kasparov had dominated through the entire match. The value of the novelty (9 ... ♞a5!) is in some measure characterized by the circumstance that the Grandmaster from Baku took almost an hour and half over the next two moves. A victory would allow me to level the score and take a psychological initiative (the same as my opponent obtained in the previous game).

1 d4   ♞f6

2	c4	e6
3	♘c3	♗b4
4	♘f3	c5
5	g3	♘c6

I played 5 ... ♘e4 straight away in the first game of this match. After 6 ♕d3 ♕a5 7 ♕xe4 ♗xc3+ 8 ♗d2 ♗xd2+ 9 ♘xd2 ♕b6 10 dc ♕xb2 11 ♖b1 ♕c3 12 ♕d3 ♕xd3 13 ed ♘a6 14 d4 White seized the initiative on the queenside, which he was able to convert to a win. Incidentally, I played the knight to e4 a move earlier in the 19th game—4 ... ♘e4. There subsequently followed 5 ♕c2 f5 6 g3 ♘c6 7 ♗g2 0-0 8 0-0 ♗xc3 9 bc ♘a5 10 c5 d6 11 c4! b6 12 ♗d2 13 ♘xd2 13 ♘xd2 d5 14 cd ed 15 e3. White again obtained a serious opening advantage which he converted into a win.

I only chose the main theoretical move 5 ... cd in the following match. Kasparov–Karpov, m (4) London 1986 went 6 ♘xd4 0-0 7 ♗g2 d5 8 ♕b3 ♗xc3+ 9 bc ♘c6! 10 cd ♘a5! 11 ♕c2 ♘xd5 12 ♕d3 ♗d7. To this day I can't remember why I refrained from playing the obvious move 12 ... ♕c7, which gives excellent chances. But now, after 13 c4! ♘e7 14 0-0 ♖c8 15 ♘b3 ♘xc4 16 ♗xb7 ♖c7 17 ♗a6! White obtained a serious queenside initiative, which decided the game in his favour.

6	♗g2	♘e4

I prepared the new move 6 ... d5 for the return match and in the second game after 7 cd ♘xd5 8 ♗d2 cd 9 ♘xd4 ♘xd4 10 ♘xd5 ♗xd2+ 11 ♕xd2 ♘c6 12 ♘f4 ♕xd2+ 13 ♔xd2 ♗d7 the situation was fully equal. However, I didn't subsequently play sufficiently accurately and contrived to lose.

7	♗d2	♗xc3
8	bc	0-0
9	0-0	♘a5! *(45)*

45
W

Thus, the Romanishin System arises, which, as we shall see, brings me a lot of trouble. I chose here **9 ... f5** in the 13th game, and after **10 ♗e3!** White had an advantage. On that occasion, though, I soon succeeded in escaping the danger zone.

Kasparov–Karpov, m (13) Moscow 1985:

10	...	♘xc3
11	♕d3	cd
12	♘xd4	♘e4
13	c5	♘xd4
14	♗xd4	b6
15	♗xe4	fe
16	♕xe4	♗a6
17	cb	ab
18	♕e5	

After 18 a4 the weak pawn on b6 would cause me certain problems.

18	...	♕f6

19	♕e3	♕h6!

The ending without queens is harmless for Black.

20	♕xh6	gh
21	♖fe1	♗c4
22	a3	b5
23	♖ad1	♖f5
24	♗b2	♖d5

Draw agreed

In the present game I found a means of emphasizing the negative side of White's plan.

10	dc	♕c7
11	♘d4	♘xd2
12	♕xd2	♘xc4
13	♕g5	f6
14	♕f4 *(46)*	

We have come to the position that made me decide to include this game in the book.

Here, after 14 ... ♘e5, the game would quite naturally conclude in a draw after only fifteen moves. The commentators quite cursorily indicated the capture 14 ... ♕xc5, and were limited to the remark that White had an initiative for the pawn. However, careful analysis shows that it is Black who retains the initiative on the capture of this pawn. White's position is most likely defensible,

but nevertheless he would have to surmount certain difficulties in order to equalize. Moreover, it must be said that Kasparov was short of time. Let's look at some variations that corroborate this evaluation of the position.

14 ... ♕xc5! Of course, not 14 ... e5? 15 ♗d5+ ♔h8 16 ♘b5.

15 ♘b3 ♕b5. White now has two paths—to invade Black's camp with his queen (16 ♕c7) or, conversely, to drive away the enemy queen (16 ♘d4). The moves 16 ♖ab1 or 16 ♖fd1 are of no independent significance, as the necessity for the rook to occupy one or the other open file comes later.

16 ♕c7 d5 17 e4 ♕c6! 18 ♕e7 de 19 ♖ad1 f5. 19 ... b6 20 ♖d4 ♖e8 21 ♖xc4 or 20 ... f5 21 ♖fd1 ♗a6 22 ♖d7 are in White's favour.

20 ♘d4. Now the transfer of the rook to d4 is harmless: 20 ♖d4 b5 21 ♖fd1 ♖e8 22 ♖d8 ♗a6 23 ♖1d7 ♕xd7! 24 ♕xd7 ♖axd8.

20 ... ♕e8! (20 ... ♕b6 is not bad either, but not 20 ... ♕d5 21 ♘f3! ef 22 ♖xd5 fg 23 ♖d8 gf(♕)+ 24 ♔xf1 ♖xd8 25 ♕xd8+ ♔f7 26 ♕c7+ or 20 ... ♕d6 21 ♘xf5!) 21 ♕c5 (21 ♕b4 ♘b6 22 ♘b5 ♕c6 23 ♖d6 ♕c4 is worse) 21 ... ♘b2 22 ♖d2 ♘d3 23 ♕a3 e5 24 ♘b3 ♗e6 25 f3 ef 26 ♗xf3 e4 with advantage to Black.

As these active operations come to no good, White does better to wait with 16 ♘d4! Now 16 ...

₩e5 is dangerous due to 17 ♘xe6!
₩xe6 18 ₩d4 ♘b6 19 a4 (19 c4
d6 20 a4 ♚h8 21 a5 ♘d7, saving
the knight) 19 ... a5 20 c4 (20
♖ab1 ♖ab 21 c4 ♚h8 22 c5 ♘a8)
20 ... ♖f7 21 c5 ₩c4 22 ♖ad1
regaining the piece and maintaining all of his trumps. It is more
judicious for Black to retreat his
queen to the outside file: a4 or a6.

16 ... ₩a4 17 ₩c7 (17 ♘f5
♘b6) 17 ... d5 18 e4 (but not 18
♘f5 ₩d7 19 ♘e7+ ♚h8 20 ₩c5
♘d6) 18 ... de 19 ♗xe4 ♘d2 20
♗xb7 ♗xb7 21 ₩xb7 ♖ab8 21
₩c7 ♖fc8 22 ₩d6 ♖b6 23 ₩e7
♖e8 and 24 ... ♘xf1. Sharp play
leads to a Black advantage—he
has extra material. Apparently it
would follow for White to delay
the advance of his e-pawn for one
move: 18 ♖fd1 ₩e8 19 e4 ♖f7 20
₩c5 b6 21 ₩b4 ♗b7. The situation remains tense, but Black can
face the future optimistically.

16 ... ₩a6 17 ₩c7 d5 18 ♖fb1
(worse would be 18 ♘f5 ef 19
♗xd5+ ♗e6 20 ♗xb7 ₩b6) 18
... ₩d6 19 ♘b5 ₩d7. Other variations are 19 ... ₩xc7 20 ♘xc7
♖b8 21 ♘a6 with a perpetual
attack on the rook, or 19 ... ₩d8
20 ₩xd8 ♖xd8 21 ♘c7.

20 ₩xd7 ♗xd7 21 ♘c7 ♖ab8
22 ♘xd5 ♘a3 23 ♖b3 ♘c2 24
♖c1 ed 25 ♗xd5+ ♚h8 26 ♖xc2
♗a4 27 c4 ♗xb3 28 ab *(47)*.

A long, almost forcing, variation has led to a position in which
Black has a small material advantage. Of course, it's not simple to
win, but he could try to do so
without any apparent risk.

Let's return to the actual events
of the game, which quickly con-
cludes in peaceful negotiations.

14 ... ♘e5
15 ♘b3 ♖b8

Black easily equalizes by such
means, but he can also discount
any serious thoughts of success.

16	₩d4	b6
17	f4	♘f7
18	♖fd1	♖fd8
19	c4	♗b7
20	♗xb7	♖xb7
21	cb	♖xb6
22	c5	♖c6
23	♖ac1	d5

The last chance to maintain the
tension lay in 23 ... e5!? There
now follow mass exchanges.

24	cd	♖xd6
25	₩e3	♖xd1+
26	♖xd1	g6
27	♖c1	♖xc1+
28	₩xc1	₩b6+
29	₩c5	

Draw agreed

Salov–M. Gurevich
Leningrad 1987

Apart from the two games from
the World Championship
matches (in the notes to which are

mentioned six more of my games with Kasparov) I decided to apportion one more supplementary game to the Nimzo–Indian Defence. My choice fell on the current encounter as it was awarded the prize as best theoretical novelty in the first half of 1987 (*Chess Informant* No. 43) which doesn't often happen for the Nimzo–Indian Defence.

1	d4	♘f6
2	c4	e6
3	♘c3	♗b4
4	e3	c5
5	♘e2	cd
6	ed	d5

Here Black often castles, allowing White to advance his own d-pawn, after kicking the bishop. According to the latest information, this isn't so terrible for Black. I think it's worth digressing and examining a few examples.

6 ... 0-0 7 a3 ♗e7 8 d5 ed 9 cd ♖e8 10 d6!? 10 g3 or 10 ♗e3 are quieter continuations leading to a probable draw. The march of the d-pawn must ultimately lead to its destruction, but White's aim in this variation is to hinder Black's development to the maximum.

10 ... ♗f8 11 g3 ♖e6*(48)*

It seems that this position was first encountered in the game Gligoric–Karpov (Bugojno 1980). There followed 12 ♗g2 ♖xd6 13 ♕c2 ♘c6 14 0-0 ♖e6 15 ♘f4 ♖e8 16 b4 d6 17 ♗b2 ♗d7 18 ♘cd5 ♘xd5 19 ♗xd5 ♖c8 20 ♕b3 ♘e7 21 ♖ad1 b5! 22 ♗g2 ♖e8 23 ♗d5 ♖e7 24 ♗g2 ♖e8 25 ♗d5 ♖e7 24 ♗g2 ♘e5! 25 ♖xd6 ♘c4 26 ♖dd1 ♕e8 27 ♗d4 ♗c6. By returning the pawn, I obtained the advantage and eventually prevailed.

Subsequently, some attempts were made to improve on White's 15th move—15 b4, 15 ♗g5—but they proved to be unsuccessful. Seemingly stronger is 12 ♗f4!, diverting the knight to the edge of the board. One possibility is **12 ... ♘h5 13 ♗e3 ♖xd6 14 ♕c2 ♖e6 15 ♗g2 ♘c6 16 0-0 ♘f6 17 b4!** (**17 ♖ad1 ♖e8 18 ♘d4 d5 19 ♗g5 Draw agreed; Petran–Utasi, Szirak 1985**) 17 ... a6 (17 ... d6 18 b5 ♘e5 19 ♘d4 ♖e8 20 ♗g5 or 17 ... d5 18 b5 ♘a5 19 ♖fd1 with strong White pressure) 18 ♘f4 ♖e8 19 ♘fd5 with advantage to White: 19 ... ♘xd5 20 ♘xd5 ♖b8 21 ♗b6 ♕g5 22 ♗c7 ♖a8 23 ♗f4 and 24 ♘c7 (analysis by Adorjan and Dory).

If the conclusion is to be made that 11 ... ♖e6 is not the way out of the situation, then one may examine two further possibilities, one bad and one good.

In the game **Korchnoi–Miles (Wijk aan Zee 1984)** Black played **11 ... ♕b6?** and didn't survive long: **12 ♗g2 ♗xd6** (12 ... ♕xd6 13 ♕xd6 ♗xd6 14 ♘b5 ♖e6 15

♗h3) 13 ♗e3 ♕a6 14 0-0 ♗e5 15
♘f4 d5 16 ♘cxd5 ♘c6 17 ♘xf6+
♗xf6 18 ♘d5 ♗e5 19 ♕h5 ♕a4
20 ♗f4 ♗d7 21 b3 ♕a5 22 b4
♕a4 23 ♖ad1 ♗xf4 24 gf ♖ad8
25 ♖d3 ♔h8 26 ♘c7 ♖e7 27 ♕c5
♖e2 28 ♖xd7 **Black resigned**.

A successful innovation was
discovered by Grandmaster
Adorjan—**11 ... b6!** Black
doesn't hurry to regain the pawn,
and carries out the development
of his queenside. Practice and
analysis by Adorjan and Dory
indicate that Black obtains excellent play after this fianchetto. I
limit myself to one example.

**Grünberg–Dory (Stockholm
1984/5): 12 ♗g2 ♘c6 13 ♘b5.**
This looks active, but in reality it
loses time. However, Black also
obtains good play after 13 0-0
♗a6 14 ♗f4 ♖c8 15 ♖e1 ♘e5 16
♕a4 ♗c4 17 ♖ed1 ♘g6 18 ♖d2
a5 19 ♕d1 b5 (Miles–Csom, Esb-
jerg 1984).

13... ♗a6 14 a4 ♖e6 15 0-0. In
the event of 15 ♗f4, fine examples
are given by Adorjan and Dory:
15... ♕e8 16 ♗f3 g5! 17 ♘c7 (17
♗xg5? ♘e5 18 ♗g2 ♗xb5 19 ab
♖xd6 20 ♕b3 ♘d3+ 21 ♔f1
♘e4! 22 ♗e3 ♘dxf2! winning) 17
... ♗xe2! 18 ♗xe2 gf 19 ♘xe8
♖axe8 20 gf ♖xe2+ 21 ♕xe2
♖xe2+ 22 ♔xe2 ♗xd6. This is
an unusual balance of forces—
three minor pieces versus two
rooks, but Black's superiority is
not in doubt.

**15 ... ♗xd6 16 ♗h3 ♗c5 17
♗xe6 fe 18 ♗f4 ♘d5 19 ♕d2 ♕f6
20 ♗d6 ♗xd6 21 ♘xd6 ♕f3 22
♘b5** (22 ♖fe1 is more solid.

There now follows a flashy finale)
**22 ... ♘e5 23 ♘ed4 ♗b7 24 ♕d1
♕g2+! 25 ♔xg2 ♘f4+ 26 ♔g1
♘h3 mate!**

So, this impetuous advance of
the d-pawn is not dangerous for
Black, but now it's time to return
to the text game, where the question of this advance was immediately dismissed.

7	a3	♗e7
8	c5	0-0
9	g3	b6
10	b4	bc
11	dc	a5
12	♖b1 *(49)*	

Everything is well known up till
now. Incidentally, Gurevich
played this position as White a
couple of months before the text
game. Gurevich–Lerner (Tallinn
1987) went 12... ab 13 ab ♘c6 14
♗g2 ♖b8 15 ♗a3 ♗a6 (and on
the other development of the
bishop by 15... ♗d7 16 0-0 ♘a7
17 ♖e1 ♘e8 18 ♘d4 ♘c7 19 f4
♗f6 20 ♕d2 ♖e8 21 ♘ce2 White
has the better chances; Marin–
Georgiev, Warsaw 1987) 16 0-0
♗c4 17 ♖e1 ♕c7 18 ♘d4 ♖fd8
19 ♘xc6 ♕xc6 20 ♗c1 ♖b7 21
♕d4. White maintained a mini-

mal advantage, but the game ended in a truce ten moves later.

Possibly, while analysing this game, this original idea occurred to Gurevich.

| 12 | ... | ♘c6 |
| 13 | ♗g2 | |

It appears that, by a transposition of moves, a position from Gurevich–Lerner will arise (13 ... ab 14 ab ♖b8 15 ♗a3), but after

| 13 | ... | ♖b8! |

... it becomes clear that this is not so. The a-pawn does not leave the board yet, and the a3 square is not available to the bishop. It must find another way.

| 14 | ♗f4 *(50)* | |

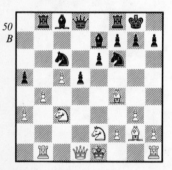

50
B

This move followed after almost an hour of reflection. The variation 14 b5 ♗xc5 15 bc ♖xb1 16 ♘xb1 ♕b6! allows Black to take too many pawns for the piece. 14 ♕a4 ab 15 ab (15 ♕xc6 ♗d7!) leads to unclear play, but Gurevich, commenting on the game, proposed 14 ♘d4. This possibility was soon to be tested and it became clear that here too Black has excellent chances.

Marin–Portisch (Szirak 1987): 14 ♘d4 ♘xd4 15 ♕xd4 ♘d7 16 0-0 ♗a6 17 ♖d1 ♗f6 18 ♕d2 ab 19 ab ♘e5 20 ♕c2 ♘c6! Black has a significant advantage, which is soon converted into a decisive one.

| 14 | ... | ab! |

Of course, not 14 ... e5 in view of 15 ♘xd5! Now Black, by sacrificing the exchange, completely demolishes his opponent's pawn chain.

| 15 | ♗xb8 | bc |
| 16 | ♕a4 | |

16 ♗d6 ♗xd6 17 cd ♕a5! 18 0-0 ♕xa3 19 ♕c2 ♕xd6 is also in Black's favour.

16	...	♘xb8
17	♖xb8	♘d7!
18	♖a8	

No better either is 18 ♖b1 ♘xc5 19 ♕c2 (19 ♕d4 c2!) 19 ... ♗a6 or 19 ... d4 with a strong initiative.

| 18 | ... | ♘xc5 |
| 19 | ♕b5 | |

19 ♕c2 d4 loses as does 19 ♕d4 ♕b6! 20 ♘xc3 (20 0-0) 20 ... ♕b7 21 ♖a5 ♘b3!

| 19 | ... | ♕d6! |

19 ... d4 is insufficient: 20 0-0 c2 21 ♖xc8 ♕xc8 22 ♘xd4, and White comes through unscathed, as 22 ... ♘d3 cannot be played in view of the counterblow 23 ♘c6! ♗xa3 24 ♕xd3 c1(♕) 25 ♖xc1 ♗xc1 26 ♘e7+. Now White cannot castle successfully because of the reply ... ♗a6, when he would be subject to a fatal attack.

20	♗f3	♗a6
21	♖xf8+	♗xf8
22	♕a5	

If 22 ♕b1 then 22 ... ♘d3+ 23
♔f1 ♕e5! decides.

22	...	♘d3+
23	♔f1	♘e5
24	♕xc3	

In the event of 24 ♔g2 ♘xf3 25
♔xf3 d4 White is doomed in view

of the defencelessness of the light
squares.

| 24 | ... | d4 |
| 25 | ♕b3 | ♗c4 |

White resigned

26 ♕b7 ♘xf3 27 ♕xf3 ♗d5.

3 The King's Indian Defence

Ftacnik–Zsu. Polgar

Czechoslovakia 1985

From the multitude of interesting games in which the King's Indian Defence is played, I have singled out five examples. My choice, in particular fell on the current encounter, which also opens the selection. Our four-volume series is drawing to a close and up till now all of the main games have been played by male chess players. It is time therefore to include a game from one of the best women chess players. Zsuzsa Polgar, the eldest sister in a unique Hungarian chess family, is a most appropriate candidate. The arrangement of a game between her and a male Grandmaster was made especially to emphasize the high level of modern women's chess. However, Polgar herself has full Grandmaster status. It remains to say that the current game is quite fascinating, and on reflection, this circumstance is what merits the inclusion of this game in the book.

1	♘f3	♞f6
2	c4	g6
3	♘c3	♝g7
4	d4	0-0
5	e4	d6
6	♗e2	e5
7	0-0	

This is the so-called Classical System of the King's Indian Defence. Besides castling, White has other possibilities at his disposal. The exchanges 7 de de 8 ♕xd8 ♖xd8 are initiated in the game Salov–Belyavsky below. In reply to 7 ♗e3 theory knows various answers—7 ... ♘g4 8 ♗g5 f6, 7 ... ♕e7, 7 ... ♘c6 and 7 ... ed. Indeed, 7 ... h6 is not bad either, bringing the square g5 under control. Here is a recent game, from which a sharp struggle arises. Even the World Champion is unable to obtain an advantage.

Kasparov–Nunn (Reykjavik 1988): 7 ♗e3 h6 8 0-0 ♘g4 9 ♗c1 ♘c6 10 d5 ♘e7 11 ♘d2 f5 12 ♗xg4 fg 13 b4 b6 14 ♘b3 g5 15 a4 ♘g6 16 a5 ♗d7 17 c5 bc 18 bc a6 19 ♘d2 ♘f4 20 ♖b1 dc 21 ♗a3 ♖f7 22 ♘c4 ♕f6 23 ♗xc5 ♗f8 24 ♗xf8 ♖axf8 25 ♖b4 h5 26 d6 ♗e6 27 ♘d5 ♗xd5 28 ed cd 29 ♖b6 ♖d7 30 ♖xa6 ♕g6 31 ♖e1 ♘d3 32 ♘xe5 ♘xe5 33 ♖xe5 ♕f6 34 ♖e2 ♖e7 35 ♖c6 ♖xe2 36 ♕xe2 ♕a1+ 37 ♕f1 ♕xa5 38 ♖xd6 ♖e8 39 ♖e6 ♖xe6 40 de ♕e5 41 ♕c1 ♔g7 Draw agreed.

I will mention the classical continuation 7 d5, which is now met significantly less often than 7 0-0. White immediately closes the centre, thus determining the subsequent course of the game. The pawn structure is favourable for a queenside assault by White, while

Black tries for counterplay on the kingside. Both of these ideas are characteristic in the majority of variations in the King's Indian Defence. However, such an early stabilization of the centre, as pointed out by Grandmaster Geller, may be considered by Black as a definite achievement. He has the possibility of his knight appearing on c5 (... ♘bd7 ... a5 ... ♘c5), impeding White's queenside attack and preparing the thematic ... f7–f5. In short, practice shows that the conservative 7 0-0, and only on 7 ... ♘c6 8 d5, is notably more dangerous for Black.

7 ...   ♘c6

Immediately opening the centre by 7 ... ed ♘xd4 ♖e8 9 f3 doesn't promise Black equality. After 7 ... c6 8 d5 cd (8 ... c5 leads to a position from the Benoni with an extra tempo for White) 9 cd ♘e8 10 a4 h6 11 a5 f5 12 ef gf 13 g3 ♘a6 14 ♘h4 f4 15 ♖a3 ♗h3 16 ♗g4 White achieves a big positional advantage. 7 ... ♘bd7 is as popular as the last move, these days almost completely replacing the more active manoeuvre of the knight to c6.

8 d5   ♘e7
9 ♘e1

Also popular is the alternative knight retreat to d2, which, incidentally occurred in my solitary King's Indian with Kasparov. Two games are devoted to the move 9 ♘d2 below. The continuation 9 b4, which in his time was preferred by Taimanov, is not dangerous for Black. Now this programmed move is more often chosen after preliminary preparation. The modest 9 ♗d2 lost its topicality as far back as 1971, after the candidates match Fischer–Taimanov, in which the American Grandmaster succeeded in winning all six games, including, as Black, with the King's Indian.

9 ...   ♘d7

Immediately preparing ... f7–f5. 9 ... c5 represents a loss of time and an unnecessary weakening, since he cannot deprive his opponent of queenside play anyway.

10 ♘d3

The continuation 10 f3 f5 11 g4 leads to sharp play with mutual chances. The move 10 ♗e3 is covered in the game Korchnoi–Hulak.

10 ...   f5
11 ♗d2   ♘f6

11 ... c5 is not such a reliable continuation (proposed by Fischer). 11 ... fe is also possible, but the new moves 11 ... ♖f7 and 11 ... ♔h8 are comparatively interesting.

12 f3   f4

The drawback of the move 12 ... c5 is shown in the game Rashkovsky–Ermolinsky (Volgodonsk 1981): 13 ♖b1 f4 14 b4 b6 15 bc bc ♖b2 g5 17 ♘f2 h5 18 h3 ♖f7 19 ♕a4 ♗f8 20 ♖fb1 ♖g7 21 ♖b8! and White has a significant advantage. The waiting move 12 ... ♔h8 is also in White's favour, as practice indicates.

13 c5

An interesting novelty was employed in the game Pavlovic–Vokac (Trnava 1988): 13 g4! Before commencing operations on the queenside White stabilizes the kingside situation. 13 ... fg (13 ... h5 14 g5! or 13 ... g5 14 ♗e1 h5 15 h3 are in White's favour) 14 hg c6 15 a4 a5 16 ♗e3 ♔h8 17 ♕d2 cd (according to Pavlovic, 17 ... c5 was necessary) 18 cd ♗d7 19 ♔g2 ♖f7 20 ♖h1 ♖c8 21 ♘f2 h5 22 ♖a3! White has an imposing advantage. Hence, Black has something to think about in this variation.

13 ... g5*(51)*

51
W

This position arose not long ago in my game with van der Wiel (Brussels 1987). Here I immediately exchanged on d6: 14 cd cd 15 ♘f2 h5 16 h3 ♘g6 17 ♕c2 ♘e8. Quite a good novelty; 17 ... g4 or the manoeuvre ... ♗g7–f6–d8–b6 are also met. 18 a4 ♗f6 19 ♖a3 ♕c7 20 ♖c1 ♗d8 21 ♘b5 ♕b8. Black should exchange queens. 22 a5 a6 23 ♘c3 b6 24 ♘cd1 ♖f7 (correct, strange as it may seem, would be to banish the knight to the corner of the board:

24 ... ♘h8!) 25 ♕b3 b5 26 ♘d3! ♘f6 27 ♘1f2 ♖c7 28 ♖c3 ♖xc3 (28 ... ♘d7 29 ♖c6!; 28 ... ♖aa7 29 ♘b4!, but 28 ... ♗d7 was best) 29 bc ♘d7 30 c4. White has the advantage. However, my opponent defended accurately, and 30 moves later a draw was secured.

14 ♖c1 ♘g6

The knight move to g6 is, in principle, obligatory. A different placement of the piece occurred in the game Neverov–Khalifman (USSR Young Masters Championship 1985): 14 ... h5 15 ♘b5 ♘e8 (15 ... g4? loses to 16 ♗b4 ♘e8 17 ♘xc7!) 16 cd! (more precise than the previously encountered 16 ♕c2) 16 ... cd 17 a4 ♖f6 18 ♘f2 ♖g6 19 h3 ♔h8 20 ♕b3 ♘g8 21 ♖c2 ♘h6 22 ♖fc1 with advantage to White.

15 cd cd
16 ♘b5 ♖f7
17 ♕c2

After 17 ♘f2? a6! 18 ♘a3 b5 Black has good play, which is corroborated by the game Gligoric–Quinteros (Novi Sad 1982): 19 ♕e1 h5 20 ♗a5 ♕f8 21 h3 g4 22 fg hg 23 ♘xg4 ♗xg4 24 ♗xg4 ♘xg4 25 hg ♗f6 26 ♕e2 ♗h4 27 ♖c3 ♗g3 28 g5 ♕e7 29 ♕h5 ♕a7+ **White resigned**.

17 ... ♘e8

17 ... g4 has been considered doubtful for a long time, but in the game Podgayets—M. Gurevich (1st League, USSR Championship 1984) this move was justified: **17 ... g4 18 ♘c7! gf 19 gf ♗h3 20 ♘e6** (in the event of 20

♘xa8 ♘xe4 21 fe ♕g5+ 22 ♔f2
♕h4+ 23 ♔g1 ♕g5+ the game
most naturally ends in perpetual
check, although in the celebrated
game Larsen–Tal (match 1969),
the ex-World Champion declared
a different check—22 ...
♕g2+—and prevailed after a
sharp struggle) **20 ... ♕b6+ 21
♖f2 ♗xe6 22 de ♖e7 23 ♕a4
♘f8! 24 ♗a5 ♕e3 25 ♗f1 ♘xe6
26 ♗d2 ♕b6**, and here White
found nothing better than to repeat moves: **27 ♗a5 ♕e3 28 ♗d2
Drawn.**

	18	a4	h5
	19	♘f2	♗f8
	20	h3	♖g7
	21	♕b3	♘h4(52)

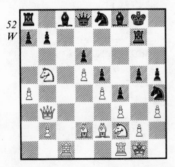

52
W

The diagram position may be
considered to be one of the King's
Indian's main themes. 21 ... ♗d7
is also met in practice. In the game
Ftacnik–Rekorelli (Czechoslovakia 1985) after 21 ... ♗d7 22
♖c2! a6 23 ♘a3 g4 24 fg ♘h4 25
a5 ♘f6 26 ♕b6 hg 27 ♕xd8
♖xd8 28 hg ♘xg4 29 ♘xg4 ♗xg4
30 ♗xg4 ♖xg4 31 ♗e1 ♖d7? 32
♗xh4 White had an advantage.
However, Black can play more
accurately: 23 ... ♘h4! 24 ♖fc1

♖b8 25 ♘c4 g4! 26 fg b5! 27 ab
♗xb5 28 ♕a3 ♕f6 with a good
position (Klunas–Lanka, USSR
1979).

| | **22** | **♖c2** | **a6** |

The game Ftacnik–Pribyl (Bra-
tislava 1983) developed differently: 22 ... g4 23 fg ♘f6 24 ♗e1
♔h8! (24 ... a6? is bad due to 25
♘c7! ♖xc7 26 ♗a5). Here 25
♕d3! is stronger than the mistaken 25 ♕c4?, retaining the advantage. 22 ... ♘f6 probably
leads to a level game: 23 ♖fc1 g4
24 fg (24 ♖c7 is also interesting)
24 ... hg 25 hg ♗xg4 26 ♗xg4
♘xg4 27 ♘xg4 ♖xg4 28 ♗e1 f3.

	23	**♘a3**	**♘f6**
	24	**♗e1**	**g4**
	25	**hg**	

A recommendation of Ftacnik
deserves consideration: 25 fg!?

| | **25** | **...** | **hg** |

More accurate than the alternative continuation 25 ... ♕e8.

| | **26** | **♘xg4(53)** | |

53
B

This position first arose in the
game Ftacnik–Lechtinsky (Czechoslovakia 1984). After 26 ...
♘xg4?! 27 fg ♗xg4 28 ♗xg4
♖xg4 29 ♕h3! ♕g5 30 ♗xh4
♖xh4 31 ♕e6+ ♔h8 32 ♘c4

♕h5 33 ♖f3 ♖e8 34 ♕f6+
White has a significant advantage.
Polgar employs a new and very
strong continuation.

26	...	♘h5!
27	a5	♘g3
28	♗xg3	fg

Black's plan is to attack on the
kingside utilizing the g3 pawn.

29 ♕b6!

29 ♕e3 ♖h7 30 f4 ♘f5 31 ef
♕h4 loses.

29	...	♕e7
30	♖fc1	♗xg4
31	fg	♘g6!

The black knight makes way
for the queen on h4 and simultaneously targets f4.

32	♗f3	♕h4
33	♔f1	♘f4!
34	♖c7	♖xc7
35	♖xc7	♗h6
36	♘c4	

Mistaken are both 36 ♖xb7
because of 36 ... ♖c8! 37 ♖b8
♕h1+ winning, and 36 ♕g1
♕h2 37 ♘c4 ♖f8 38 ♘xd6 ♘e2!
etc.

36	...	♖f8
37	♘xd6	♘xg2! (54)

The struggle has reach its cli-
max. Black proceeds with a dangerous attack on the king, but
White manages to hold her off.

38	♘f5	♕h1+
39	♔e2	

39 ♕g1 loses to 39 ... ♘e3+
40 ♘xe3 ♖xf3+.

39	...	♕e1+
40	♔d3	♕d2+
41	♔c4	♕c2+
42	♔b4	♕xb2+
43	♔c4	♕c2+
44	♔b4	♗d2+!
45	♔a3	♗c1+
46	♔b4	♕b2+
47	♔c4	♘e3+

Black declines the perpetual
check and goes for the better endgame.

48	♘xe3	♕xb6
49	ab	♖xf3
50	♘g2	♖f2
51	♔b3!	

White generates the threats
♖c2 or d5–d6, and therefore
Black is forced to go into a rook
ending.

51	...	♖b2+
52	♔a3	♖xg2+
53	♖xc1	♖e2
54	♖g1	g2

Commenting on the game, Polgar evaluated this position as
drawn. However, Ftacnik quickly
established that after 54 ...
♖e3+ 55 ♔b2 (55 ♔b4 doesn't
save him either) 55 ... ♔f7 56
♔c2 (and here 56 g5 doesn't
change matters) 56 ... ♔f6 57
♔d2 ♖xe4 58 ♖xg3 ♖d4+ 59
♖d3 ♖xd3+ 60 ♔xd3 a5 61 ♔e4
a4 62 g5+ ♔xg5 63 ♔xe5 a3
Black could win.

55	g5	♔f7

56	♔b4	♚e7
57	♔c5	♖c2+
58	♔b4	♚d6
59	g6	♖e2
60	♔a5!	♖a2+
61	♔b4	♖e2
62	♔a5	

Draw agreed

Korchnoi–Hulak
Zagreb 1988

1	♘f3	♘f6
2	c4	g6
3	♘c3	♗g7
4	e4	0-0
5	♗e2	d6
6	d4	e5

A slightly unusual order of moves has led to the standard position of the Classical System. This is, perhaps, the most popular system used in the King's Indian Defence today, so therefore we devote much attention to it (I recall how it was encountered in the Seville contest, where the current opening was played only once in my four matches with Kasparov).

What a pity that many King's Indian variations remain only in books: the Four Pawns Attack (according to modern thinking it is not considered dangerous for Black), the system with the development of the bishop to g2, the Averbakh System (the earlier appearance of the bishop to g5), the Benoni-type formation and others. As Kozma Prutkov said, 'it is impossible to comprehend the immensity'.

The choice of the text game is explained above all by the fact that it was awarded first prize in the competition for the most important theoretical game in one of the latest editions of *Chess Informant*—No. 44.

7	0-0	♘c6
8	d5	♘e7
9	♘e1	

We devote two games to the knight retreat to e1, and two—they come later—to the retreat to d2. Bent Larsen, who is inclined to experiment in the opening, quite recently played quite a surprising move here: 9 ♔h1. One may react to it in the usual manner (9 ... ♘d7 or 9 ... ♘e8), but Black replied 9 ... ♘h5 and after 10 g3 f5 11 ef ♘xf5 12 ♘g5 ♘d4 13 ♗d3 ♘f6 14 f3 c6 play was level, and matters concluded in a draw.

9	...	♘d7
10	♗e3	

As we know, the main moves here are 10 ♘d3 and 10 f3. The bishop manoeuvre to e3 has rarely been met in recent years. In principle, considering that White concentrates his main strength on the queenside, the g1–a7 diagonal is quite suitable for his dark-squared bishop. However, practice shows that there are certain problems associated with this position. Black's move f5–f4 gains a tempo, and subsequently, when his g-pawn goes to g3, he gains another, still more important tempo. Here is one classic example.

Larsen–Torre (Bayang 1973): 10 ... f5 11 f3 f4 12 ♗f2 g5 13 ♘d3 ♘f6 14 c5 ♘g6. In the game Taimanov–Aronin (Moscow 1962), to which the history of the move 9 ♘e1 leads us, Black chose the unsuccessful 14 ... h5 and after 15 ♖c1 g4 16 ♕b3 ♗h6 17 cd cd 18 ♘xe5! appeared to be in a critical position.

15 a4 h5 16 cd cd 17 a5 g4 18 ♘b5 g3! 19 ♗xa7. Black also has a dangerous attack after 19 hg fg 20 ♗xg3 h4 21 ♗f2 ♘h5. 19 ... ♘h7 20 h3 ♕h4 21 ♗b6 ♗xh3! 22 gh ♕xh3 23 ♖f2 ♘h4 24 ♕f1 gf+ 25 ♘xf2 ♕g3+, and Black has a winning position.

Hence, in recent times White has preferred to develop his bishop to d2 or just leave it at home. However, Korchnoi manages to find a new idea, namely the 'defective' move ♗e3, which also led to the conferment of the prize mentioned above.

10	...	f5
11	f3	f4
12	♗f2	g5

Taking into account White's next move, Korchnoi suggests 12 ... a6.

| 13 | ♘b5! *(55)* |

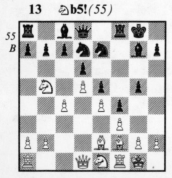

This knight move also constitutes a valuable novelty. Up till now, apart from 13 ♘d3, 13 b4 has also been played. Here is one recent example.

D. Gurevich–Hellers (New York 1987): 13 b4 ♘f6 14 c5 ♘g6 15 cd cd 16 ♖c1 ♖f7 17 a4 h5 18 a5 ♗d7 19 ♘b5 ♗xb5 20 ♗xb5 g4 21 ♕h1 g3 22 ♗g1 gh 23 ♗f2 h4 24 ♔xh2. In the game D. Gurevich–Schmidt (Beer Sheva 1986) after 24 ♘d3 ♘h5 25 ♖e1 ♘g3+ 26 ♔xh2 ♘f8 27 ♗g1 h3! 28 gh ♘h7 29 ♗f2 ♕h4 30 ♕a4 ♖d8! Black obtained a winning position.

24 ... ♘h5 25 ♖g1 ♘g3 26 ♘d3 ♗f8 27 ♗e1 ♖h7 28 ♘f2 h3! 29 gh ♕h4 30 ♖c3 ♕h5 31 ♗f1 ♔h8 32 ♕d3. According to Hellers, 32 ♕c2 ♘h4 33 ♗g2 ♖d8 34 ♘g4 (34 ♖c8 ♕xf3!!) 34 ... ♗e7 35 ♗xg3 fg+ 36 ♔xg3 ♖f8 leads to unclear play.

32 ... ♗e7 33 ♘h1 ♖g8 34 ♗xg3. It was necessary to take with the knight first and only then with the bishop.

34 ... fg+ 35 ♘xg3 ♕h4!, and Black converted his initiative five moves later: 36 ♘h1 ♕f4+ 37 ♘g3 ♘h4 38 ♕e3 ♕xe3 39 ♖xe3 ♗g5 40 ♘f5 ♘xf5 White resigned.

The appearance of the knight on b5 diverts Black from his kingside operations. Of course, it's not possible to win a game with one move, and sticking with the move ♗c1–e3, in another game with **Hellers (European Club Championship 1987)**, **Gurevich**

employed yet one more novelty—
13a4!?—and only on the reply **13
... h5** (13 ... a6 is also possible)
did he play **14 ♘b5**. There subsequently followed **14 ... ♘f6!?**
(this pawn sacrifice can hardly be
correct) **15 ♘xa7 ♗d7 16 ♘b5 g4
17 fg hg 18 ♗h4 ♘xe4 19 ♗xg4
♘f6 20 ♗xd7 ♕xd7 21 ♖a3 ♘f5
22 ♗f2 e4 23 ♘c2 ♖ae8 24 ♗e1
f3 25 gf e3 26 ♘bd4 ♘xd4 27
♘xd4 ♘h5 28 ♘e6** (Korchnoi
pointed out that 28 ♔h1 leads to
a win) **28 ... ♖xe6 29 de ♕xe6 30
♕d5 ♕xd5 31 cd e2 32 ♖f2 ♗d4
33 ♔g2 ♘f4+ 34 ♔g3 ♘h5+**. In
time trouble Black announces
perpetual check. He would have
now held the advantage by continuing 34 ... ♗e5+.
35 ♔g2 ♘f4+ Draw agreed.

13 ...   a6

In the game Cebalo–Vukic
(Yugoslavia 1987) Black decided
not to allow the knight to go to a7
and played 13 ... b6 14 b4 a6 15
♘c3. Worse would be 15 ♘a3 h5
16 c5 b5 17 ♘ac2 ♘f6 18 a4 ba 19
♖xa4 ♘g6 20 b5 g4 21 ♘b4 g3!
22 hg fg 23 ♗xg3 h4 24 ♘c6 ♕d7
25 ♗h2 ♗h6! 26 f4! ♘xf4 27 ba
♕g7 28 ♗xf4? ♗xf4, and Black
won (Huzman–Smirin, Sver-
dlovsk 1987); 28 ♔h1 would lead
to complex play. Hence White
loses two tempi by retreating the
knight to c3. However, the tearing
up of his 'roots', the pawn pair a6
and b6, does nothing to improve
Black's position, and therefore
White does not begrudge the time
spent.
15 ... ♘g6 16 ♘d3 ♖f7 17 a4

♗f8 (halting the advance of the
queenside pawns does not meet
with success: 17 ... a5 18 ba
♖xa5 19 ♘b4!; 18 ... ba 19 c5) 18
a5 ♖b8 19 ab cb (it is better to
take on b6 with the knight) 20 c5
h5 21 ♕c2. Now Black succeeds
in obtaining his standard counterplay on the kingside, and the
game subsequently concluded in a
win for him after a string of
mutual mistakes.

However, Vukic proposes that
by continuing 21 ♘a4! b5 22 ♘c3
♖g7 23 cd ♗xd6 24 ♘c5, White
would have created a big advantage.

14   ♘a7

This is the gist of Korchnoi's
plan. Black can count on nothing
on the kingside without his light-
squared bishop, and therefore it is
necessary to take on a7. However,
does he not also win two pieces
for a rook?! The fact of the matter
is that while the bishop is rounded
up, the white pawns break
through the queenside.

14	**...**	**♖xa7**
15	**♗xa7**	**b6**
16	**b4**	**♗b7**
17	**c5**	

On almost the very same day
the game Agnos–Zueger (London
1987) was played, in which White
played 17 ♕a4 and also quickly
obtained a decisive advantage: 17
... ♘c8 18 c5 dc 19 ♗xa6 ♗xa6
20 ♕xa6 ♘d6 21 ♘d3 c4 22 ♘c5!
bc 23 bc ♘c8 24 c6 ♘db6 25
♗xb6 ♘xb6 26 a4 ♕a8 27 ♕b5
♕a7 28 ♔h1 ♖a8 29 a5 ♗f8 30

d6! ♗xd6 31 ab! ♕xa1 32 ♕xc4+
♔g7 33 b7 etc.

| 17 | ... | dc |

17 ... bc is no better either: 18
bc ♕a8 19 ♗b6 cb 20 c6.

| 18 | ♖c1 | ♘c8 |

Korchnoi gives this variation in
his notes to the game: 18 ... cb 19
♕a4 a5 20 ♗b5 ♘f6 21 ♕c2 ♕a8
(21 ... ♘c8 22 ♗b8; 21 ...
♘exd5 22 ed ♘xd5 23 ♗c4 ♖f7
24 ♘d3 ♖d7 25 ♖fe1) 22 ♕xc7
♖c8 23 ♕xe7 ♖xc1 24 ♕e6+
♔h8 25 ♕xb6 winning.

19	bc	♗a8
20	c6	♘f6
21	♗xb6	♘xb6
22	♗xa6	

One of White's bishops is
doomed, but in return, the other
is allowed to dominate the board
completely.

| 22 | ... | g4 |
| 23 | ♘d3 | g3 |

There would yet be some tension created on the kingside after
23 ... h5. Now this very part of
the board is blockaded, and the
queenside battle is lost for Black.

24	h3	♘e8
25	♘c5	♕b8
26	a4	♘d6
27	a5	♘bc8
28	♔h1	♕a7
29	♕c2	♘e7
30	♖b1	♘g6
31	♖fc1	♗f6
32	♗f1	♗xc6
33	dc	♕xa5
34	♖a1	♕b4
35	♘e6	

Black resigned

Salov–Belyavsky
Vilnius 1987

1	c4	♘f6
2	♘c3	g6
3	e4	♗g7
4	d4	d6
5	♘f3	

The Sämisch Variation—5 f3—
is met significantly less often these
days than the Classical System—5
♘f3 etc. The next game won the
best game competition in *Chess
Informant* 39 (the first half of
1985), and the victim happens to
be one of the participants in the
text game.

**Belyavsky–Nunn (Wijk aan Zee
1985): 5 f3 0-0 6 ♗e3 ♘bd7 7 ♕d2
c5 8 d5 ♘e5**. Up till now 8 ... a6
or 8 ... ♖e8 have been played
here. The thrust of the knight to
the centre seems unjustified, as it
doesn't hold out on e5 for long.
Could one have guessed that the
horseman would deliver the decisive blow!?

9 h3. White takes control of the
g4 square in order to drive the
knight away conveniently, but
spends a priceless tempo on this.
A few days later, at this very
tournament, Timman continued
against Nunn 9 ♗g5 and after 9
... a6 10 f4 ♘ed7 11 ♘f3
obtained the better game.

**9 ... ♘h5 10 ♗f2 f5 11 ef
♖xf5!**(56) **12 g4**. White's position is sufficiently sound after 12
♘e4, but why not take the piece
now? **12 ... ♖xf3! 13 gh ♕f8! 14
♘e4 ♗h6 15 ♕c2 ♕f4!** Not a
position, but an entire kaleido-

scope of pieces. A romantic in the 20th century!

16 ♘e2 ♖xf2! 17 ♔xf2 ♘f3+ 18 ♔d1 ♕h4 19 ♘d3 ♗f5 20 ♘ec1 ♘d2! Cutting across the communications of White's pieces.

21 hg hg 22 ♗g2 ♘xc4 23 ♕f2 ♘e3+ 24 ♔e2 ♕c4 25 ♗f3 ♖f8 26 ♖g1 ♘c2 27 ♔d1 ♗xd3 White resigned.

Three years later these opponents did battle again in a King's Indian Defence, and the Grandmaster from Lvov took his revenge.

Belyavsky–Nunn (Reykjavik 1988): **5 f3 0-0 6 ♗e3 ♘c6**. This time Black chooses another topical continuation. **7 ♕d2 a6 8 ♘ge2 ♖b8 9 ♘c1 e5 10 ♘b3 ed 11 ♘xd4 ♘xd4 12 ♗xd4 ♗e6 13 ♗e2**. Theory considers this position as advantageous to White, and the present game once again confirms this evaluation. **13 ... c6 14 a4 d5 15 cd cd 16 e5 ♘d7 17 f4 f6 18 ef ♘xf6 19 ♖d1 ♕d7 20 0-0 ♖bd8 21 ♗d6 d4 22 ♕xd4 ♕xd4+ 23 ♗xd4**, and White eventually converted his extra pawn.

Along with the moves 6 ... ♘bd7 and 6 ... ♘c6, Black has at his disposal 6 ... e5. It was used twice quite recently by Kasparov, with which he achieved these brilliant victories.

Timman–Kasparov (Reykjavik 1988): **6 ... e5 7 d5 c6 8 ♗d3 b5!** Curiously, this move was invented by Timman himself 15 years ago (in a game with Spassky, Amsterdam 1973). This theme is well known in other games, but White, it seems, never accepts the pawn sacrifice. Playing as White, Timman chooses the more principled continuation, but his opponent quickly seizes the initiative.

9 cb cd 10 ed e4! 11 ♘xe4 ♘xd5 12 ♗g5 ♕a5+ 13 ♕d2 ♕xd2+ 14 ♗xd2 ♗xb2 15 ♖b1 ♗g7 16 ♘e2 ♘d7 17 ♘xd6 ♘c5 18 ♗c2 ♗e6 19 ♘e4 ♖ac8 20 0-0 ♘xe4 21 ♗xe4 f5 22 ♗d3 ♘b6 23 ♘c1 ♖fd8 24 ♗g5 ♖d7 25 ♖e1 ♔f7. White's extra pawn is of no significance, and Black's positional advantage is conspicuous despite its harmless appearance. **26 ♗e2 h6 27 ♗h4 ♘d5 28 ♗d1 ♗d4+ 29 ♗f2 ♗xf2+ 30 ♔xf2 ♘c3 31 ♗b3 ♗xb3 32 ♖xb3 ♘d1+ 33 ♖xd1 ♖xd1**. It's all over, and White soon resigned.

Gheorghiu–Kasparov Thessaloniki 1988: 7 ... c6 8 ♕d2 cd 9 cd ♘bd7 10 ♘ge2 a6 11 ♘c1 ♘h5 12 ♗d3 f5 13 ♘1e2 ♘df6 14 ef gf 15 ♘g3 e4! As in the previous game, this central pawn thrust allows Black to seize the initiative.

16 ♘xh5 ♘xh5 17 fe f4 18 ♗f2 ♗g4 19 h3 ♗d7 20 0-0-0 ♗e5 21

♔b1 ♛f6. Again, White doesn't benefit from his extra pawn, and Black's pressure grows with every move.

22 ♗e2 ♘g3 23 ♗xg3 fg 24 ♗f3 ♖ac8 25 ♘e2 ♛g6 26 ♖c1 ♖xc1+ 27 ♛xc1 ♖c8 28 ♛e3 ♛f6 29 ♛d2 ♖c5 30 ♘c1 ♗f4 31 ♛b4 ♗b5 32 ♘b3 ♗d3+ 33 ♔a1 ♖c2 34 ♖b1 ♗e5 35 ♘c1 ♗xb2+! 36 ♛xb2 ♛xb2+ White resigned.

The King's Indian Defence isn't met so often now at the highest level: it is more difficult for Black to reckon on equality (only not on account of those games examined!) than, let's say, the Queen's Indian Defence. But the most devoted adherents of this opening always expect a reward for their boldness. This, of course, not only concerns the World Champion, but also chess players of all standards.

We now return to the main game.

5	**...**	**0-0**
6	**♗e2**	**e5**
7	**de**	**de**
8	**♛xd8**	**♖xd8***(57)*

What may one say about the exchange variation? Objectively speaking, it is very dangerous for Black, although it may not be to the taste of many 'King's Indians'. Adherents of this opening strive intensely for their desired intricate battle with rich tactical possibilities, and here he is forced into a 'boring' endgame after only a few moves, with the knowledge that a certain accuracy will be demanded of him for a level game.

Belyavsky rarely chooses the King's Indian Defence as Black, and Salov, expecting some kind of opening novelty from his opponent, presents his surprise first, avoiding the well-trodden theoretical paths.

9 ♗g5

It goes without saying that White cannot win a pawn—if he could it would simply refute the move ... e7–e5: 9 ♘xe5 ♘xe4! 10 ♘xe4 ♗xe5 11 0-0 (11 ♗g5 ♖d4) 11 ... ♘c6 12 ♖e1 ♔g7 13 a3 ♗f5 14 ♘g3 ♗e6 with the better game for Black. All of this was seen in the old game Sanchez–Geller (Stockholm 1952).

In the event of 9 ♘d5 best of all would be 9 ... ♖d7! 10 ♘xe5 ♘xd5 11 ♘xd7 ♘b4 12 ♘xb8 ♘c2+ 13 ♔d1 ♘xa1 14 ♗f4 ♗xb2 15 ♗xc7 a5, preparing a4 and ♘b3. Black also has an excellent game here.

9 ... ♖e8

9 ... ♘bd7, 9 ... ♘a6 and 9 ... c6 are rarer continuations. The last of these, up until recently, was condemned by theory on the basis of the variation 10 ♘xe5 ♖e8 11

♗f4 (the moves 11 0-0-0 or 11 f4 are not dangerous for Black) 11 ... ♘xe4 12 ♘xe4 ♗xe5 13 ♘d6! However, in the game Bouaziz–Nunn (Szirak 1987) there followed 11 ... ♘a6!, and after 12 0-0-0 ♘c5 13 f3 ♘h5 14 ♗e3 ♘xe4 15 ♘xe4 ♗xe5 16 ♗d4 ♗f5 17 ♗xe5 ♖xe5 18 ♘c3 ♘f4 19 ♗f1 ♖ae8 Black obtained a clear advantage.

10   ♘d5

An active move. On 10 ♖d1 or 10 0-0-0 Black has no difficulties.

10	...	♘xd5
11	cd	c6
12	♗c4	cd

Similarly, striking on the flank with 12 ... b5 is insufficient for equality: 13 ♗b3 ♗b7 14 ♖c1 a5 15 a3 ♖a6 16 0-0 a4 17 ♗a2 ♘d7 18 dc ♖xc6 19 ♖xc6 ♗xc6 20 ♖c1 (Miles–Marinovic, Bled 1979).

13   ♗xd5   ♘a6

If the knight was heading for b4, it would be equally suited by the staging posts a6 or c6, but Black's idea consists of the transfer of the knight to c7. In the event of 13 ... ♘d7 White retains a positional advantage.

14   0-0-0(58)

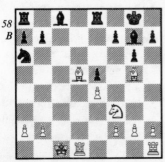

The game Shabalov–Khalifman (USSR 1986) developed interestingly: 14 ♔e2 ♘c7 (more precise than 14 ... ♘b4 15 ♗c4 ♗g4 16 ♖hc1 ♘c6 17 ♔f1 ♗xf3 18 gf ♘d4 19 ♔g2, which led to a White advantage in a string of games) 15 ♗b3 ♗d7 (more accurate than 15 ... ♗e6 16 ♖hd1 ♗xb3 17 ab ♘e6 18 ♗e3 ♘d4 19 ♗xd4 ed 20 ♔d3! with advantage to White; Andersson–Bouaziz, Hastings 1979/80) 16 ♘d2 ♗c6 17 ♗e3 ♘e6 18 ♖hd1 ♔f8 19 ♗xe6 ♖xe6 20 a4 f5 21 b4 a6 22 ♘b3. White holds a small advantage which Black succeeded in nullifying.

14	...	♘c7
15	♗b3	♗e6
16	♗xe6	♘xe6
17	♗e3	f5
18	♔b1	b6

Salov pointed out, when commenting on the game, that only this move is new; 18 ... f4 was played previously.

19   ♖he1

A minimal advantage is retained by White after 19 ♖d6 ♖ad8 20 ♖hd1 ♖xd6 21 ♖xd6 f4 22 ♗c1 ♘c5 23 ♘d2.

19	...	♖ad8
20	♘g5	♘f8
21	♘f3	♘e6
22	♘g5	♘f8
23	♗c1	

White refrains from repeating moves, but Black's position is sufficiently solid.

23	...	h6
24	♖xd8	♖xd8
25	♘f3	f4

26	b3	g5
27	h3	♘e6
28	♗b2	♘c5!

Now the chances are on the side of full equality.

29	♖e2	♖e8
30	♘e1	

White could suddenly be losing in the event of 30 ♗c3 ♖c8 31 ♗xe5 ♘d3!

30	...	♔f7
31	f3	♖d8
32	♔c2	♔e6
33	♖d2	♖xd2+
34	♔xd2	♗f8
35	♘d3	♘xd3
36	♔xd3	a6
37	a4	b5
38	♗c3	♗c5
39	♗e1	♔d6
40	ab	ab
41	♗a5	♔e6
42	♗c7	♗b4
43	♔c2	♔f6
44	♔d3	

Draw agreed

Gavrikov–Kasparov
Moscow 1988

I will illustrate the modern treatment of the Classical System with the move 9 ♘d2 by means of two of Kasparov's games from the 55th USSR Championship (and, as usual, various examples in the notes): in one of them he plays as Black, and the other, as White. The solitary King's Indian from my matches with Kasparov is covered in the first of these games.

1	d4	♘f6
2	c4	g6
3	♘c3	♗g7
4	e4	d6
5	♗e2	0-0
6	♘f3	e5
7	0-0	♘c6
8	d5	♘e7
9	♘d2	

On the immediate 9 b4 there follows 9 ... ♘h5 and the threat on ... ♘f4 forces White to play g2–g3, which leads to dynamic play, quite favourable for Black. So, before such an advance of the b-pawn, it makes sense to retreat the White knight. The two games which are devoted to the move 9 ♘e1 are given above.

9	...	a5

Now Black has to take care to blockade the queenside. Attempts to commence immediate operations on the kingside by 9 ... ♘d7(e8) 10 b4 f5, as shown by many years' practice, more often lead to success for White. Black has three ways to help develop a queenside initiative: 9 ... a5, 9 ... c5 and also the advance of both pawns by two squares. We dwell at more length on the move 9 ... c5 in the notes to the next game.

A confusing path was chosen deliberately by Kasparov in our game, which we will now look at (one more example of the 'double blockade' will be examined below). In both of the main games Black limits himself to the manoeuvre ... a7–a5.

10	a3 *(59)*

The main move, which prepares b2–b4. Kasparov didn't once risk the King's Indian Defence in the first three of our matches and I almost discounted the possibility of its appearance in the fourth. So, when my opponent's choice nevertheless fell on the current opening, it came as a small surprise to me. This, in some measure, explains my wish to depart from the central trend—10 a3—and to decide in favour of the rarer and more solid 10 b3; now the b-pawn will got to b4 with a loss of tempo. Subsequently, I intended to play more positively, but, alas, Kasparov did not repeat his experiment (either in Seville, or in our later encounters).

Karpov–Kasparov, m (17) Seville 1987: 10 b3 c5! Black utilizes the loss of tempo b2–b3 and establishes a strong blockade on the queenside. In the game Lputyan–Dorfman (Moscow 1986) after 10 ... ♘d7 11 ♗a3 (this is the idea of the move b3: the pawn makes way for the bishop, which then advances further) 11 ... f5 12 b4 ab 13 ♗xb4 ♔h8 (13 ... ♗h6 14 ♘b3! ♘f6 15 ♗f3 g5 16 ef ♗xf5 17 c5! g4 18 ♗e2 ♔h8 19

♘a5 and White has a clear advantage; Gleizerov–Gurevich, USSR 1987) 14 a4 ♘g8 15 ♘b3 b6 16 a5 ♘c5 17 ♖a3! ♗d7 18 ♗xc5 bc 19 a6 ♘f6 20 a7 White had a significant initiative, and he quickly prevailed. Incidentally, the only mention of the move 10 b3 in the *Encyclopaedia of Chess Openings* is given in the old game Korchnoi–Geller (match 1971): 10 ... ♘d7 11 ♗a3 ♘c5 12 b4 ab 13 ♗xb4 ♘a6 14 ♗a3 b6 15 ♘b3 f5 with approximate equality.

11 a3 ♘e8 12 ♖b1 f5 13 b4 ab 14 ab b6 15 ♕b3 (15 ♕c2 is worth considering) **15 ... ♘f6 16 ♗d3 ♗h6 17 ♖b2***(60)*. Black has solved his opening problems, but, all the same, White has a minimal advantage.

17 ... ♖a1 18 ♕c2 ♗f4. 18 ... ♗xd2 can hardly be good, since White has 19 ♕xd2! f4 20 ♘a2 with the further ♖b3 and ♕b2. After the transfer of the bishop to f4, some commentators mistakenly considered that Black could scarcely take the initiative. A fine variation was suggested in the press room by Tal: 19 ♘b3 ♘exd5 20 ♘xd5 ♗xh2+ 21 ♔h1

♘g4 22 g3 f4 23 f3 ♗xg3 24 ♖g1
(24 fg ♕h4+ 25 ♔g1—25 ♔g2
♕h2+ 26 ♔f3 ♗xg4+ 27 ♔xg4
♕h5 mate—25 ... f3) 24 ...
♕h4+ 25 ♔g2 ♕h3+ 26 ♔xh3
♘e3 mate. A flashy combination,
but easily refuted: 21 ♔xh2
♘g4+ 22 ♔g3 h5 (22 ... f4+ 23
♔f3) 22 f3.

19 ♘f3. Leading to an endgame
with a microscopic advantage for
White. He could have counted on
more by continuing 19 bc bc 20
♖b1 ♖xb1 21 ♘dxb1.

**19 ... fe 20 ♘xe4 ♘xe4 21
♗xe4 ♖xc1 22 ♖xc1 ♗xc1 23
♕xc1 ♘f5 24 ♕g5.** 24 ♘g5 ♘d4
25 bc bc 26 h4 h6 27 ♘e6 ♗xe6
(27 ... ♘xe6 28 de ♕xh4 29 e7!
♕xe7 30 ♕xh6) 28 de ♕xh4 29 e7
♖e8 30 ♗xg6 ♖xe7 31 f3! ♕g5
32 ♕xg5 hg 33 ♖b6 is unclear.

**24 ... ♘d4 25 ♕xd8 ♘xf3+
26 ♗xf3 ♖xd8 27 bc bc 28 ♖b8
♖f8 29 ♖b6 ♖f6 30 ♖b8 ♖f8 31
♖b6 ♖f6 32 ♗e4 ♗f5!? 33 ♗xf5
♖xf5 34 g3 ♖f6 35 h4 h6 36 ♔g2
♔g7 37 f3 ♔g8 38 ♔f2 g5 39 hg
hg 40 ♔e3 ♔g7 41 ♖b8 ♔h7 42
♖d8.** Allowing Black to force a
draw. More accurate was 42
♖b7+ ♔g6 43 ♖d7 or 42 ♔e4.

42 ... ♔g7*(61)*. 42 ... g4!
secures the draw immediately: 43
f4 ef+ 44 gf g3 45 ♖a8 g2 46 ♖a1
♖g6 47 ♖g1 ♖g3+ 48 ♔f2 ♖c3
49 ♖xg2 ♖xc4 50 ♔f3 ♖d4.

43 ♖a8. After the game, Kasparov uneasily related how, just
over an hour before the start of
play, he had discovered a dangerous manoeuvre for White. In his
search for a defence, he was quite

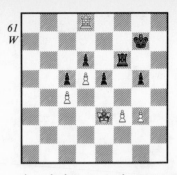

61
W

convinced there wasn't one, and
he was even 18 minutes late for
the resumption. Of course, when
at the last moment a previously
unnoticed variation is discovered,
it is easy to become frustrated and
to exaggerate its significance. In
reality, a rook ending under these
conditions is not won for White,
although a certain accuracy is
demanded from Black. Here are
the main variations:

43 ♖d7+. Apparently, my
opponent also had this move in
mind. 43 ... ♔g6 44 g4 ♔h6 45
♔e2 ♔g6 46 ♔d2 ♔h6 47 ♔c2
♖xf3. It is important not to allow
the white king to the queenside. In
the event of 47 ... ♔g6 48 ♔b3
♖xf3+ 49 ♔a4, it's not difficult
to see how a queen ending eventually arises with an extra pawn
for White. This, probably, would
also have been feared by Kasparov. Now a simple draw is
achieved.

48 ♖xd6+ ♔g7 49 ♖c6 (49
♖e6 ♖f4 50 ♔b3 ♖xg4 51 ♖xe5
♔f6 52 ♖e6+ ♔f7 53 ♖c6 ♖d4
54 ♖xc5 g4 55 ♖a5 g3 56 ♖a1 g2
♔b4 ♖g4 57 58 ♖g1 ♔e7 with a
draw) 49 ... ♖f4 50 ♖xc5 ♖xg4
51 ♔d3 (51 ♖c6 ♖d4) 51 ... ♖f4

(51 ... ♖d4+ 52 ♔e3 ♔f6 53
♖c6+ ♔f5 54 d6 ♖e4+ 55 ♔f3
♖f4+ 56 ♔g3 ♖g4+ 57 ♔h3
♖h4+ 58 ♔g3 ♖g4+ 59 ♔f3
♖f4+ 60 ♔e3 ♖e4+ 61 ♔d3
♖d4+ with perpetual check, and
62 ♔c3 is generally bad for White
due to 62 ... g4) 52 ♖c7+
♔f6(f8) with a draw.

Returning to the game: **43 ...
♔f7 44 ♔e4**. Nothing is gained by
44 ♖a7+ ♔g6 45 ♖e7 (45 g4
♖f7 46 ♖a8 ♖f4 47 ♖d8 ♖xc4
48 ♖xd6+ ♔f7 49 ♖e6 ♖d4 50
♖xe5 ♔f6 51 ♖f5+ ♔g6) 45 ...
g4 (but not 45 ... ♔h6 46 ♖e6
♔g7 47 ♔e4 ♔f7 48 ♖xf6 ♔xf6
49 g4 ♔g6 50 ♔d3! ♔f6 51 ♔c3
e4 52 fe ♔e5 53 ♔b3 ♔d4 54 e5!
♔xe5 55 ♔a4 with a win) 46 f4 ef
47 gf g3 with a draw, as the attempt to win by 48 ♖e6? con-
cludes lamentably for White: 48
... ♖xe6 49 de ♔f6 50 f5 d5! 51
cd ♔e7!

**44 ... ♔g7 45 ♖a7+ ♔g6 46
♖e7**. The counterblow ... g5–g4
also saves Black after other rook
moves: 46 ♖b7 g4! 47 f4 ef 48 gf
♖f7!; 46 ♖d7 g4 47 f4 ef 48 gf g3
49 ♖a7 ♖f8! (but not 49 ... g2?
50 ♖a1 or 49 ... ♔h5 50 ♖h7+)
50 ♖a3 ♖e8+ 51 ♔f3 ♔f5 52
♔xg3 ♖e4.

44 ... g4! I would have retained
some chances of success after 46
... ♔h6 47 ♖e6 ♔g7 48 ♖xf6
♔xf6 49 g4 ♔g6 50 ♔d3 ♔f6 51
♔c3 e4 52 fe ♔e5 53 ♔b3, and
although the d- and c-pawns
queen at the same time, an endgame arises in which White has
chances to win. Now there is

nothing left for me to do but enter
into peaceful negotiations: **Draw
agreed.**

I hope that the reader did not
get tangled in the web of diverse
variations. It's time for me now to
return to the game Gavrikov–
Kasparov.

10 ... ♘d7

The move 10 ... ♘d7 was also
chosen in the same tournament, in
the game Salov–Khalifman: 11
♖a2!? (the rook is defended by
the knight, while 11 ♖b1 is not
bad either, intending not to lose
time with b2–b3) 11 ... ♘e8 (11
... a4 12 b4 ab 13 ♕xb3 ♗c8 14
a4; 11 ... ♘c8 12 b4 ab 13 ab
♘b6 14 ♕c2, preparing c4–c5 or
♘b5; White has the initiative in
both cases) 12 b4 f5 (12 ... ab 13
ab ♖xa2 14 ♘xa2 f5 15 c5, and
White is better; Lputyan–Lanka,
Novosibirsk 1986) 13 c5 ab 14 ab
♖xa2 15 ♘xa2 ♘f6 16 ♘c3 ♔h8
(16 ... fe is better) 17 f3 f4 18 ♘c4
♘c8 19 ♘a5 b6 20 ♘c6. White's
chances are greater, though play
subsequently became level and he
only won because of a gross
blunder by his opponent.

Although there also exists a
rule which recommends you not
to advance a pawn in an area of
the board which is under attack
by your opponent, here the creation of a pawn shield—**10 ... c5**—
is worthy of attention. Let's look
at one example of this advance.

**Pekarek–Vokac (Kecskemet
1988): 11 ♖b1 b6 12 b4 ab 13 ab
♘e8 14 bc bc 15 ♘b3 ♔h8** (15 ...
f5 16 ♗g5 ♗f6 17 ♗d2 ♖f7 18 f3

f4 19 ♖a1 ♖b8 20 ♘b5 with advantage to White; Eingorn–Marinovic, Bor 1985; it would follow for Black to develop his bishop to d7 on either the 17th or 18th move) **16 ♗d2 ♘g8 17 ♖a1 ♖xa1 18 ♕xa1 f5 19 ♕a8 ♘ef6 20 ef gf 21 ♕b8**. It would also follow to delay the queenside pawn exchanges, which allow the white pieces to penetrate behind enemy lines. However, Black has counterplay.

21 ... ♕d7 22 ♕b6 ♘e4. Commenting on this encounter, Pekarek quotes another of his games: 22 ... ♘e7 23 ♘a5 ♘e4 24 ♘xe4 fe 25 ♗e3 ♗h6 26 ♘c6 ♕f7 27 ♘a7 ♗g4!, and Black has the initiative (Pekarek–Schmidt, Prague 1988).

23 ♘xe4 fe 24 ♗e3 ♘f6 25 ♘d2 ♖g8 26 ♖a1 ♗f8 27 g3 ♕h3 (losing a tempo; the queen could go straight to f5) **28 ♕d8 ♕f5 29 ♖a7 ♗d7** *(62)*.

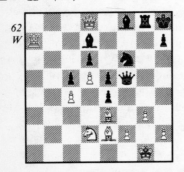

It is due to this position that we have gone to so much detail in the present game. The situation is tense enough, but White essentially needs to find one blow to decide the contest: **30 ♗g4!!** Truly

a study move: the bishop is *en prise* to a number of pieces! **30 ...
♘xg4** (30 ... ♖xg4 31 ♕xf8+ ♖g8 32 ♕xd6; 30 ... ♕xg4 31 ♕xf6+ ♗g7 32 ♕xd6) **31 ♕xd7 ♕h5 32 ♘f1 ♖g7 33 ♕c8 ♖g8 34 ♕e6 ♕g6 35 ♖f7 ♕h5 36 ♖f5 ♕g6 37 h3 ♘xe3 38 ♘xe3 ♗h6 39 ♖f6 ♗xe3 40 ♖xg6 ♗xf2+ 41 ♔xf2 ♖xg6 42 ♕f7 e3+ 43 ♔e2 ♖xg3 44 ♕f8+ ♖g8 45 ♕xd6 Black resigned**.

We return once more to the game Gavrikov–Kasparov.

11	♖b1	f5
12	**b4***(63)*	

12	...	♔h8

A few rounds later, in the game Kasparov–Smirin, which follows this one, Black played the immediate 12 ... b6.

13	♕c2	

A new move, possibly specially prepared by Gavrikov for this clash with the World Champion. In the case of 13 f3 f4 14 ♘b3 ab 15 ab g5 16 c5 ♘f6 17 ♗d2 h5 Black obtains the typical kingside counterplay associated with this variation (Dokhoyan–Loginov, USSR 1987). He doesn't have bad prospects either after 13 c5 dc 14

bc ♘xc5 15 a4 ♘xe4 16 ♘dxe4 fe
17 ♗a3 (Rashkovsky–Loginov,
Tashkent 1987) or 13 ♘b3 ab 14
ab fe 15 ♘xe4 ♘f6.

13	...	b6
14	♘b3	ab
15	ab	fe
16	♘xe4	♘f6
17	♗d3	♘xe4

White has a minimal advantage
after 17 ... ♘f5 18 ♗g5.

| 18 | ♗xe4 | ♘f5 |

Soon after, an interesting idea
was tried out in the game Ruz-
hana–A. Kuzmin (Blagoveshensk
1988): 18 ... ♘g8!? 19 ♗d2 ♕h4
20 f3 ♘f6 21 ♖a1 ♗d7, and
chances are probably equal.

| 19 | ♕d3 | |

19 c5 ♗a6 20 ♖d1 ♗b5 leads
to unclear play.

19	...	♕h4
20	g3	♕f6
21	f3	♗d7
22	♗d2	♘d4?!

22 ... ♖a3 is more accurate,
and in the event of 23 ♖a1 ♖fa8
24 ♖xa3 ♖xa3 25 ♖a1 a drawn
result is imminent.

23	♘xd4	ed
24	♖a1	

White has a small advantage,
but Kasparov gradually neutral-
izes it.

24	...	♗h3
25	♖xa8	♖xa8
26	♖d1	♗f5
27	♖e1	h5
28	♔f2	♗xe4
29	♕xe4	♖a3

Correct would be to push the
rook one square further: 29 ...
♖a2 30 ♖e2 ♔h7.

30	♕f4!	♕xf4
31	gf	

White has somewhat increased
his advantage, but it is nevertheless insufficient for a victory over
Kasparov.

31	...	♗f6
32	♖e8+	♔g7
33	♖c8	♖a7
34	♔e2	♗h4
35	♔d3	♗f2
36	♗c1	♖a1
37	♖xc7+	♔f6
38	♗d2	

Makarichev points out that 38
♗b2 ♖d1+ 39 ♔c2 ♖e1 40 ♗c1
♗e3 41 ♗xe3 ♖xe3 42 ♔d2 ♖c3
also leads to equality, but there is
also 38 ♔c2! d3+ 39 ♔d2 and
the further ♗b2 still gives White
something to hope for.

38	...	♖a3+
39	♔e4	♖a2
40	♔d3	♖a3+

Draw agreed

Kasparov–Smirin
Moscow 1988

Playing as Black, Kasparov has
gained many stunning victories
with his pet King's Indian
Defence. However, this time he
plays a brilliant game with White.

1	♘f3	♘f6
2	c4	g6
3	♘c3	♗g7
4	e4	d6
5	d4	0-0
6	♗e2	e5
7	0-0	♘c6
8	d5	♘e7
9	♘d2	a5

The third time this system has

been encountered in the USSR championship, and each time Black responded to the retreat of ·knight to d2 with the advance of his a-pawn. It is difficult to explain such consistency, as up till now the advance of the c-pawn clearly led in popularity. Perhaps the reason for this is that in recent times Black, all the more frequently, is finding discomfort in this variation. Before going any further, let's look at some most interesting examples of play with the traditional manoeuvre ... c7–c5.

9 ... c5 10 ≡b1. 10 a3 is another way of preparing an attack, but after 10 ... ♘e8 11 b4 b6 the move ≡a1–b1 is still necessary for White. He often captures *en passant*, but this is not really dangerous for Black: 10 dc bc 11 b4 d5 (11 ... ♘h5 is not bad either) 12 ≡e1 (White gains nothing either with the other well-known continuations 12 b5 and 12 ♗a3) 12 ... ≡e8! 13 b5 ♗e6 14 ♗a3 ♕a5 15 ♗b2 ♘xe4 16 ♘dxe4 de 17 ♘xe4 cb 18 cb ♕b4! 19 ♕c2 ≡ac8 20 ♗c3 ≡xc3 21 ♘xc3 ≡c8 22 ♕a4 ♕xc3 23 ♕xa7 ♘d5! Black has a big advantage, which he easily realizes (Plachetka–Georgiev, Dubai 1986).

10 ... ♘e8. The move 10 ... a5 doesn't have any independent significance; look, for example, at the game Pekarek–Vokac above. Another well-known move 10 ... ♘d7 was cast into doubt in the game Lputyan–Khalifman

(USSR Championship 1987): 11 ♘b5!! ♕b6 12 b4! cb 13 a3 ba *(64)*.

14 c5!! ♘xc5 (14 ... dc 15 d6 ♘c6 16 ♘c7 ♕xb1 17 ♘xb1 a2 18 ♗b2 ab(♕) 19 ♕xb1 ≡b8 20 ♘d5 etc.) 15 ♗xa3 ♕d8 16 ♘xd6 b6 17 ♘2c4 ♗a6 18 ♗xc5 bc 19 ♘b7 ♗xb7 20 ≡xb7 ♘c8 21 d6 ♘b6 22 ♘a5 ♘c8 23 ♘c4 ♘b6 24 ♕d2 and Black resigned ten moves later.

11 b4 b6 12 bc. 12 a4 was seen in the famous game Larsen–Fischer (Denver 1971). After 12 ... f5 13 a5 ♘f6 14 ♕a4 ♗d7 15 ♕a3 ♗h6 16 ♗d3 ♕c7 17 bc bc 18 ef gf White has the freer game on the queenside, but Black has fully equal chances in the centre and on the kingside.

12 ... bc. The other capture 12 ... dc is scarcely better. **13 ♘b3 f5**. In the game Lerner–Renet (Geneva 1988) after 13 ... a5 14 a4 ♘c7 15 ♘xc5 dc 16 d6 ♘e6 17 de ♕xe7 18 ♘d5 ♕a7 19 ♗e3 ♘d4 20 ♗xd4 ed 21 f4 White took an initiative and won the game.

14 ♗g5. More accurate than

the standard 14 f3, for example: 14 ... ♔h8 15 ♗d2 ♘g8 16 ♕c2 ♘h6 17 ♖b2 ♘f6 with equality (Stein–Panno, Las Palmas 1973).

14 ... ♔h8. The black king prudently withdraws to the corner of the board. Let's examine other possibilities: 14 ... ♗f6 15 ♗d2 ♔h8 16 ♗d3 ♗g7 17 f3 ♘g8 18 ♘e2 f4 19 ♘a5 g5 20 ♘c6 ♕f6 21 ♕e1 g4 (12 ... h5 is more precise) 22 fg ♗xg4 23 ♘g3 ♘h6 24 ♗e2 ♕h4 25 ♘h1 ♕g5 26 ♖b3, and Black's counterplay is stopped (Eingorn–Hebden, Moscow 1986).

14 ... ♖f7 15 ef ♗xf5 16 ♗d3 h6 17 ♗xe7 ♖xe7 18 ♕c2 ♖f7 19 ♘e4 ♘f6 20 ♘g3 ♗xd3 21 ♕xd3 ♔h7 22 ♘d2 ♖b8 23 ♖b3 ♖fb7 24 ♖a3 a5 25 ♘de4 ♘xe4 26 ♘xe4 ♖b4 27 g3 a4 28 h4 ♔h8 29 ♔g2 ♕f8 30 ♖e1 ♖8b7 31 ♖e3 ♖d7 32 ♖f3 ♕e8 33 ♕c2 ♖d8 34 h5 g5 35 ♘f6 ♗xf6 36 ♖xf6 ♕xh5 37 ♕f5 ♔g7 **Black resigned** (Chernin–Gunawan, **Belgrade 1980**).

After 14 ... h6 15 ♗xe7 ♕xe7 16 ♘a5 ♘f6 17 ♘c6 ♕d7 18 ef gf 19 ♖b3 e4 20 ♕c1 ♗b7 21 ♕f4 ♗xc6 22 dc ♕xc6 23 ♘b5 White has strong pressure, but in the game Pekarek–Sznapik (Warsaw 1987) Black managed to extricate himself from a ticklish situation 23 ... ♘h7 24 ♘xd6 ♕d7 25 ♖d1 ♕e6 26 ♖d5 ♖ad8 27 ♖g3 ♔h8 28 ♗h5 ♖d7 29 ♖g6? (29 ♗g6 is correct) 29 ... ♖f6! 30 ♖xg7 ♖xg7 31 ♘e8(65).

31 ... ♖b7! A winning manoeuvre, which White obviously

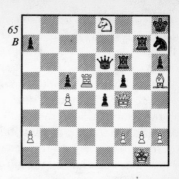

overlooked. **32 ♘xf6 ♕xd5! White resigned**.

15 ♗xe7. The interesting variation 15 ef gf 16 ♘xc5!? should have forced a draw in the game Farago–Watson (Beer Sheva, 1987): 16 ... dc 17 d6 ♘xd6 18 ♘d5 ♖e8 (18 ... ♖f7? 19 ♗h5) 19 ♘xe7 ♖xe7 20 ♕d5 ♗b7 21 ♖xb7 ♘xb7 22 ♕xd8+ ♖xd8 23 ♗xe7 ♖d2 and, as Farago points out, after 24 ♖b1! ♖xe2 25 ♔f1 ♖xa2 26 ♖xb7 ♔g8 27 ♗xc5 a peace treaty may be signed. White played the unfortunate 24 ♗h5 and Black seized the initiative: 24 ... e4 25 ♖b1 ♖xa2 26 g4 ♖a1 27 ♖xa1 ♗xa1 etc.

15 ... ♕xe7 16 ♘a5 ♘f6 17 ♘c6 ♕f7 18 ♗f3 g5. This position arose in the game Littlewood–Nunn (London 1987). Here, after 19 ef ♗xf5 20 ♖b3 g4 21 ♗e2 ♗h6 Black obtained an excellent game and eventually won. However, Nunn established that by continuing 19 ♘b5! g4 (19 ... ♕d7 20 ef; 19 ... ♘e8 20 ♗h5) 20 ♘xd6 ♕d7 21 ♘xf5 gf 22 ♘xe5 ♕e8 23 ♘xf3 ♗xf5 24 ef White obtains four pawns for the bishop and retains the advantage.

We now return to the main game:

10 a3 ♘d7
11 ♖b1

Defeat in the current game didn't deter Smirin from continu-ing the search and soon after the Championship he adopted this variation again, highly success-fully. The game Guseinov–Smirin (Klajpeda 1988) ended in a rout: **11 ♘a4 f5 12 b4 ♘f6 13 ef gf 14 ba f4 15 ♘b3 ♘f5 16 ♘c3 ♘h4 17 f3 ♔h8 18 ♖a2 ♖g8 19 ♗d3 ♗f8 20 ♔h1 ♘h5 21 ♘e4 ♘f5 22 ♘f2 ♕h4 23 ♖e1 ♗e7 24 ♔g1 ♗d7 25 a4 ♖g7 26 ♘g4 ♖ag8 27 ♗xf5 ♗xf5 28 ♘h6 ♗f8 29 ♘d2 ♗d7 30 ♘g4 ♖fg8 31 h3 ♘g3 32 ♘e4 h5 33 ♘h2 ♗xh3 34 ♘xg3 ♖xg3 35 ♖ee2 ♗f5 36 ♗a3 ♖h3 37 g4 fg White resigned.**

11 ... f5
12 b4 b6

It is necessary to prevent the advance of White's c-pawn. In the game Lputyan-Zapata (Belgrade 1988) the continuation 12 ... ab 13 ab ♗h6, and then 14 ef gf 15 c5! dc 16 bc ♘xc5 17 ♘c4 ♗xc1 18 ♕xc1 ♘g6 19 ♖d1 led to an unpleasant position for Black. There followed 19 ... ♘e4 20 ♘xe4 fe 21 ♕e3 ♘f4 22 ♗f1 ♕g5 23 ♕g3 ♕xg3 24 hg ♘g6 25 d6 ♗g4 26 ♖e1 cd 27 ♘xd6 ♗e6 28 ♖xb7 e3 29 f3 ♖a3 30 ♖bb1 ♖fa8 31 ♗c4 ♘f8 32 ♔h2 ♗xc4 33 ♘xc4 ♖c3 34 ♘xe3, and White easily won the ending with his extra pawn.

In the game Gavrikov–Smirin (Klajpeda 1988) Black deferred

... b7–b6 by one move—12 ... ♔h8 13 ♕c2 b6—and a position arose that we saw in the game Gavrikov–Kasparov. Instead of 14 ♘b3 ab 15 ab fe 16 ♘xe4, as played by Gavrikov against the World Champion, there followed: 14 f3 f4 15 ♘b3 ab 16 ab g5 17 c5 ♘f6 18 ♘b5 g4 19 cd cd 20 ♕c7 gf 21 gf ♕e8. Black leaves the centre and queenside in the lap of the gods, but in return develops a decisive offensive on the kingside. 22 ♔h1 ♘h5 23 ♖b2 ♗h3 24 ♖e1 ♕g6 25 ♗f1 ♘g3+ 26 hg ♕xg3 27 ♕c3 ♖ac8 28 ♕d2 ♗xf1 29 ♖xf1 ♕h3+ 30 ♔g1 ♗f6 31 ♘xd6 ♖g8+ 32 ♕g2 ♖cf8, and Smirin won easily.

13 f3 f4
14 ♘a4

Possibly 14 ♘b3 ab 15 ab g5 16 c5 is more accurate.

14 ... ab
15 ab g5
16 c5 ♘f6
17 cd cd
18 b5 ♗d7
19 ♘c4 ♘c8
20 ♗a3 ♘e8(66)

It seems as though Black has positioned his pieces ideally: all the key squares on the queenside are covered and he can set about an assault on the hostile king. However, Kasparov demonstrates a simple but elegant way of parrying this assault.

21 g4!   fg

Otherwise Black has nothing to reckon on: 21 ... h5 22 h3, and the whole flank is sealed tight.

22 hg   g4!

22 ♗c1

Black could count on an attack if the pawn sacrifice were to be accepted. Now, by bringing in the bishop, White takes the initiative in the area usually dominated by his opponent.

23 ...   gf
24 ♗xf3   ♘f6
25 ♗g5   ♖a7
26 ♖f2   ♖b7

Unleashing the queen would lose: 26 ... ♕e8 27 ♘axb6 ♘xb6 28 ♘xb6 ♗xb5 29 ♗xf6 ♗xf6 30 ♗h5.

27 ♖b3   ♖a7
28 ♖b1   ♖b7
29 ♖b3   ♖a7
30 ♖b4

Of course, a draw is out of the question. White's prophylactic manoeuvre frees his queen.

30 ...   ♔h8

The World Champion's trainer, Nikitin, pointed out that the immediate 30 ... ♕e8 was necessary, and after 31 ♘axb6 ♘xb6 32 ♘xb6 ♗xb5 33 ♕b1 Black could still hold on.

31 ♕f1!   ♗xb5
32 ♖xb5   ♖xa4
33 ♗g2!

It is a rare event when, in a King's Indian, a crushing kingside attack is carried out by White.

33 ...   h6
34 ♗h4   ♕e8
35 ♗xf6!   ♖xf6
36 ♖xf6   ♕xb5(67)

67
W

The first impression is that Black has wriggled out (37 ♖f8+ ♗xf8 38 ♕xf8+ with perpetual check), but Kasparov has calculated the combination right to the very end.

37 ♖e6!   ♔g8
38 ♗h3!

The black king is trapped in a mating net.

38 ...   ♖xc4
39 ♖xh6!

A flashy final blow.

39 ...   ♗xh6

Black does not succeed in winning the queen: 39 ... ♕c5+ 40 ♔h1 ♘c1 41 ♗e6 mate.

40 ♗e6+   ♔h8
41 ♕f6+

Black resigned, since mate is unavoidable: 41 ... ♔h7 42 ♕f7+ ♗g7 43 ♗f5+ ♔h8 44 ♕h5+ ♔g8 45 ♗e6+ ♔f8 46 ♕f7 mate.

4 The Queen's Indian Defence

Miles–Belyavsky
Tilburg 1986

An interesting debate surrounding one of the sharpest variations of the Queen's Indian Defence is concluded in this game.

1	d4	♘f6
2	c4	e6
3	♘f3	b6
4	♘c3	♗b4
5	♗g5	♗b7
6	e3	h6
7	♗h4	g5

In the 18th game of the return match I operated here with the more restrained 7 ... ♗xc3+ 8 bc d6 9 ♘d2 g5 10 ♗g3 ♕e7, but I wasn't able to solve my opening problems. We shall return to this position later.

8	♗g3	♘e4
9	♕c2*(68)*	

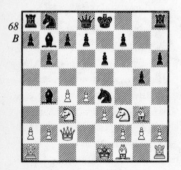

This move was also met in the fascinating game Kasparov–Timman, the fourth of a training match (Hilversum 1985). It was awarded the prize for best novelty in the second half of 1985 by *Chess Informant*. Curiously, a year later the text game also won the very same competition! How do these games differ? We will try to provide the answer to this question.

Before we go any further, I will point out that the other common move in the present variation—9 ♘d2—is less dangerous for Black. Kasparov played this in the second game of the match mentioned above and achieved victory in a sharp struggle. But Timman did not consider the opening to be at fault, and in the fourth game again invited the knight move. His opponent was the first to divert and played his queen to c2. Kasparov returned to the move 9 ♘d2 in a game with Miles (Dubai 1986) and prevailed once more in a sharp battle. Black's play was later improved upon.

9	...	♗xc3+
10	bc	d6
11	♗d3	f5

The exchange on g3 is covered in the game Timman–Sax (Brussels 1988).

12	d5	♘c5

The move 12 ... ♕f6 is also encountered; here is one of the latest examples on this theme.

Salov–Timman (St John 1988): 12 ... ♕f6 13 ♗xe4 fe 14 ♕xe4 ♕xc3+ (Timman had prepared this new move for the 3rd game of his Candidates match; 14 ... ♘d7 was previously played) 15 ♔e2 ♕b2+. The queen loses time here in order to divert the knight from the centre. After 15 ... ♕f6 16 ♘d4 White has a clear advantage. 16 ♘d2 ♕f6 17 h4 g4 18 h5 ♘d7 19 ♗h4 ♕f5 20 ♕xe6+ ♕xe6 21 de ♘c5 22 e7 ♔d7 23 f3 ♖ag8 24 e4 gf+ 25 gf ♖g2+ 26 ♔e3 ♖hg8 27 ♖af1 ♘e6 28 ♖f2 ♖xf2 29 ♔xf2 ♘f4 30 ♗f6 ♗c6 31 ♘b3 ♔e8 32 ♘d4 ♗d7 33 ♘b5 ♔f7 34 ♗h4 ♖g2+ 35 ♔e3 ♘e6 36 ♘c3 c5. 36 ... ♖c2 37 ♔d3 ♖b2 leads to equality. Here, by continuing 37 ♘e2, White retained winning chances, though he subsequently let them slip and the game ended in a draw.

The position after 12 ... ♘c5 was known before the game Kasparov–Timman, when White answers 13 ♘d4. In the game Psakhis–Agzamov (Sochi 1985) after 13 ... ♕f6 14 0-0 ♘ba6 15 f4! gf!? a sharp struggle ensued, eventually concluding in a draw. The try 14 h4!? undertaken in the game **Georgiev–Kudrin (Amsterdam 1985)**, proved unsuccessful: 14 ... ♘ba6 15 ♘xe6 ♘xe6 16 de ♔e7! 17 ♗xf5 ♘b4 18 ♕d2 ♕xf5 19 cb ♗xg2 20 ♖h2 ♗f3 21 c5? (the exchanges on g5 and h8 lead to a draw) 21 ... bc 22 bc ♖ab8! 23 cd+ ♔xe6 24 ♖c1 ♖b1 25 ♔f1 ♕d3+! 26 ♔g1 ♕xd2 27 ♖xb1 ♕d3 28 ♖f1 ♖b8 **White resigned.**

13 h4!

The h-pawn is pushed immediately. This important novelty was used by Kasparov in the fourth game of the same match with Timman, and it created a decisive impression on the *Chess Informant* adjudicators. White stabilizes the kingside situation before commencing central operations.

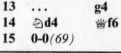

13 ... g4
14 ♘d4 ♕f6
15 0-0 *(69)*

69
B

15 ... ♘xd3

Timman also opted for this exchange, but only in the sixth game of the match. He continued 15 ... ♘ba6 in the fourth, which went 16 ♘xe6 ♘xe6 17 ♗xf5! (in the event of 17 de 0-0 18 e7 ♖f7 Black's chances are no worse) 17 ... ♘g7 18 ♗g6+ ♔d7 19 f3! In such a way White exploits the position of the presumptious pawn which he lured to g4 by means of h2–h4. Here it is already clear why Kasparov's opening surprise was rated so highly. 19 ... ♖af8 20 fg ♕e7 21 e4 ♔c8 22 ♕d2 ♔b8. Yet another critical moment. Here Kasparov continued 23 ♖xf8+, and after 23 ... ♖xf8 24 ♕xh6 ♗c8! 25 ♖e1

♗xg4 26 c5 ♕f6 27 cd ♗h5! 28 e5 ♕xg6 29 ♕xg6 ♗xg6 30 e6 ♘c5 31 d7 ♘xd7 32 ed ♖d8 33 ♖e6 ♗h5 34 ♗e5 ♖xd7 35 ♖h6 ♗f7 36 ♗xg7 ♗xd5 37 ♗e5 ♗xa2 a fascinating opening dialogue eventually leads to an opposite-coloured bishop ending, the game ending in a draw. According to Kasparov, White could have developed an initiative by continuing 23 ♕d4! ♘e8 ♖xf8 ♖xf8 25 ♖f1. This variation was encountered in the fifth game of the Candidates match **Salov–Timman (St John 1988)**, only instead of the exchange on f8 Salov played 24 ♖f7. There followed: 24 ... ♖xf7 25 ♕xh8 ♖f8 26 ♕xh6 ♘c5 27 h5 ♘d7 28 ♗f5 ♗c8 29 ♖f1 ♘e5 30 ♗xc8 ♖xf1+ 31 ♔xf1 ♔xc8 32 g5 ♔d7 33 ♔g1 ♕f7 34 g6 ♕f6 35 ♕h7+ ♔d8. White has more than sufficient compensation for the piece, both materially and positionally, but he played the unfortunate 36 ♗xe5 and history repeated itself from the third game of the match: Black getting out of trouble with 36 ... ♕xe5 37 g7 ♕g3 38 g8(♕) ♕e1+ 39 ♔h2 ♕h4+ 40 ♔g1 **Drawn** by perpetual check. While discussing the game, Timman noted that the immediate 36 g7! would have maintained some advantage for White: 36 ... ♘xg7 37 h6 ♘e8 38 ♕f5! ♗f7 (38 ... ♕xh6 39 ♗f4 loses as does 38 ... ♕xf5 39 ef ♘f6 40 ♗h4 ♔e7 41 h7 ♘f7 42 g4) 39 ♕h5 ♕xh6 40 ♗h4+ ♔c8 41 ♕xf7 ♕xh4·42 ♕xe8+ ♔b7. Black establishes the draw.

The attempt 22 ... ♘c5 (instead of 22 ... ♔b8) also falls short. In the game Miles–Timman (Tilburg 1986) there followed 23 ♖xf8 ♖xf8 24 ♕xh6 ♕f6 25 ♗f5 ♘xf5 26 ♕xf6 ♖xf6 27 ef ♗a6 28 ♗f2 and White won quickly.

16	♕xd3	e5
17	♘xf5!	♗c8(70)

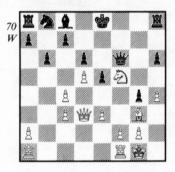

70
W

The sixth game of Kasparov–Timman is repeated up till now. White suggested here the positional knight sacrifice 18 ♘d4! (Black has good play after 18 e4 ♗xf5 19 ef ♘d7 or 19 f4 gf 20 ♖xf3 ♘d7 21 ♖xf5 ♕g6). After 18 ... ed 19 cd ♕f5 20 e4 ♕g6 21 ♕c3 0-0 22 ♖fe1 ♘d7 23 e5. White's central pawn storm would bring him victory. However, a year later in the game **Gligoric–Popovic (Yugoslav Ch. 1986)** Black introduced a valuable improvement: 19 ... 0-0! 20 f3 (20 f4! c5! is unclear) 20 ... ♕g7! 21 ♔h2 (21 fg ♖xf1+ 22 ♖xf1 ♗xg4 23 e4 ♘d7 is in Black's favour) 21 ... ♘d7 22 e4 ♘f6 23 f4 ♘xe4 (according to Gligoric, his opponent could have fought for the initiative by way of 23 ...

♘h5) **24 ♕xe4 ♗f5 25 ♕e3 ♖fe8 26 ♕d2 ♖e4 27 ♖ad1 ♖ae8 28 ♖fe1 ♕d7 29 ♖xe4 ♖xe4 Draw agreed**.

Hence the novelty 13 h4, as a result of inspirational clashes between a few Grandmasters was seen for a time as not too dangerous for Black. But it seems that our text game dots all the 'i's. From diagram 70 White presented his opponent with yet another surprise. There followed:

18 f4!!

And it turns out that Black is utterly helpless.

18 ... ♕xf5

Miles analysed other possibilities in his notes and found nothing better. Here are the main variations given by the English Grandmaster.

18 ... ♗xf5 19 e4 with the further 20 fe;
18 ... gf 19 ♖xf3! ♗xf5 (19 ... ♘a6 or 19 ... ♘d7 20 ♘e7! ♕xe7 21 ♕g6+ with a rout) 20 ♖xf5 ♕g7 21 ♗xe5! de 22 d6! with a decisive initiative, for example: 22 ... ♘c6 23 ♕d5 ♕d7 24 ♖xe5+ ♘xe5 25 ♕xe5+ ♔f7 26 ♖f1+ ♔g8 27 ♖f6! etc. 22 ... c6 23 ♕e4 ♘d7 24 ♕xc6 ♖d8 25 ♖af1 ♖g8 26 ♕d5 ♕g6 27 ♖f6!, and it's all over.

19	**e4**	**♕h5**
20	**fe**	**de**
21	**c5!**	**♔d8**

21 ... bc is no better either. 22 ♕b5+ ♔d8 23 ♕xc5 ♘d7 24 ♕c6 ♖b8 25 ♖f5 ♕e8 26 ♗xe5.

22	**d6!**	**♕e8**

If 22 ... c6 then 23 d7! with the idea of ♕d6 and ♖f5.

23	**dc+**	**♔xc7**
24	**♕d5**	**♘c6**
25	**♖f7+**	**♗d7**
26	**♖af1!**	**♖d8**
27	**♖1f6**	**♔c8**
28	**cb**	**ab**
29	**♕b5**	

Black resigned

Neither 29 ... ♘b8 30 ♕xb6, nor 29 ... ♕xf7 30 ♕a6+ ♔c7 31 ♗xe5+ ♘xe5 32 ♕a7+ ♔c8 33 ♖xb6 saves matters.

Timman–Sax
Brussels 1988

1	**d4**	**♘f6**
2	**c4**	**e6**
3	**♘c3**	**♗b4**
4	**♘f3**	**b6**
5	**♗g5**	**h6**
6	**♗h4**	**♗b7**
7	**e3**	**g5**
8	**♗g3**	**♘e4**
9	**♕c2**	**♗xc3+**
10	**bc**	**♘xg3**

One could maintain the knight in the centre by means of 10 ... f5 or 10 ... d6 11 ♗d3 f5. The variations which arise as a result of 12 d5! are examined in detail in the notes to the game Miles–Belyavsky (Tilburg 1986). The exchange on g3 is also possible on the next move: 10 ... d6 11 ♗d3 ♘xg3 etc.

11 fg!(71)

71
B

This move is contrary to general principles (a pawn should capture towards the centre), but it is highly thematic in the current position to seize the half-open f-file. The traditional 11 hg is not so dangerous for Black. I recall two of my games, played in the early eighties.

Langeweg–Karpov (Amsterdam 1981): 11 hg ♘c6 12 ♘d2 ♕e7 13 ♕b2 g4 14 ♘b3 ♕g5 15 c5 ♖b8 16 ♕a3 h5 17 ♖h4 ♗a8 18 ♗e2 f5 19 ♖d1 ♕e7 20 ♕a4 (20 ♔d2! is better, swinging the second rook over to the h-file) 20 ... ♔f7 21 c4 a5 22 a3 ♘e5! 23 d5 bc 24 ♘c1 d6 25 ♕xa5 ed 26 cd ♘g6 27 ♖h1 h4 28 gh ♘xh4 and Black soon won.

A year later I tried to play this variation as White and ran into difficulties—only a miracle gave me the draw.

Karpov–Speelman (London 1982): 11 hg ♕e7 12 ♗d3 ♘c6 13 ♖b1 0-0-0 14 c5 d6 15 cb cb 16 c4 ♔b8 17 ♘d2 (17 0-0 or 17 ♖b5 are more solid) 17 ... h5! 18 ♕a4 h4 19 gh gh 20 ♖b5 f5 21 ♗e2 ♕g7 22 ♗f3 e5! 23 d5 e4! Strange

as it may seem, Black has obtained a winning position, playing almost only with pawns. 24 dc. The bishop cannot retreat so White must give up the exchange. 24 ... ef 25 gf (25 cb fg 26 ♖g1 h3) 25 ... ♗xc6 ♖xb6+ ab 27 ♕xc6 ♕c7 28 ♕a4 d5 29 c5 ♕xc5 30 ♖xh4 ♖xh4 31 ♕xh4 ♖g8! 32 a4 ♕a5 33 ♔d1 ♖g1+ 34 ♔c2 ♕c5+ 35 ♔d3 ♖c1 36 ♔e2 ♕c8 37 f4. Black wins here by way of 37 ... ♖c2! 38 ♕f6 ♕c4+, but after 37 ... ♕a6+ 38 ♔f3 I was able to save it.

11 ...   g4

In the event of **11 ... d6 12 ♗d3 ♘d7** another popular position is reached (the usual order of moves being 10 ... d6 11 ♗d3 ♘xg3 12 fg ♘d7). Further play could proceed thus: **13 0-0 ♕e7 14 ♖f2!?** White prepares to double his rooks on the f-file, at the same time awaiting his opponent's reaction (14 ♗e4, 14 ♕a4 and 14 a4 are other continuations) **14 ... 0-0-0** (14 ... 0-0 15 e4 is more dangerous for Black) **15 ♗e4.**

After this, as the black king is transferred to the queenside the exchange of light-squared bishops would be more advantageous for White. The move **15 ♖af1** would be a waste of time in the present situation: **15 ... ♖df8 16 ♗e4 f5 17 ♗xb7+ ♔xb7 18 ♘d2 ♖f6 19 ♕a4 h5 20 ♖b1 h4** with active play for Black: **21 c5 dc 22 ♘b3 ♕d6 23 g4** (23 ♘a5+ ♔a8 24 ♘c6 ♔b7 leads to a draw) **23 ... ♔a8! 24 e4 fe 25 ♖xf6 ♘xf6 26 dc ♕d3 27 ♖c1 ♕e3+ 28 ♔h1 h3**

White resigned (Hjartarson–Hellers, Gausdal 1987).

15 ... f5 16 ♗xb7+ ♚xb7 17 e4 with better chances for White (Timman–Miles, Tilburg 1985).

12 ♘h4

The piece sacrifice leads to unclear play: 12 ♘e5 h5 13 ♗d3 d6 14 ♗e4 c6 15 ♘xf7 ♚xf7 16 0-0+ ♚e7 17 ♗g6 ♚d7 18 ♕e4 ♚c7 19 ♖f7+ ♘d7 20 c5 ♚b8 21 ♖af1 bc 22 ♕xe6 (Toshkov–Kengis, Jurmala 1987).

12 ... ♕g5

12 ... ♘c6 was played earlier. After 13 ♕f2 ♕e7 14 ♗d3 0-0-0 15 0-0 ♕a3 16 ♕c2 f5 17 ♖ab1 ♖hg8 White has a clear advantage (Vaganian-Ribli, London 1984).

13 ♕d2 ♘c6
14 ♗d3(72)

72
B

14 ... ♘e7

Although Timman confidently won this game, he apparently decided that the situation is not so dangerous for Black and a few rounds later (the event was the first World Cup tournament) chose this variation as Black against Salov, having firstly

played 14 ... f5 from the diagram position and only on 15 0-0 did he play 15 ... ♘e7. White employed the novelty 16 a4! in this position (16 ♖f4 0-0 17 ♖af1 d5 18 cd ♘xd5 19 ♖4f2 ♘f6 with good play for Black; Stanishevsky–Farago, Warsaw 1987) 16 ... a5. And now, although White lost time on the displacement of his rook on f4, the game ended in peace after mutual inaccuracies. Meanwhile, as Salov remarked after the game, the move 17 ♖ab1 with the threat c4–c5 would give White a tangible advantage; for example, Black's pursuit of a pawn would end sadly: 17 ... ♗c6 18 d5 ♗xa4 19 ♖a1 ♗b3 20 ♖fb1.

Notice that in reply to 14 ... f5, as also in the text game, 15 e4! is strong for White.

15 e4!

Castling may hand the initiative to his opponent: 15 0-0 0-0 16 ♖f2 f5 17 ♖af1 ♖f7 18 d5 ♖af8 19 ♗c2 e5 20 ♕e2 d6 21 e4 f4 22 ♘f5 ♘xf5 23 gf.ef 24 ef f3 25 ♕d2 ♕xd2 26 ♖xd2 ♗c8! However, in the game **Lalic–Sax (Seville 1987)** the players soon agreed a draw: 27 gf ♗xf5 28 fg ♗xc2 29 ♖xf7 ♖xf7 30 ♖xc2 ♖f4 31 h3 ♖xc4 (31 ... ♚g7 would have caused White some discomfort) 32 ♚f2 ♖c5 **Draw agreed.**

15 ... ♘c6

The endgame 15 ... ♕xd2+ 16 ♚xd2 ♘c6 17 ♖hf1 ♘a5 18 ♖f4 ♗a6 19 ♖af1 is clearly in White's favour.

16 ♕f2! 0-0-0
17 0-0 ♗a6

18	♕e2	♕a5
19	♕c2	e5
20	♘f5	

: White's advantage is unquestionable, and he plays out the second half of the game vigorously.

20	...	♗b8
21	♖ab1	♗a8

21 ... ed is no better either: 22 cd ♘b4 23 ♕c3 ♘c6 24 ♕b2.

22	a3!	d6
23	♔h1	♗c8
24	♕b2	♗d7
25	♘e3	♗b8
26	♘d5	ed

26 ... ♗e8 would be the only way to retain chances of saving the game.

27	cd	h5
28	♖xf7	♗e6
29	♖g7	♖dg8
30	♘b4!	

The rest, as they say, is a matter of technique.

30	...	♘d8
31	♖xg8	♖xg8
32	c5	dc
33	dc	♗c8
34	♖c1	♕a4
35	♕c3	♕d7
36	♘d5	♖g7
37	cb	ab
38	♗b5	♕xb5
39	♕xg7	♘e6
40	♘xc7!	♕g5
41	♕xg5	

Black resigned

Bareev–Gavrikov
Minsk 1987

We will conclude our account of the variations bordering between the Nimzo–Indian Defence (with the black bishop on b4) and the Queen's Indian Defence (the black b-pawn taking one step forward) in this game (played in the USSR Championship). A position is encountered here that is reminiscent of one obtained in the Nimzo–Indian.

1	d4	♘f6
2	c4	e6
3	♘f3	b6
4	♘c3	♗b4
5	♗g5	♗b7
6	e3	

6 ♕c2 is a less well researched continuation. Here is a very recent game on this theme.

Gelfand–Miles (Amsterdam 1988): 6 ♕c2 h6 7 ♗h4 g5 8 ♗g3 ♘e4 9 ♗e5 ♗xc3+. Strange as it may seem, this exchange in the present variation is a new move, 9 ... f6 is normally played, and after 10 d5 ed 11 cd ♗xc3+ 12 ♗xc3 ♗xd5 13 0-0-0 ♘xc3 14 ♕xc3 ♗f7 15 h4 White has a strong attack (Portisch–Timman, Hilversum 1984); the immediate exchange of bishop for knight forces White to take on c3 with a pawn.

10 bc f6 11 ♘d2. In the event of 11 ♗g3 d6 12 e3 f5 a well-known position arises with an extra tempo for Black, and after 11 d5 ed 12 cd ♗xd5 we have in front of us the position examined in the previous notes, but the fact that

White has captured on c3 with a pawn lessens his chances: 13 ♖d1 ♗b7 14 ♗g3 ♘a6 15 ♘d4 ♕e7 16 f3 ♘xg3 17 ♕g6+ ♕f7 18 ♕xf7+ ♔xf7 19 hg ♘c5 (Bellon–Anand, Biel 1988).

11 ... fe 12 ♘xe4 ed 13 cd ♕e7 14 e3*(73)*

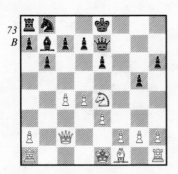

14 ... ♘c6. Correct was 14 ... ♗xe4 15 ♕xe4 ♕b4+, keeping the white king in the centre. After 16 ♔d1 ♘c6 17 ♖b1 (17 ♕g6+ ♔e7 18 ♕g7+ ♔d6) 17 ... ♕a4+ 18 ♕c2 ♕xc2+ 19 ♔xc2 a roughly equal endgame arises.

15 ♗e2 0-0-0 16 a3 e5. And after 16 ... d5 17 cd ed 18 ♘d2 ♘a5 19 ♘f3 White's chances are better.

17 d5 ♘a5 18 0-0 ♔b8 19 ♖fb1 d6. The pawn structure and active knight guarantee White the advantage, which he duly converts. **20 ♕c3 ♔a8 21 ♖b2 ♗c8 22 a4 ♖hf8 23 ♖b5 ♗f5 24 ♘d2.** 24 ♘g3 ♗d7 25 ♖xa5 ba 26 c5 is significantly stronger, for example: 26 ... ♕f7 27 c6 ♕xf2+ 28 ♔h1 ♗c8 29 ♖b1 with unavoidable mate.

24 ... ♗d7 25 ♖xa5 ba 26 c5 ♕f7 27 c6 ♕xf2+ 28 ♔h1 ♗h3

29 ♗f1 ♗g4 (29 ... ♖b8 30 gh ♖b4 was correct) **30 ♗a6 ♗c8 31 ♗c4 ♗f5?** (after 31 ... ♗g4 Black could hold out) **32 ♖f1 ♕h4 33 ♕xa5 ♗e4 34 ♕xc7 ♖xf1+ 35 ♘xf1 ♗xg2+ 36 ♔g1 ♖b8 37 ♗a6 Black resigned**.

6 ...   h6
7   ♗h4   ♗xc3+

The pin on the knight at f6 is unpleasant and it's difficult to get rid of it without the traditional ... g7–g5. But one needn't hurry with this move. After 7 ... g5 8 ♗g3 ♘e4 9 ♕c2 Black is faced with difficulties; Miles–Belyavsky (Tilburg 1986).

In the game Azmaiparashvili–Makarichev (Moscow 1986) Black played 7 ... 0-0, showing that he is not afraid of the pin. After 8 ♕c2 d6 9 ♗d3 ♘bd7 10 ♘d2!? c5 (10 ... ♗xg2 11 ♖g1 ♗b7 12 0-0-0 with unclear play) 11 0-0! White has the preferable position.

In the game Greenfeld–Plaskett (Hastings 1985/6) Black played 7 ... c5, although after 8 ♗d3 d6 9 0-0 ♗xc3 10 bc ♕c7 11 ♘d2 ♘c6 12 a4 0-0-0 13 a5!, at the cost of a pawn, White develops an initiative on the queenside. In the game Lputyan–Razuvayev (Irkutsk 1986) after 8 dc ♗xc5 9 ♗e2 ♗e7 the battle assumes a manoeuvring character, but here the proceedings are also dictated by White: 10 0-0 0-0 11 ♘d4 a6 12 ♗f3 ♕c7 13 ♖c1 ♗xf3 14 ♕xf3 ♘c6 15 ♗g3 ♘e5 16 ♕e2 ♖fc8 17 b3 d6 18 f4 ♘c6 19 f5! with an attack.

8   bc   d6

· It would seem to be an insignificant inaccuracy made by Black in the game Rashkovsky–Belyavsky (Minsk 1987): 8 ... ♛e7. However, it leads to an important loss of tempo: 9 ♗xf6!? ♛xf6 10 ♗d3 d6 11 0-0 0-0 12 ♘d2 e5 13 ♛g4 ♛e7 14 ♖ae1 ♘d7 15 ♗c2 c5 16 f4, and White has the advantage.

9 ♘d2

White immediately commences energetic play in the centre while preventing Black creating a kingside initiative. The popularity of this move grew after Kasparov's use of it in the return match (this game is discussed below). Black obtains sufficient counterplay after the traditional 9 ♗d3, for example: 9 ... ♘bd7 10 0-0 ♛e7 11 ♘d2 g5 12 ♗g3 h5 13 f3 (13 h4 ♖g8 14 f3 0-0-0 15 hg ♖xg5 16 ♗h4 is more accurate, Petursson–Greenfeld, Hastings 1985/6) 13 ... h4 14 ♗f2 (14 ♗e1 0-0-0 15 ♛e2 ♚b8 16 a4 a5 17 ♘b3 c5, and Black has no problems; Johansen–Hjartarson, Dubai 1986) 14 ... c5 15 h3 ♘h5 16 ♖e1 0-0-0 17 ♛a4 ♚b8 18 ♖ab1 ♖c8 19 ♖b2 f5 20 ♗e2 ♘hf6 21 e4 g4!, and Black's counterattack on the kingside is more effective than White's initiative on the queenside (Segal–Trepp, Dubai 1986).

9 ... g5

The moment has come to expel the bishop. After 9 ... ♘bd7 10 f3 ♛e7 11 ♛a4 play lies in White's favour: 11 ... e5 12 ♗e2 a5 13 e4 0-0-0 14 ♘b3 ♖de8 15 0-0 c5 16 ♖ab1 (Dokhoyan–Solozhenkin,

Minsk 1986) or 12 e4 g5 13 ♗f2 ♚f8 14 ♗e2 ♘h5 15 0-0 ♘f4 16 ♖fe1 ♖g8 17 ♘f1 f5 18 c5! (Salov–Dokhoyan, Irkutsk 1986).

10 ♗g3 *(74)*

74
B

In my game with Kasparov (game 18 of the third match) I used a new move here: 10 ... ♛e7, but it turned out to be just a loss of time. After 11 a4 a5 12 h4! ♖g8 13 hg hg 14 ♛b3 ♘a6 (14 ... ♘c6; 14 ... ♘bd7 15 c5!) 15 ♖b1! ♚f8 16 ♛d1! White's initiative has become serious. I won't begin to annotate this long game, which was riddled with a multitude of mistakes; I will just describe the subsequent course of events.

Kasparov made an inaccuracy on his 23rd move, and I could have forced a draw. Declining this, I quickly fell into a difficult situation once more. Kasparov missed a win on move 38, and on the 39th played a move which allowed me to get the upper hand. Then I played imprecisely, but nevertheless retained winning chances. Towards the end of play, Kasparov didn't defend in the best way (apparently, he could have achieved a draw), and finally his king found itself in a mating net.

I describe the course of this game in this manner because, as you see, the outcome of the game was akin to the throwing of dice. I think that the majesty of the occasion played a decisive role here. I also won the two 'neighbouring' games, the 17th and 19th, thanks to opening preparation of certain positions. It was simple to guess which ones (of this you may be sure, after consulting the section devoted to the Grünfeld Defence). This string of three victories allowed me to level the score, which Kasparov obviously hadn't expected. I hope that it's understood by the reader that no phantasmagoria occurred in these games, and that no 'external forces' interfered with play. Meanwhile a witch-hunt was going on at that time in Kasparov's team: his second of long-standing, Vladimirov, was declared a spy, working for me. It wouldn't do for a pure chess book to encroach on the subject of moralities, but I suggest it is quite sufficient to say that this idea of a 'Vladimirov Variation' is completely refuted.

Before we return to the text game, a few (chess now!) points connected with the game just described. Instead of 11 ... a5 Black would do better to prefer 11 ... c5 or 11 ... ♘c6. But White could also have earlier played the stronger 11 h4! immediately. In the game Bareev–Dolmatov

(Minsk 1987) after 11 ... ♖g8 12 hg hg 13 ♗e2! ♗xg2 14 ♖h6 g4 15 ♗h4 ♘bd7 16 ♕a4 ♔f8 17 0-0-0 ♔g7 18 ♖h5! he obtained a big advantage.

10	...	♘bd7
11	h4	♖g8

In the game Ftacnik–Short (Dubai 1986) Black succeeded in equalizing by means of 11 ... ♗e7 12 ♖b1 ♘e4 13 ♘xe4 ♗xe4 14 ♖b2 ♕g8 15 hg hg 16 ♖xh8 ♕xh8 17 ♕g4 ♘f6.

| 12 | hg | hg*(75)* |

A dynamic equilibrium is maintained, though it's not easy for White to open up the game in order to exploit the power of his two bishops. The only problem for Black is to secure his king.

13   ♕a4

A novelty. Black has no difficulties after 13 ♕c2 ♗e7 14 e4 0-0-0 15 ♗e2 e5 16 f3 ♖h8 (Miles–Sokolov, Bugojno 1986). 13 f3 doesn't look bad for White: in the game Legky–Schneider (USSR 1986) there followed 13 ... ♕e7 14 ♕a4! a5 15 0-0-0 0-0-0, and here White could maintain a small advantage by continuing 16 ♗d3, and if 16 ... e5, then 17 ♗f5.

| | 13 ... | ♚e7 |

On 13 ... ♛e7 then 14 c5! bc 15 ♖c1 is not bad. But now with the king on e7 the standard 14 c5 dc 15 ♛a3 would have allowed White to achieve the better chances.

| 14 | f3 | ♖h8 |
| 15 | ♖g1 | |

Now Black's king will go back to its place, and he can feel quite confident. It would have followed for White to exchange on h8 and again consider the break c4–c5.

15	...	♚f8!
16	♗d3	♛e7
17	0-0-0	a6
18	♖h1	♚g7
19	♗f2	c5
20	e4	♘h5
21	g3	♖ac8 *(76)*

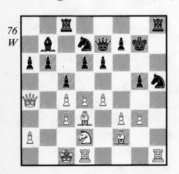

76
W

A critical moment. Bareev proposes that Black retains the initiative after 21 ... b5!, but now the advantage gradually returns to White.

| 22 | ♚b1 | ♗c6 |

Now 22 ... b5 doesn't suit: 23 cb ab 24 ♗xb5.

| 23 | ♛a3 | ♖b8 |

24	♖h2	♘hf6
25	♖xh8	♖xh8
26	g4!	♗b7
27	♛c1	♘f8
28	♘f1	♘6d7
29	♘g3	♘g6?

A serious inaccuracy. Bareev recommends 29 ... f6 30 ♘h5+ ♚f7 31 f4 gf 32 ♛xf4 cd 33 cd d5.

30	♘h5+	♚f8
31	♗e3	f6
32	e5!	♛f7
33	♘xf6	♘xf6
34	ef	♗xf3
35	♖g1	cd

35 ... ♖h3 loses after 36 ♗xg5 ♗xg4 37 ♖xg4 ♖xd3 38 ♗h6+ ♚e8 39 ♛c2.

36	cd	e5
37	♗xg5	e4
38	♛e3	ed?

The decisive mistake, although also after the better 38 ... ♛e6 39 ♗c2 ♛xc4 40 ♗h6+ ♚e8 41 g5 White's advantage is without dispute.

39	♛xf3	♛xc4
40	♛a8+	♚f7
41	♛b7+	♚e6
42	♖e1+	♘e5
43	d5+	

Black resigned

Kasparov–Karpov
Game 2,
World Championship 1
Moscow 1984

This drawn game, played at the start of our first marathon, oozed such tension and caused so much agitation, that the resulting game was second to none, the more so as both contestants, in turn, were close to victory.

1	d4	♘f6
2	c4	e6
3	♘f3	b6
4	g3	♗b7
5	♗g2	♗e7
6	0-0	0-0
7	d5	ed
8	♘h4! *(77)*	

An original invention by Polugaevsky, the patent of which was obtained in his Candidates match with Korchnoi (Buenos Aires 1980). The opening surprise then provided the Moscow Grandmaster with a brilliant victory, and his idea was regarded as highly dangerous for Black. But later, when the analysts got down to work, they discovered several paths to equality, and the new plan occupied a modest place in opening classification. Kasparov undertook an attempt to perfect Polugaevsky's opening. White conducts the programmed manoeuvre d4–d5 and now he must develop an initiative in the centre. Strange as it may seem, this is the best way of all to further the aim of the knight raid on the edge of the board. The previously met 8 ♘d4 is not dangerous due to 8 ... ♘c6 or 8 ... ♗c6.

8	...	c6
9	cd	♘xd5
10	♘f5	♘c7

In the stem game Polugaevsky–Korchnoi, after 10 ... ♗c5 11 e4 ♘e7 12 ♘xg7!! ♔xg7 13 b4! ♗xb4 14 ♕d4+ White obtained a strong attack and won a brilliant victory.

Subsequently, various continuations were tried instead of 10 ... ♗c5—10 ... ♘f6, 10 ... ♗f6—but finally the knight retreat to c7 was found to be the most solid response.

| 11 | ♘c3 | |

More precise than the immediate 11 e4.

| 11 | ... | d5 |

In a game with **Timman (Tilburg 1983)** I once again retreated the knight—11 ... ♘e8—and after **12 ♗f4 ♘a6 13 ♕d2 d5 14 e4 ♘ac7 15 ♖ad1 ♗f6 16 ed ♘xd5 17 ♘xd5 cd 18 ♘e3 ♘c7 19 ♗xc7 ♕xc7** we agreed a **draw**. However, this time I didn't wish to choose a passive route.

| 12 | e4 | ♗f6 |
| 13 | ♗f4 | |

The game **Kasparov–Marinovic (Malta 1980)** had a flashy end: **13 ed cd 14 ♗f4 ♘ba6 15 ♖e1 ♕d7? 16 ♗h3 ♔h8 17 ♘e4! ♗xb2 18 ♘g5 ♕c6 19 ♘e7 ♕f6 20 ♘xh7! ♕d4 21 ♕h5 g6 22 ♕h4 ♗xa1 23 ♘f6+ Black resigned.** Soon after

a solid defence was found—15 . . .
♘c5!

13 ...   ♗c8

In the game **Hort–Olafsson**
(**Buenos Aires 1981**) after 13 . . .
♘d7 14 ed cd 15 ♖e1 ♘c5 16
♗d6 ♖e8 17 ♕g4 g6 18 ♗xc7
♕xc7 19 ♘xd5 ♗xd5 20 ♗xd5
♖xe1+ 21 ♖xe1 ♖d8 22 ♖d1
the protagonists signed a peace
treaty. The immediate 14 ♖e1 is
strongest for White, retaining the
e-pawn. If now 14 . . . d4, then
both 15 ♘xd4 and 15 e5! are
possible.

14 g4!

Of course, not 14 ♘d6 because
of the reply 14 . . . g5! Now the
knight is defended and the e-pawn
is freed of its duty.

14 ...   ♘ba6
15 ♖c1   ♗d7

This move could have led to
unpleasant consequences for me.
Curiously though, our game only
gathered momentum. It was also
evident that nobody had yet
formed any theoretical conclu-
sions, and in an international
tournament in Holland at this
time an improvement for Black
was demonstrated. An excellent
example of how theory can be
poles apart from practice.

Hence, in the game Sosonko–
Tukmakov (Tilburg 1984) there
followed: **15 . . . ♗xf5! 16 gf ♗g5
17 ♗xc7** (a sharper game arises
after 17 ♗xg5 ♕xg5 18 f4 ♕h4,
or 17 ♕g4 ♗xf4 18 ♕xf4 de 19
♖fd1 ♘d5 20 ♘xd5 cd 21 ♗xe4
♕f6) **17 . . . ♘xc7 18 f4 ♗e7 19 ed**
(19 e5 deserves attention) **19 . . .**

♗c5+ **20 ♔h1 cd 21 ♘xd5 ♘xd5
22 ♕xd5 ♕xd5 23 ♗xd5 ♖ad8
24 ♖cd1 ♖fe8 25 ♗c6 ♖xd1 26
♖xd1 Draw agreed**.

16 ♕d2   ♘c5(78)

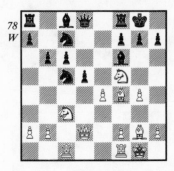

The first crucial moment. In the
event of 17 ♗xc7 ♕xc7 18 ed
♗xf5 19 gf ♖ad8 20 b4 ♘b7 21
♘e4 Black would be in quite a
tight spot. Kasparov counts on a
kingside attack, and the position
is acutely sharpened.

17 e5   ♗e7
18 ♘xe7+

18 ♗g3 ♖e8 19 ♘xe7+ ♕xe7
20 f4 ♗xg4 21 21 f5 is stronger,
maintaining an initiative.

18 ...   ♕xe7
19 ♗g5   ♕e6
20 h3   ♕g6
21 f4

A sharp position arises after 21
♗e7 ♕d3 22 ♖fd1 ♕xd2 23
♖xd2 ♖fe8 which is difficult to
evaluate.

21 ...   f6
22 ef   gf
23 ♗h4   f5(79)

The second critical moment.
After 24 gf, with the subsequent
♖f1–f3–g3, Black would then
have to worry about his king.

79
W

24 b4 fg!

And now it is Black who takes the initiative.

25 hg

My plan was based on the variation 25 bc gh 26 ♖f2 hg 27 ♖xg2 ♗g4! and ... h7–h5 and Black should win.

23 ... ♘d3

26 ♖f3

The advantage now lies in my favour. With this exchange sacrifice Kasparov strives to the limit to set fire to the situation on the board.

26	...	♘xc1
27	f5	♕g7
28	♕xc1	♖ae8
29	♕d2	d4
30	♘e2	♘d5
31	♘xd4	♔h8

The following moves were made in extreme time trouble, and therefore neither of us were playing to the best of our capabilities.

32	g5	♖e4
33	♗f2	♕e5
34	♖g3	♖f4
35	f6	♗e8
36	b5	

To all appearances the losing move. 36 ♘f3 would lead to unclear play.

36	...	c5
37	♘c6	♕a1+
38	♗f1	♖f5
39	g6	♗xg6
40	♖xg6	♖5xf6

The last move of the time control. With the flag hanging, I let victory slip, as I have a forced winning manoeuvre with this very rook, but by other means: 40 ... ♖xf2! After 41 ♔xf2 (41 ♕xf2 hg) 41 ... ♘xf6 White is helpless.

41 ♖xf6 ♕xf6

During analysis of the adjourned position we thoroughly researched the continuations 41 ... ♖g8+ and 41 ... ♘xf6, but Black finds clear paths to safety after all variations.

42	♕e1!	♖g8+
43	♔h2	♕f4+
44	♗g3	♖xg3
45	♕xg3	♕xf1
46	♕b8+	♔g7
47	♕g3+	

Draw agreed

It could possibly have finished: 47 ... ♔f7 48 ♘d8+! ♔f8 49 ♕d6+ ♘e7 50 ♘e6+ ♔f7 51 ♘g5+ ♔e8 52 ♕b8+ with perpetual check.

Karpov–Korchnoi
Amsterdam 1987

I have played close to 100 games against Korchnoi (I have only played Kasparov more often). However every time the confrontations have led to a tense battle. The given game is outwardly simple, though White's instructive strategic policy is to exchange both pairs of bishops with subsequent play against his opponent's weakened pawns.

1	d4	♘f6
2	c4	e6
3	♘f3	♗b4+

3 ... b6 is the more popular continuation. The bishop check on b4 forms a certain blend of two defences—the Queen's Indian and the Nimzo-Indian—and bears the name of the Bogo-Indian.

| 4 | ♗d2 | c5 |

Here are played 4 ... a5, 4 ... ♗e7, 4 ... ♗xd2+ and most common of all 4 ... ♕e7. The move of the c-pawn was dreamt up in the 70s by International Master Vitolinsh. If I intentionally used only my own games to illustrate the modern state of the Grünfeld Defence in this volume, such was not the aim in the other openings. However, while examining the material connected with the Vitolinsh variation, I was convinced that the text game is one of the most important for the evaluation of the present position.

| 5 | ♗xb4 |

The most principled continuation. The moves 5 a3, 5 e3, 5 g3 and 5 dc don't promise White any major achievements.

| 5 | ... | cb |
| 6 | g3*(80)* |

White has a wide choice here: 6 a3, 6 e3, 6 ♕c2, 6 ♕b3 and 6 ♘bd2. Practice indicates that the fianchetto is not a bad way to fight for the initiative. Here are some quite recent examples,

80
B

which show that other continuations are not dangerous for Black.

Timman–Nikolic (Tilburg 1987): 6 ♕c2 d6 7 e4 e5 8 c5 0-0 9 cd ed 10 ♘bd2 Draw agreed. After 10 ... ♖e8 11 ♗b5 ♗d7 12 ♗xd7 ♕xd7 13 0-0 ♘c6 14 ♖fe1 ♘g4 Black has a comfortable game.

Stohl–Lanc (Trnava 1987): 6 ♕b3 a5 7 a3 ba 8 ba a4 9 ♕b2 0-0 10 e3 d6 11 ♘c3 ♘c6 12 ♗e2 ♗d7 13 0-0 ♘a5 14 ♘d2 ♕e7 15 ♖fc1 e5 16 d5 b6! with abundant counterplay.

Petursson–Korchnoi (Reykjavik 1987): 6 a3 ba 7 ♖xa3 0-0 8 e3 b6 9 ♗d3 ♗b7 10 ♘c3 d6 11 ♕b1 a5 12 b4 ab 13 ♖xa8 ♗xa8 14 ♕xb4 e5 15 d5 ♘a6 16 ♕b1 ♘c5 17 ♗c2 ♗b7 with double-edged play.

Speelman–Nikolic (Brussels 1988): 6 e3 0-0 7 ♗d3 d6 8 0-0 ♖e8 9 h3 b6 10 ♘bd2 ♗b7 11 ♘g5 ♘bd7 12 ♖c1 ♖c8 13 ♕b3 a5 14 ♘ge4 ♕c7 15 a3 ba 16 ♕xa3 ♗xe4 17 ♘xe4 ♘xe4 18 ♗xe4 ♘b8! 19 b4 ♘c6 20 ba ♘xa5 21 ♗d3 e5. Black has practical counterplay.

| 6 | ... | b6 |

Black also does best to bring his

bishop to the long diagonal. The moves 6 ... d5 and 6 ... d6 don't justify themselves.

	7	♗g2	♗b7
	8	0-0	0-0
	9	♕b3*(81)*	

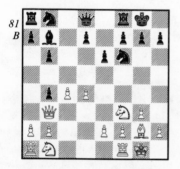

9 ♘bd2 has been most frequently encountered up till now, but this queen thrust is more logical, in my opinion.

	9	...	a5
	10	a3	♘a6

The action revolves around the point b4, to which the black knight would not object as an outpost. But after 10 ... ba 11 ♘xa3 ♘a6 12 ♘c2 the b4 square is under firm control, and the knight on a6 does nothing for Black's position.

	11	♘bd2	♕e7

Here on 11 ... ba there would now follow 12 ba, and by controlling the b4 square White would have an undisputed advantage.

In the game Hulak–Torre (Zagreb 1987) the queen was placed on c7: 11 ... d6 12 ♖fd1 ♕c7 13 ♘e1 ♗xg2 14 ♘xg2 ♖fe8 15 ♘e3 ♖ab8 (a similar position arose in my game with Korchnoi)

16 ♖ac1 ♕d7 17 ♕d3 ♕b7 18 ♘c2 ba 19 ♕xa3 ♘e4 20 b4! ab 21 ♘xb4 ♘xb4 22 ♕xb4 ♘xd2 23 ♖xd2, and the weak b6 and d6 pawns are a constant cause of concern for Black.

	12	♖fd1	d6
	13	♘e1	♗xg2
	14	♘xg2	♖fd8
	15	♘e3	♕e8

With the aim of closing up the queenside by way of 16 ... a4 and 17 ... b3 and freeing his knight for more useful duties.

	16	♕d3*(82)*	

The advantage in space and the active knight (compared with his colleague on a6) are the main positional trumps which determine White's advantage. Black doesn't easily find counterchances and it would follow to adopt waiting tactics, for example 16 ... ♕c6 or 16 ... ♖a7, providing for the necessity of swinging his second rook over to a central file.

	16	...	e5?

Played too sharply. 'A game of one move', Korchnoi said to me afterwards, criticizing his error. But a game is rarely lost due to one positional blunder. You can be sure that there was also a second.

17 ♘e4! ♘xe4

The knight doesn't have a good retreat square, and 17 ... ♕e6 18 ♘xf6+ ♕xf6 19 ♘d5 leads to the loss of a pawn.

18 ♕xe4 ed?

Of course, Black's position is scarcely attractive—his forces are split and his light squares are weak—but one might yet hold out by the means of 18 ... ♕e6; for example, the straightforward 19♕b7 ed 20 ♖xd4 wouldn't do because of 20 ... ♘c5 and 21 ... ♘b3 with unclear play. I had intended to play 19 ♘d5 ed 20 ♕xd4 ♖ab8 ab ♘xb4 22 ♘xb4 ab 23 e3, maintaining my advantage. The text move leads forcibly to a hopeless position.

19 ♕xe8+ ♖xe8
20 ♖xd4 ♖ad8
21 ♖ad1 ♖e6
22 ♔f1 b3

The chronically weak b6 and c6 pawns are beyond salvation, and must perish sooner or later. Leaving one of these to its fate, Korchnoi attempts to activate his knight, which has sat on the edge of the board for too long.

23 ♘d5 ♘c5

23 ... ♖b8 doesn't change things: 24 ♘c3 ♖d8 25 ♘a4.

24 ♘xb6 h6
25 f3 g5
26 ♖1d2 ♔g7

Both knights, white and black, guard the a4 square, but now, having defended his b2 pawn, the

white knight sets out on a programmed tour.

27 ♘d5 ♘a4
28 ♘c7 ♖f6
29 ♘b5 ♔f8
30 ♘xd6 ♖fxd6

Desperate, but the continuation 30 ... ♘xb2 31 c5 costs Black a piece.

31 ♖xd6 ♖xd6
32 ♖xd6 ♘xb2
33 ♖d8+ ♔g7
34 ♖b8 ♘xc4

34 ... a4 doesn't work in view of 35 ♖b4, and the unfortunate knight is crippled. Now there is only one concern for White—not to fall for the fork.

35 a4 ♔f6
36 e4 ♔e5
37 ♔e2

Black resigned

Karpov–Andersson
USSR v Rest of the World
London 1984

The Swedish Grandmaster Ulf Andersson is one of the most skilful defenders in chess. One does not often break down his fortifications. Here again in this match, playing him on top board, I only triumphed once in four games, and that victory was only achieved after a most difficult struggle.

1 d4 ♘f6
2 c4 e6
3 ♘f3 ♗b4+
4 ♗d2 ♗xd2+

White quite often endeavours to protect the bishop with 4 ♘bd2, but if he now offers to exchange it, then his opponent replies 4 ... a5, 4 ... c5, 4 ... ♕e7 or generally retreats 4 ... ♗e7. One tempo is not so important in such a position.

5 ♕xd2 0-0
6 e3

By fianchettoing his bishop—6 g3—White can also organize strong pressure on the queenside. 6 ... d5 7 ♗g2. This position is characteristic of the Catalan Opening, but with the absence of the dark-squared bishops. 7 ... ♘bd7 8 0-0 c6 9 ♖c1 ♕e7 10 ♕e3. Andersson championed this system of development as Black in Brussels, in the World Cup. In the game Speelman–Andersson there followed 10 ... ♖d8 11 cd ♘xd5 12 ♕a3 ♗f8 13 ♕d3 ♘5f6 14 ♖d1 ♗g8 15 ♘c3 b6 16 e4, and, having seized the centre, White has a small but persistent advantage.

In the game Portisch–Andersson after 10 ... b6 11 cd ♘xd5 12 ♕g5 ♗b7 13 ♕xe7 ♘xe7 14 ♘bd2 ♖fd8 15 ♘c4 c5 16 ♘d6 ♗xf3 17 ♗xf3 ♖ab8 18 ♘b5 White had the better endgame.

Finally, in the game Karpov–Andersson the difficulties for Black in the endgame, characteristic of this system, were again emphasized. The order of moves was somewhat different: 5 ... d5 6 g3 ♘bd7 7 ♗g2 c6 8 ♘a3 ♘e4 9 ♕d3 ♕a5+ 10 ♘d2 ♘xd2 11 ♕xd2 ♕xd2+ 12 ♔xd2 ♔e7 13

♖hd1 ♘f6 14 ♖ac1 ♗d7 15 ♖c3 b5 16 cb cb 17 ♖c5 with a clear advantage for White. This time my opponent held on for a draw.

We played the Bogo-Indian again soon after, in Thessaloniki, and this time I managed to prevail. The text game is quite lengthy, although there are many interesting moments (that is also why it was selected among the main material for this book), but the game from the Olympiad is shorter and also turned out to be interesting. We will look at this game, with its elegant finale, which, up to the present day, has settled the dispute with Andersson over the current variation of the Queen's Indian Defence.

Karpov–Andersson (Thessaloniki 1988): 6 g3 d5 7 ♗g2 ♘bd7 8 0-0 c6 9 ♖c1 ♕e7 10 ♕e3 ♖e8 11 ♘bd2 e5 12 de ♘xe5 13 ♕xe5 ♕xe5 14 ♘xe5 ♖xe5 15 cd ♘xd5 16 e4 ♘b6 17 f4 ♖e7 18 a4 a5 19 ♘b3. White's apparently insignificant advantage acquires visible contours. 19 ... f6 20 ♖a3! ♗e6 21 ♘c5 ♗f7 22 ♖d3! ♖ae8 23 ♗h3! ♘c8 24 ♗d7 ♖d8 25 ♖cd1 ♘b6 26 ♗g4 ♖xd3 27 ♖xd3 ♗f8 28 ♖d8+ ♖e8 29 ♖d4 ♖b8 30 ♖d7! h5 31 ♗h3 ♔e8 32 ♖c7. It seems that it's time for Black to surrender, but my opponent finds an amusing possibility; by sacrificing a piece he sharpens the battle. 32 ... ♘a8! 33 ♖xb7 ♖xb7 34 ♘xb7 ♘b6 35 ♘d6+ ♔e7 36 ♘xf7 ♘xa4! 37 ♘h8 ♘xb2 *(83)*.

38 e5! I was able to calculate to the finish. Other continuations

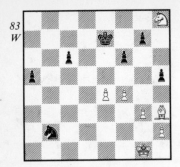

83
W

don't bring success. 38 ... a4 39
♘g6+ ♚e8 (39 ... ♚f7 40 e6+
♚xg6 41 f5+ and e6–e7–e8(♕))
40 ♗e6 ♘d3 41 ♗g8!! fe (otherwise 42 e6 followed by 43 ♗f7+
and e6–e7–e8(♕)+) 42 ♘xe5
♘b4 43 ♘c4, and Black soon
resigned.

6	**...**	**d5**
7	**♘c3**	**♘bd7**
8	**cd**	

8 ♖c1 dc 9 ♗xc4 c5 10 0-0 was
previously encountered, and here
10 ... cd, 10 ... ♕c7 or 10 ...
♘b6 with a solid position for
Black. But I decided to go over to
a formation characteristic of the
Carlsbad Variation, though it dif-
fers from the original by the absence of dark-squared bishops.

8	**...**	**ed**

White has a significant advantage after 8 ... ♘xd5 9 ♖c1.

9	**♗d3**	**♖e8**
10	**0-0**	**♘e4**
11	**♕c2**	**♘df6**
12	**b4**	

The start of the standard
minority pawn attack on the
queenside.

12	**...**	**c6**

After 12 ... ♗f5 13 b5! White's
pressure grows.

13	**♘e5**	

Now on 13 b5 there follows 13
... c5! 14 dc ♘xc5 15 ♘d4 ♗g4
with full equality.

13	**...**	**♗f5**
14	**♘a4!**	

On 14 f3 ♘xc3 15 ♗xf5 is the
reply 15 ... ♘b5, and as for 14 a4
with the aim of taking away the
b5 square from the knight, 14 ...
♗g6 15 a5 a6 leads to equality.

14	**...**	**g6**

If 14 ... ♗g6 now, then 15
♘xg6 hg 16 b5 is good.

15	**♕b2**	**a6**
16	**♖fc1**	

I planned a convenient re-
grouping of my pieces, so that in
the event of 16 ... ♘d6 17 ♗f1 to
continue my assault on the
queen's flank unhindered.

16	**...**	**♖e7**
17	**♘c5**	**♘xc5**
18	**bc**	**♗xd3**
19	**♘xd3** *(84)*	

84
B

19	**...**	**♖c8**
20	**♖c3**	**♖cc7**
21	**♖b3**	**♘e8**
22	**♕e2**	**f6**
23	**♕f3**	**♖f7**
24	**♚f1**	**♘g7**
25	**♚e2**	**♖ce7**
26	**♚d1!**	

Now planning a pawn attack on the kingside, White evacuates his monarch as a preliminary.

26	...	♛c8
27	♖ab1	h5
28	h3	♞e6
29	h4	♔h7
30	♛h3	♛e8
31	♔c2	♖d7
32	♔b2	♞g7
33	♞f4	♖fe7
34	♔a1	♛f7
35	♖g1	♞e6
36	♞d3	♞g7
37	g4	hg
38	♖xg4	♞h5
39	♖b1	♛e6
40	♛f3	♖g7
41	♖bg1	

The game was adjourned here. Not much has changed over the last 20 moves. Black has a sound position at present, so that one had to breach his greatly fortified position during play.

41	...	♖de7
42	♔b2	♔h6

An interesting moment. On 42 ... f5 there follows 43 ♖4g2! (more accurate than 43 ♖g5 ♛e4 44 ♛xe4 ♖xe4 45 ♞e5 ♖xh4 46 ♞xg6 ♖g4) 43 ... ♛e4 44 ♛d1! ♛xh4 45 ♖h1 ♛e4 (45 ... ♛f6 46 ♞f4) 46 ♖xg6! (46 ♞f4 ♔g8!) 46 ... ♔xg6 (46 ... ♖xg6 loses, 47 ♛xh5+ ♔g7 48 ♛h8+ ♔f7 49 ♖h7+) 47 ♛xh5+ ♔f6 48 ♞f4! with a big advantage.

43	♔c3	♛f7
44	♞f4	

After 44 ♔d2 ♖e4 45 ♞f4 (45 ♖xe4 de 46 ♛xe4 ♛xa2+) 45 ... ♞xf4 46 ♖xf4 ♖xf4 47 ♛xf4

White has a clear advantage, though 46 ... ♖e6 is better.

44	...	♞xf4
45	♖xf4	♖e6
46	♔d2	

The knights are exchanged, and I set about realizing a new plan, now in an endgame with the heavy pieces. Before anything it is necessary to return the king to its rightful flank.

46	...	♛e7
47	♔e2	♔h7
48	♔f1	♔h6
49	♖g3	♔h7
50	♖fg4	

Perhaps it would be more accurate to play 50 ♔g2 ♔h6 51 ♔h2 ♔h7 52 ♖fg4 ♛f7 53 ♖xg6 ♖xg6 54 ♛f5 ♔h6 55 ♖xg6+ ♛xg6 56 ♛xe6 ♔h5 57 ♔h3!

50	...	♛f7
51	♖f4	

What a pity that the fine riposte 51 ♖xg6 is refuted—51 ... ♖xg6 52 ♛f5 ♔h6! 53 ♖xg6+ ♛xg6 54 ♛xe6 ♔h5! with a draw.

51	...	♔h6
52	♔g1	♔h7
53	♔h2	♔h6
54	♛g2	♔h7
55	♔g1	♖e8
56	♛f3	♖f8
57	♔f1	♛e7
58	♛d1	♛e8
59	♛b1	♔h6
60	♔e2	♛d8
61	♖fg4	♖fg8
62	♔f1	♛e8
63	♛d1	♛e6
64	♛f3	♖f7
65	♔g1	♖fg7
66	a3	♖e7

67	♔h2	♖f7
68	♖f4	♔h7
69	♕d1	♔h6
70	♕d3	♕e8
71	e4!	

The break in the centre—one of White's chief resources; here it is finally accomplished.

71	...	de
72	♖xe4	♕d7

Of course, not 72 ... ♖e7 73 ♕e3+.

73	♕e3+	♔h7
74	♖e6	♖gg7

On 74 ... ♕d5 there follows 75 ♖d6 ♕h5 76 ♖xf6 ♖xf6 77 ♕e7+.

75	♖f3	f5

The f6 pawn cannot be defended, for example: 75 ... ♕d8 76 ♖d6 ♕f8 77 ♕f4.

76 h5!

Exploiting one more trump of my position.

76	...	gh

But not 76 ... g5 77 ♖d6.

77 ♕h6+

On 77 ♖h3 ♔g8 78 ♖xh5 then 78 ... ♖h7 would be bad: 79 ♖e8+ ♖f8 80 ♕g5+ ♕g7 81 ♖xf8+ ♔xf8 82 ♕d8+ ♔f7 83 ♕d7+ ♔g6 84 ♖xh7 with a winning pawn endgame, but there is the reply 78 ... ♖f8.

77	...	♔g8
78	♖fe3*(85)*	

One more remarkable moment arises at the finish of this marathon game. Now Black has a few possibilities at his disposal. The capture 78 ... ♕xd4 looks natural, but it turns out to be suicidal: 79 ♖e8+ ♖f8 80 ♖xf8+ ♔xf8

85
B

81 ♕h8+ ♔f7 82 ♕e8+ ♔f6 83 ♕e6+ ♔g5 84 ♖g3+ ♔h4 (84 ... ♔f4 85 ♕e3+ ♕xe3 86 fe+ and 87 ♖xg7) 85 ♕xf5! This quiet move after a series of checks threatens mate on h3, and on 85 ... ♖xg3 the final pinprick is inflicted by a pawn: 86 fg mate!

78 ... ♖e7! is strongest of all (78 ... ♖f8 79 ♕xh5 ♖h7 80 ♖h6) 79 ♖xe7 ♖xe7 80 ♕g6+ ♔h8!, and if now 81 ♖e5 (81 ♕f6+ ♖g7) then Black gets the draw straight away—81 ... ♕xd4! 82 ♖xe7 ♕h4+ and 83 ... ♕xe7, or 82 ♕xh5+ (82 ♕h6+ ♔g8 83 ♕g5+ ♖g7 84 ♖e8+ ♔f7 85 ♖e7+ ♔f8) 82 ... ♖h7 83 ♖e8+ ♔g7 84 ♖e7+ ♔f6! 85 ♖xh7 ♕xf2+ with perpetual check. However, chances of victory are retained after 81 ♖h3. A rare occasion when the most fascinating events of the game take place after eighty moves of the struggle.

78	...	♕c7+
79	♔h3	♖e7
80	♖xe7	♖xe7
81	♕g6+	♔f8
82	♕f6+	♔e8
83	♕h8+	♔d7

84	♖xe7+	♔xe7
85	♕g7+	

Black resigned

With the last pieces exchanged he is in no position to save the pawn ending.

Dzhandzhava–Chernin
Lvov 1987

A variety of a fashionable system of Petrosian, as played here, is encountered quite often in practice, and the reason the choice fell on this particular game is that in 1987 it was noted by *Chess Informant* as one of the most valuable contributions to theory.

1	d4	♘f6
2	c4	e6
3	♘f3	b6
4	a3(86)	

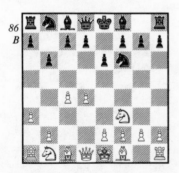

4 ♘c3 ♗b7 5 a3 is a more common move order. White's purpose is to prevent the riposte ... ♗f8–b4 for the combination of the two defences—the Queen's Indian and the Nimzo–Indian. The loss of time on the advance of the a-pawn invites the natural reaction from Black—immediate counterplay in the centre by ... c7–c5 or ... d7–d5. The second path is the most prevalent, and the text game is devoted to it. Pressurizing the centre by means of ... c7–c5 is usually put into effect (as also in the text game) after the preliminary 4 ... ♗a6 5 ♕c2 ♗b7 6 ♘c3, and now that the queen has appeared on c2 Black plays 6 ... c5. The immediate 4 ... c5 is also encountered. Black played twice thus in the semi-final Candidates match Yusupov–Timman (Tilburg 1986): 4 ... c5 5 d5 ♗a6. After 5 ... ed 6 cd g6 7 ♘c3 ♗g7 8 e4 0-0 9 d6 ♗b7 10 ♗d3 c4 11 ♗c2 ♘a6 12 ♗g5 h6 13 ♗h4 ♖e8. Black has a good game (Ftacnik–Shapiro, New York 1986).

The modest 9 h3 is more logical. After 9 ... d6 10 ♗d3 ♕e7 11 0-0 ♗a6 12 ♗xa6 ♘xa6 13 ♖e1 ♕b7 14 ♗f4 ♖fd8 15 ♕e2! ♘c7 16 ♖ac1 ♘h5 17 ♗g5 White has the advantage (Epishin–Yudashin, USSR 1987).

6 ♕c2 ed 7 cd g6 (7 ... ♘xd5 loses to 8 ♕e4+) 8 ♘c3 ♗g7 9 g3 0-0 10 ♗g2 d6 11 0-0 ♖e8 12 ♖e1. Timman chose this move in the fifth game of the match, but in the third he played 12 ♗f4 ♕e7 13 ♖fe1 ♘bd7 14 ♖ad1 ♘e4 15 ♕a4 ♗xc3 16 bc ♗b7, and Black obtained sufficient counter-chances. In the fifth there now followed 12 ... ♘bd7 13 h3 ♘e5 14 ♘xe5 ♖xe5 15 e4 ♖e8 16 ♗e3. In the position, reminiscent of the King's Indian structure, White strives to eliminate his

opponent's counterplay and arranges his pieces on their optimal squares. On f4 the bishop obstructs the path of the f-pawn and could lose time after ... ♘f6–h5.

16 ... ♘d7 17 f4 c4 18 e5! de 19 d6 ♖c8. Opening the game by 19 ... ef 20 ♗xf4 is disadvantageous for Black. After 20 ... ♖c8 21 ♘d5 ♘e5? 22 ♕a4! ♗b7 23 ♘e7+ ♖xe7 24 de ♕xe7 25 ♗xb7 he incurs material loss, and on other continuations on the 21st move would have an adverse effect on the strength of the d6 pawn, supported by the bishop.

20 f5 ♘c5. Timman probably didn't find a basis for sacrificial play by 20 ... e4, in as far as after 21 ♘xe4 the reply 21 ... c3! seizes the initiative. All the same, Black's position doesn't look too bad, but the unfortunate positioning of his bishop makes it very dangerous on strategic considerations.

21 ♗xc5 ♖xc5 22 ♘e4 ♖a5. On 22 ... ♖c8 then 23 ♕a4 ♗b7 24 d7 wins. Therefore the rook is forced to move offside, which allows White to concentrate all his energy on the exploitation of the strength of the passed d-pawn.

23 g4! ♕d7 24 ♖ad1 ♖c8. Defending the c4 pawn and preparing 25 ... ♗b7. On 24 ... gf 25 gf ♕xf5 then 26 d7 ♖d8 27 ♖f1 ♕g6 28 ♖d6 or 27 ... ♕e6 28 ♘g5 are winning. However, despite the obvious merits of White's position, as usual, exceptional accuracy and energetic play is demanded of him.

25 fg hg 26 ♕f2 ♗b7 27 ♘f6+ ♗xf6 28 ♗xb7 ♕xb7 29 ♕xf6 ♕d7 *(87)*.

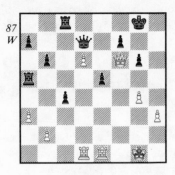

87
W

A key moment. Presumably, the Dutch Grandmaster, in his preliminary calculations, considered only 30 ♖xe5 ♖xe5 31 ♕xe5 ♖e8! with good drawing chances, but a surprise awaits: 30 ♕e7! ♖d8 31 ♖f1! ♖c5 32 ♖xf7 ♕xe7 33 ♖xe7 b5 34 ♖xa7, and White eventually won this rook ending.

4	...	♗a6
5	♕c2	♗b7
6	♘c3	c5
7	d5	

Other possibilities: 7 dc bc 8 ♗f4 ♗e7 9 ♖d1 0-0 10 e3 d6 11 ♖d2 ♕b6 12 ♗e2 ♖d8 13 0-0 ♘bd7 14 ♖fd1 ♘f8 with equality (Lobron–Polugayevsky, Biel 1986); here 8 ♗g5 is no better either: 8 ... ♗e7 9 e3 d6 10 ♗e2 ♘h5 11 ♗xe7 ♕xe7 12 b4 ♘c6 13 bc dc 14 ♖b1 ♘f6 15 0-0 0-0 16 ♖b5 ♖ac8 with a quick draw (Yusupov–Timman, m(3) Hilversum 1986);

7 e3 g6 8 ♗e2 ♗g7 9 0-0 0-0 10 ♖d1 cd 11 ♘xd4 a6 12 e4 ♕c7 13 ♗e3 d6 14 ♖ac1 ♘bd7 15 f3

♖ac8 16 ♕d2 ♖fd8 17 ♗f1 ♕b8 18 ♔h1 ♘e5 19 ♘a4 ♘ed7 20 b4 with a minimal advantage to White (Portisch–Timman, Tilburg 1986).

7 e4 is worthy of special consideration. Let's examine some examples.

7 ... cd 8 ♘xd4 ♗c5 9 ♘b3. In the game Timman–Polugayevsky (Reykjavik 1987) White, for a change, retreated his knight to f3, after 9 ♘f3 ♘c6 10 ♗f4 ♘h5 11 ♗d2 a6 12 b4 ♗d6 13 g3 ♘f6 14 ♗e2 ♖c8 15 0-0 ♘e5! his opponent seized the initiative.

9 ... ♘c6 10 ♗g5*(88)*. After 10 ♗d3 d6 11 0-0 0-0 12 h3 h6 13 ♗f4 e5 14 ♗d2 a5 Black has fully equal chances (Psakhis–Salov, Minsk 1987).

88
B

10 ... a6. In the game Gurevich–Lerner (Moscow 1987) White obtained the better game after 10 ... h6 11 ♗h4 d6 12 0-0-0, but Black recently found an improvement: 11 ... ♘d4 12 ♘xd4 ♗xd4 13 f3 ♗xc3 14 bc ♕c7 and everything is fine for him (Glek–Aseev, Frunze 1988).

11 0-0-0 ♕c7 12 ♔b1 0-0-0. We are now following the game Kas-

parov–Van der Wiel (Amsterdam 1988), in which Black adopts queenside castling for the first time. In the game Novikov–Chernin (Lvov 1987) White seized the initiative after 12 ... ♗e7 13 f4 ♘g4 14 ♗xe7 ♘xe7 15 ♕d2 ♘f6 16 ♗d3 d6 17 ♖he1 0-0-0 18 ♘d4 ♔b8 19 ♖c1 ♖c8 20 f5!

13 ♕d2 d6 14 f3 h6 15 ♗f4 ♘e5 16 h4 ♔b8 17 h5 ♖d7 18 ♖c1 ♖c8 19 ♗e2 ♔a7 20 ♖hd1 ♖dd8 21 g4 ♘g8 22 ♗g3 ♘e7 23 f4 ♘5c6 24 ♗f3 ♖b8 25 ♗h4 ♖d7*(89)*.

89
W

White dominates the whole board, though Black's position still looks sound enough. However, with the help of a temporary piece sacrifice, Kasparov finds a means of breaking down the enemy defences.

26 ♘b5+! ab 27 cb ♘a5 (♘d8 would be a more solid retreat) **28 ♘xa5 ba 29 ♖xc5 dc 30 ♕xd7 ♕xf4 31 ♖d6 Black resigned**.

We shall now return to our main game, Dzhandzhava–Chernin.

7 ...   ed
8 cd   ♘xd5

Should Black accept the pawn

sacrifice? The idea of ... ♗c8–a6 is correct, 'inviting' the queen to c2, so as to impede the advance d4–d5. In the game Ermolinski–Yudashin (Leningrad 1984) after 8 ... ♘xd5 9 ♗g5 ♗e7 10 ♘b5 0-0 11 ♘d6 ♗xg5 12 ♘xb7 ♕e7 13 ♕f5 ♘f6 14 ♕xg5 d5 15 ♘h4! White had the better chances. Material balance is now re-established: 15 ... ♕xb7 16 ♘f5 ♘e8 17 ♘e7+ ♚h8 18 ♕xd5 ♕xd5 19 ♘xd5, but due to the more effective bishop (19 ... ♘c6 20 0-0-0 ♖d8 21 g3 etc.) White's position is preferable. However, Chernin demonstrates an effective method of getting rid of all his problems in one stroke.

9 ♗g5   ♗e7
10 ♘b5

The move 10 ♕e4 is considered to be refuted—after 10 ... ♘xc3! 11 ♕xb7 ♘c6 12 ♗xe7 ♚xe7! 13 bc ♖b8 14 ♕a6 b5 15 a4 ♖b6 White loses his queen.

10 ...   0-0
11 ♘d6

Hence White has created a certain pressure on the centre in return for the sacrificed pawn, but ...

11 ...   ♘e3!! *(90)*

The tactical skirmish ends sadly for White.

12 fe

12 ♗xe3 is bad: 12 ... ♗xd6 13 ♘g5 g6 14 0-0-0 ♗e5 and 15 d5, and Black has a clear advantage. Perhaps 12 ♕d3 is worth considering: 12 ... ♗xf3 13 ♗xe3 ♗g4 14 ♕e4 ♗xd6 15 ♕xa8 ♕f6 with counterplay for the exchange.

12 ...   ♗xf3
13 ef

13 ♗xe7 ♕xe7 14 ♘f5 ♕e4! loses for White.

13 ...   ♗xg5
14 ♗c4   ♘c6
15 f4

Allowing Black to play another trick, this time decisively. 15 ♕e4 would be sounder: 15 ... ♕e7 15 ♕xe7 ♗xe7 17 0-0-0 ♗xd6 (or 17 ... ♘e5) 18 ♖xd6, while in the case of 15 h4 ♗xe3 16 ♘xf7 ♖xf7 17 ♗xf7+ ♚h8 Black's advantage is again evident.

15 ...   ♗xf4!
16 ♘xf7

16 ef ♕e7+ 17 ♘e4 ♘d4 18 ♕d3 ♖ae8 etc. is no better either.

16 ...   ♕h4+
17 g3

If 17 ♚e2 then 17 ... ♕h5+ 18 g4 ♕xg4+ 19 ♚d2 ♗xe3+ 20 ♚xe3 ♕d4+ and d5 with a rout.

17 ...   ♗xg3+
18 ♚d2   ♗f2
19 ♚d1   d5

White resigned

Miles–Polugayevsky
Sarajevo 1987

1	d4	♘f6
2	c4	e6
3	♘f3	b6
4	a3	♗b7
5	♘c3	d5
6	cd	♘xd5

This position has become so popular recently that it would be impossible to include all the interesting material that arises. As usual, we will strive to select the most important examples.

7 ♕c2*(91)*

This is now the main continuation in the Petrosian System, and it has now wholly supplanted the previously employed 7 e3. I will limit myself to one effective example (the best game in *Chess Informant* for the second half of 1983).

Kasparov–Portisch (**Niksic 1983**): **7 e3 ♘xc3**. Possibly a rash exchange; 7 ... ♗e7, 7 ... g6 or 7 ... ♘d7 are more solid. The last of these moves was seen in the game **Kasparov–Karpov, m(10) Moscow 1984/5**, having opened our peaceful sequence of 1984: **7**

... ♘d7 **8 ♗d3 ♘5f6 9 e4 c5 10 d5 ed 11 ed ♗d6 12 0-0 0-0 13 ♗g5 ♕c7 14 ♗f5 a6 15 ♕d2 Draw agreed**.

8 bc ♗e7 9 ♗b5+ c6 10 ♗d3 c5 11 0-0 ♘c6 12 ♗b2 ♖c8 13 ♕e2 0-0 14 ♖ad1 ♕c7 15 c4 cd 16 ed ♘a5 17 d5! A favourite device of Kasparov's in similar situations. **17 ... ed 18 cd ♗xd5 19 ♗xh7+! ♔xh7 20 ♖xd5 ♔g8***(92)*.

21 ♗xg7!! This modern treatment of the famous double bishop sacrifice on h7 and g7, was actually first seen in the game Lasker–Bauer in 1889.

21 ... ♔xg7 22 ♘e5! ♖fd8 23 ♕g4+ ♔f8 24 ♕f5! f6 25 ♘d7+ ♖xd7 26 ♖xd7 ♕c5 27 ♕h7 ♖c7 28 ♕h8+. After 28 ♖d3 Black finds the flashy counter-combination: 28 ... ♕xf2!! 29 ♔xf2 (29 ♔xf2 ♖c1+ 30 ♔g3 ♖xh7 31 ♖xf6+ with a draw imminent.

28 ... ♔f7 29 ♖d3 ♘c4 30 ♖fd1 ♘e5 31 ♕h7+ ♔e6 32 ♕g8+ ♔f5 33 g4+ ♔f4 34 ♖d4+ ♔f3 35 ♕b3+ Black resigned, in view of the unavoidable mate.

7	...	♘xc3

In another game with Kasparov (Kasparov–Karpov, m(32) Moscow 1984/5) I played, as in the 10th, 7 ... ♘d7, but this time matters didn't turn out so successfully: 8 ♘xd5 ed 9 ♗g5 f6 10 ♗f4 c5 11 g3 g6 12 h4 ♕e7 13 ♗g2 ♗g7 14 h5, and White obtained serious pressure. I was subsequently able to scrape out of it, but blundered in time trouble, and White eventually won. So, with that adventure, Kasparov succeeded in winning his first game in the fourth month of the contest.

With the queen on c2 the knights are exchanged. This is the most tested route, although the moves 7 ... ♗e7 and 7 ... c5 are frequently met. We won't devote much time to them here, but will make an exception only for the World Champion (with some accompanying examples). However, 7 ... c5 8 e4 ♘xc3 9 bc leads by transposition to the text game.

Kasparov–Van der Wiel (Amsterdam 1988):

7 ... c5 8 dc. After 8 ♗g5 ♗e7 9 ♗xe7 ♕xe7 10 ♘xd5 ed 11 e3 0-0 12 ♗d3 g6 13 dc bc 14 0-0 ♘d7 15 b4 d4! Black has full value (Miles–Hansen, New York, 1987).

8 ... ♗xc5 9 ♗g5 ♕c8. 9 ... ♗e7 is more solid: 10 ♗xe7 ♕xe7 11 ♘xd5 ed 12 e3 0-0 13 ♗d3 ♖c8 14 ♕e2 ♘d7 15 0-0 ♘c5 16 ♘d4 ♗xd3 17 ♕xd3 ♖c5 with a fine game for Black (Ehlvest–Korchnoi, Zagreb 1987). However, in the game Gurevich–

Ionescu, Moscow 1987) White's play was improved upon—13 ♗b5 d4?! 14 ♘xd4 ♗xg2 15 ♖g1 ♗e4 16 ♘f5 ♗xf5 17 ♕xf5—and he obtained the advantage.

10 ♖c1 h6 11 ♗h4. White's attempts to obtain the advantage after 11 ♗d2 have been successfully neutralized.

11 ... a5 12 ♘a4 ♘d7 13 e4! (13 e3 0-0 14 ♗b5 ♗a6 15 ♗xa6 ♕xa6 16 ♕e2 ♕xe2+ 17♔xe2 ♖fc8 leads to equality; Salov–Timman, Belgrade 1987).

13 ... ♘c7 14 ♘xc5 bc 15 ♗e2 ♗a6 16 0-0 0-0 17 ♖fd1 f6 18 ♗c4 ♗xc4 19 ♕xc4 ♖f7 20 ♗g3 e5 21 ♘h4 ♕e8 22 ♘f5 ♕e6 23 ♕e2 ♖b8 24 ♖d6 ♕e8 25 ♖cd1. White has a big advantage, which Kasparov easily converts into the full point.

8 bc

8 ♕xc3 doesn't present Black with any particular difficulties since it is difficult to utilize the c-file, for example: 8 ... ♗e7 (the other moves 8 ... ♘d7, 8 ... ♗d6 and 8 ... h6 are also quite adequate) 9 ♗f4 ♗d6 10 ♘e5 0-0 11 e3 ♘d7 12 ♗b5 ♗xe5 15 de a6 14 ♗e2 ♘c5 15 f3 a5 16 0-0 a4! 17 e4 ♗a6 18 ♗xa6 ♖xa6 19 ♖ad1 ♕e8, and Black has no problems (Petrosian–Anand, Moscow 1987).

In the event of **8 bc ♗e7**, the game **Kasparov–Ehlvest (Belfort 1988)** is of interest: 9 e3 ♕c8 10 ♗b2 c5 11 ♗b5+ ♘c6 12 0-0 0-0 13 ♗d3 ♔h8 14 ♕e2 ♕c7 15 ♖ad1 ♖ad8 16 e4 ♘a5 17 ♖fe1 ♗f6 18 e5 ♗e7 19 ♘d2 cd 20 cd

♗d5 21 ♘e4 f5 22 ef ♗xf6 23 ♘xf6+ ♖xf6 24 ♗c1 ♖df8 25 f3 ♘c6 26 ♗e4 ♗xe4 27 fe e5 28 d5 ♘d4 29 ♕d3 ♕f7. White has a small advantage after 29 ... ♘c2 30 ♖f1 ♕c5+. The game now is instantly concluded. **30 ♗b2!** ♘f3+ 31 gf ♖xf3 32 ♖e3 ♕g6+ 33 ♔h1 ♖f2 34 ♖g1 ♕h5 35 ♖h3 **Black resigned.**

9 e4   ♘d7*(93)*

93
W

Alternatively, Black has 9 ... ♘c6 10 ♗b2 cd 11 cd ♖c8 12 ♖d1.

A problematical position. Although both kings are yet to castle, Black's king nevertheless looks to be in great danger after the advance of White's pawn centre. In his turn, White must always consider the possibility of his opponent's counterplay down the c-file. Up till now 12 ... a6 has been encountered here, but in the game Lputyan–Belyavsky (Minsk 1987) the Lvov Grandmaster chose 12 ... b5!?, forcing White to think about the unfortunate position of his queen on c2, since 13 ♗xb5? is not possible due to 13 ... ♕a5+.

Lputyan decided to sacrifice his queen—13 d5 ♘d4 14 ♘xd4 ♖xc2—but after 15 ♗xb5+ ♔e7 16 d6+ ♔f6! 17 ♘xc2+ ♔g6! he was back to square one. 17 ♘c6+! was stronger: 17 ... ♖xb2 18 e5+! ♔g6 19 ♗d3+ f5 20 ♘xd8 ♗d5 21 ♘xe6!? ♗xe6 22 g4 with unclear play, in which White has compensation for the sacrificed material.

The move 12 ... b5 provokes White into concrete play in the centre, and therefore 13 ♕d2! ♕b6 14 d5 ♖d8 15 ♕e2! is worth consideration.

Instead of 12 ... b5 Lputyan suggested 12 ... ♗d6, with the following variations: 13 d5?! ed 14 ed 0-0! 15 dc ♗xc6! (15 ... ♖e8+ 16 ♗e2 ♗xc6 17 ♘e5! ♗xg2 18 ♕f5!) 15 ♗c4! ♖e8+ 17 ♔f1 ♗b5 18 ♘d2 ♕h4!

If an improvement is not found for White, then possibly he should try 13 ♕d2 0-0 14 ♗d3 with the usual dynamic position in which White has the freer game.

These examples are restricted to the possibilities of the plan with 9 ... ♘c6, but it goes to show that Black can already fight for active counterplay in the early stages, not waiting for White to create an attack on the kingside.

10 ♗f4

Only this continuation, which hinders Black's regrouping on the c-file, allows White to hope for the realization of his intentions. Black has no problems in the event of 10 ♗d3 ♕c7 11 ♕b1.

10 ...   cd

All the more often, in recent

times, Black tries to prepare for castling kingside first and plays 10 ... ♗e7. In the game Lputyan–Adorjan (Hastings 1986/7) White impulsively played 11 d5, and after 11 ... ed 12 ed 0-0! (12 ... ♗xd5 13 0-0-0!) 13 ♖d1 (13 c4 b5!) 13 ... g5! he was forced to think about the safety of his own king. After 14 ♗e3 g4 15 ♘d2 f5 Black takes the initiative completely.

> **11   cd   ♖c8**
> **12   ♕b3** *(94)*

In the game Anastasian–Mikhalchishin (Pavlodar 1987) Black had no problems after 12 ♕a4 a6 13 ♗d3 b5 14 ♕b3 ♗e7 (14 ... ♘f6!?) 15 0-0 0-0. Korchnoi came up with the queen move to b3 against Portisch in the Candidates tournament in Montpellier.

> **12   ...   ♗e7**

It would be dangerous to accept the pawn sacrifice: 12 ... ♗xe4 13 ♗b5 with a strong attack. 12 ... ♕f6 is anti-positional: 13 ♕e3! ♕g6 14 ♗d3 ♗e7 15 0-0 0-0 16 e5! ♕h5 17 ♗e4 ♗xe4 18 ♕xe4 ♖c7 19 ♖fc1 ♖fc8 20 ♖xc7 ♖xc7 21 ♕a8+ ♘f8 22 d5! etc.

(Gelfand–Mikhalchishin, Minsk 1986).

> **13   ♗d3   ♘f6**

This is the first time Polugayevsky has used this move. The system was considered unpleasant for Black up till now; for example, in the above-mentioned game Portisch–Korchnoi (Montpellier 1985) after 13 ... 0-0 14 0-0 ♘b8 15 ♖ad1 ♗d6 16 ♗d2! ♖c7 17 ♖fe1 ♗a6 18 ♗b1 ♖c8 19 h4! White achieved an irresistible attack on the kingside. The knight thrust to f6 on the 14th move is not so convincing any more: 14 ... ♘f6 15 ♖fe1 ♘h5 16 ♗d2 g5 17 ♖ad1 ♘g7 18 ♗b1 f5 19 d5 with a clear advantage to White (Khalifman–Blatny, Groningen 1986/7).

> **14   d5**

The English Grandmaster reflected for more than an hour on this move. It's difficult to say with certainty whether his solution is better.

In the game Khalifman–Anand (Moscow 1987) White played 14 ♗b5+ ♔f8 15 0-0, having sacrificed a pawn in the hope of causing discomfort to the black king. However, after 15 ... ♘xe4 16 ♖ac1 g5! 17 ♖xc8 ♗xc8 18 ♗c1 ♔g7 the correctness of White's sacrifice has yet to be proved. 19 ♗c6 ♘d6 20 ♗b2 ♗f6 21 ♘xg5 ♗xg5 22 d5+ ♔g6 23 ♕d3+ f5 24 de ♖f8 Black has a clear advantage.

In the game Browne–Miles (New York 1987) White chose 14 ♕b5+, and after 14 ... ♕d7 (14

... ♗c6 15 ♕b1!?) 15 ♘e5 ♕xb5 16 ♗xb5+ ♔f8 17 f3 his central pawn is solidly defended, though chances are level.

14 ♕b1 0-0 15 0-0 h6, threatening ... ♖c8–c3, leads to sharp play. It's not so easy for White to organize play in the centre and on the kingside.

14	...	ed
15	♖d1	0-0
16	0-0	*(95)*

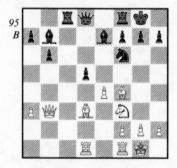

16	...	de!
17	♗xe4	♘xe4
18	♖xd8	♖fxd8

Black has sufficient material equivalent for his queen plus excellent coordination between his pieces with a pair of active bishops.

19	♖e1	♘c5
20	♕a2	

Miles doesn't want to withdraw from the point f7. Here Black makes the decision to give up the better of his bishops for the knight in order to ruin his opponent's pawn structure on the kingside.

20	...	♗xf3

21	gf	♗f8
22	♗e3	♖d3
23	♖c1	♖cd8
24	♖c4	♘e6
25	a4	♗c5!
26	♗xc5	bc

In the transformation to an ending, Black's advantage now acquires distinct contours.

27	♔g2	g6
28	♖e4	♖3d6
29	f4	♖b8
30	h4	h5
31	♔h2	♖b4

Perhaps 31 ... a5 would have reached the goal more quickly.

32	♖xb4	cb
33	♕c4	♖d4
34	♕c8+	♔g7
35	a5	♖xf4
36	♕b7	♖xh4+
37	♔g2	♖g4+
38	♔f1	h4!

It becomes clear that the most dangerous man on the board is this pawn.

39 f3

The immediate capture of the pawn by 39 ♕xa7 was more solid; after 39 ... h3 40 ♕b8 ♘f4 41 ♕e5+ ♔h7 42 ♕f6 h2 43 ♕xf7+ ♔h6 44 ♕f8+ White could have a perpetual check.

39	...	♖g5
40	♕xa7	h3
41	♕b8	♖xa5
42	♕xb4	♖f5
43	♕c3+	♔g8
44	♔g1	*(96)*

Another trap. 44 ... ♘g5 suggests itself, but it is answered by 45 ♔h1! and the f3 pawn is immune: 45 ... ♖xf3 46 ♕xf3!

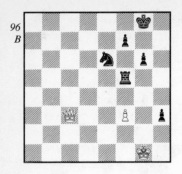

96
B

♘xf3 stalemate; 45 ... ♘xf3 46
♕g7+! ♚xg7 stalemate.

44	...	♘f4
45	♚h2	♖d5
46	♕c8+	♚g7
47	♕c3+	♚h7
48	♕f6	♖f5
49	♕d4	♘e6
50	♕e3	♘g5
51	f4	♘e6
52	♚xh3	♖xf4

The ending of rook, knight and
two pawns versus queen has
already been met in practice, and
it is established that the queen
doesn't have much chance of
defending.

53	♕a7	g5
54	♕e7	♚g6
55	♕d6	♖e4
56	♕c6	♖e3+
57	♚g2	g4
58	♚f2	♖f3+
59	♚g1	♚g5

It's not in the scheme of things
here to comment on each move
separately, in as far as Black has a
simple plan: he will push his g-
pawn, activate his king and then
bring up the second pawn.

| 60 | ♕d5+ | ♚h4 |
| 61 | ♕e5 | ♘f4 |

62	♕h8+	♘h5
63	♕h7	♖f4
64	♕h8	g3
65	♕h7	f6
66	♕h6	♖g4
67	♚g2	♖g7!

67 ... ♖g5 is not good
enough—68 ♕h7 ♚g4 69 ♕d7+
f5 70 ♕d1+.

68	♕d2	♖g5
69	♕c1	♖e5
70	♕h6	♚g4!
71	♕g6+	♖g5
72	♕c2	♘f4+
73	♚g1	♖d5
74	♕c8+	f5
75	♕c2	♖e5!
76	♕d1+	♖e2
77	♚h1	♚h3
78	♕xe2	g2+

White resigned

Karpov–Sokolov
*Game 10, Super-Final Match
Linares 1987*

Sokolov has a narrow, though
good, opening repertoire, in
which the Queen's Indian Defence
occupies a prominent place. But
this opening dates back to my
youth as a favourite of mine, so
that my advantage in experience,
to such an extent, possibly had a
say in our match.

1	d4	♘f6
2	c4	e6
3	♘f3	b6
4	g3	♗a6

A continuation that has, in recent years, become more popular
than the straightforward 4 ...
♗b7.

5 b3

White settles for the most radical of the many methods of defending the c-pawn (♕a4, ♕b3, ♕c2 and ♘bd2).

5 ...   ♗b4+
6 ♗d2   ♗e7
7 ♘c3

In my duels with Kasparov (first and third matches) the current variation was encountered 11 times. On this there invariably follows 7 ♗g2. Such was also played by Yusupov against Sokolov in the final Candidates match. In some cases a change in the order of moves is of no significance, while in others it has an essential influence on the course of the game. In all five games of the Super-Final that I played as White, only the Queen's Indian was played, from which the present position arose automatically. It must be said that the result surpassed all my expectations—I won three of the games and drew the other two. However, I would explain this success as not only successful opening play but also in the endgame.

7 ...   0-0(97)

Sokolov continued here 7 ... d5 in the second, fourth and sixth games, and after 8 cd ♘xd5 9 ♗g2 0-0 10 ♘xd5 ed 11 0-0 ♘d7 matters had led to a position well-known from the first Karpov–Kasparov match. In such a situation the transposition of White's moves (♗g2 and ♘c3) is of no matter. Here though, after Black has castled kingside, the placement of the knight on c3 is not so inoffensive for Black, with White taking the centre with e2–e4. Although Sokolov managed to cope with all of his opening problems in the preceding four games, the unpleasant psychological after-taste of two defeats forced him to abandon the tried and tested deployment of his forces.

8 e4   d5

8 ... ♗b7 has also been met on more than one occasion. Here is one illustration on that theme. Pinter–Adorjan (Szirak 1986): 9 ♗d3 d5 10 cd ed 11 e5 ♘e4 12 0-0 c5 13 ♖c1 cd 14 ♘xd4 ♘d7 (a new move, better than the well-known 14 ... ♗a3) 15 ♗f4 ♘dc5 16 ♗b5, and the game is roughly level. In Pinter's opinion, 16 ♗b1 with the further ♕g4 and ♖fd1 is to White's advantage.

9 cd   ♗xf1
10 ♔xf1   ed
11 e5   ♘e4
12 ♕e2(98)

In the second game, after prolonged thought, I played here 12 ♖c1, preventing the immediate re-grouping: ... ♕d7 and ... ♘b8–c6–d8–e6. However, the

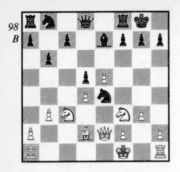

98
B

loss of time was telling, and Black obtained a fully satisfactory position, continuing ... c7–c5 before ... ♞b8–c6—12 ♖c1 c5 13 ♔g2 ♞c6 etc. This time I managed to find a more precise way of arranging my pieces. The placing of my queen on e2, apart from anything else, has the important merit of preventing the advance ... f7–f5. Here is a valuable example for comparison.

Van der Sterren–Magerramov (Baku 1986): 12 ♔g2 f5 13 ef. If the pawns weren't exchanged then black could face the future boldly with a well supported knight in the centre. **13 ... ♗xf6 14 ♖e1** (14 ♕c2 is no better either: 14 ... ♞c6!) **14 ... ♞c6!** (stronger than 14 ... ♗xd4) **15 ♖c1 ♞xd4 16 ♞xd4 ♗xd4 17 ♞xe4 de 18 ♗e3 ♗xe3 19 ♖xe3 ♕g5** (the exchange of queens also leads to equality) **20 h4 ♕f5 21 ♕e2 ♖f7 Draw agreed**.

Returning to the text game, I will say that with the queen on e2 the manoeuvre ... f7–f5 is not now so convincing: after 12 ... f5 13 ef the knight on e4 is forced to abandon the centre, and both the

e-file and the e5 square are at White's disposal.

12	...	♞xc3
13	♗xc3	♕d7
14	♔g2	

14 ... ♕h3+ was threatened.

| 14 | ... | ♞c6 |

The idea of this somewhat artificial knight manoeuvre, which has recently been brought into fashion, is to transfer it to e6 for a blockade of White's pawn centre. All the same, the natural 14 ... c5 seems more solid.

However, while subsequently reflecting on the present position, and on this variation in general, I came to the conclusion that Black does not necessarily have to move ... ♞b8–c6, or urgently advance his c-pawn, and that the knight could set out for the centre via the square a6. Here is a most recent example on this theme, in which I now play with the other colour (the slight transposition of moves is not significant).

Nikolic–Karpov (Tilburg 1988): 12 ♔g2 ♕d7 13 ♖c1 ♞xc3 14 ♖xc3 a5 15 h4 ♗b4 16 ♖c2 ♞a6 17 ♗e3 ♗e7 18 ♞g5 h6 19 ♖cc1 ♗a3 20 ♖a1 ♖fe8 21 ♕f3 c5 22 ♖ad1 ♞c7 23 ♞h3. It would be dangerous to accept this knight sacrifice, but, on the other hand, situated on g5 it doesn't create any specific threats to Black's position. 23 ... cd 24 ♗xd4 ♗c5 25 ♕d3 ♖ad8 26 f4 ♗xd4 27 ♕xd4 ♞b5 28 ♕d3 d4 29 ♞f2 ♞c3. Black has fully equal chances and the agreement of a draw soon followed.

15 ♖he1

The introduction to a natural plan: White will thrust forward with his f-pawn, simultaneously controlling the e-file. 15 ♖ac1 has previously been played here, which allowed Black to construct a solid defence with 15 ... ♘d8 16 ♗b2 ♘e6 17 ♖hd1 ♖ae8.

15 ... ♘d8

16 ♘g1! (99)

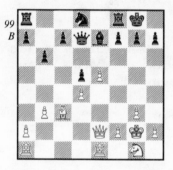

First White loses time on the transfer of his king, and now also the knight abandons an active post. But all this is subject to a definite idea. Now the plan behind the move 15 ♖he1 becomes clear. From the square e1 the rook prevents the advance ... f7–f5, without which the black knight cannot look forward to a quiet life on e6. And in the event of the immediate 15 ... f5 16 ef ♗xf6 17 ♘f3 this knight proves to be generally out of the action.

16 ... c5

This is correct. 16 ... ♘e6 is not possible due to 17 f4 f5 18 ef ♖xf6 19 f5! winning a piece.

17 f4 cd

Black decides that he can't do

without the opening of the c-file and so immediately sees to it himself. There is risk attached to the try 17 ... ♘c6 18 ♘f3 g6—the potential of a White offensive associated with the preparation of f4–f5 is very high.

18 ♗xd4 ♕f5

19 ♖ad1 ♗b4

20 ♖f1 ♘e6

It appears that Black is just about to seize the initiative, but as is often the case, he misses out by one tempo. If, let's say, the rook were on c8, White wouldn't have the possibility of 21 ♕d3 due to 21 ... ♖c2+ 22 ♖f2 ♕xd3 23 ♖xd3 ♘xd4 24 ♖xd4 ♖xf2+ and 25 ... ♗c5.

21 ♕d3! (100)

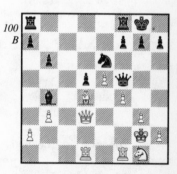

Wrecking the light square blockade. The ending may still not be won, but the siege of the isolated d5 pawn with the promise of d4 as an outpost gives Black little to be happy about.

21 ... ♕xd3

22 ♖xd3 ♖ac8

23 ♘f3

Of course, not the hasty 23 f5?? ♘xd4 24 ♖xd4 ♖c2+ 25 ♖f2 in view of 25 ... ♖xf2+ and 26 ... ♗c5.

23   ...   ♖c2+

Perhaps 23 ... g6 24 ♖f2 ♖fd8 would be better. After 25 ♗b2 with the threat 26 a3 (25 ... ♘c5 26 ♘d4!) and 27 ♖fd2 Black would have to give up a pawn, but 25 ... d4! 26 ♘xd4 (26 ... ♗c3 was threatened) 26 ... ♗c5 27 ♖fd2 ♗xd4 28 ♗xd4 ♘xd4 29 ♖xd4 ♖xd4 30 ♖xd4 ♖c2+ drawing chances would be maintained. This variation was given by Grandmaster Makarichev (I point out that I have used a number of his analyses in the notes to the text game).

24   ♖f2   ♖fc8

24 ... ♖xf2+ wouldn't make sense because of 25 ♗xf2 attacking the d5 pawn.

25   f5!

At last White's phalanx of pawns begin its advance.

25   ...   ♘xd4
26   ♘xd4   ♖xf2+
27   ♔xf2   ♖c1
28   g4

It may appear that the active position of Black's rook gives him sufficient counterchances. But this is not so: the pawn advance creates the prerequisite for a dangerous attack on the enemy king. Hence, 28 ... ♖a1 would lose almost immediately due to 29 ♘c6!

28   ...   ♔f8
29   ♔f3   ♖f1+
30   ♔g3   ♖c1

Further checks come to nothing: 30 ... ♖g1+ 31 ♔f4

♖f1+ 32 ♘f3, but he already has to reckon on the direct threat 31 ♘c6.

31   ♔f4

In the event of 31 g5 ♖g1+ 32 ♔f4 ♖f1+ 33 ♘f3 or 31 ... ♔e8 31 ♘g3 the position is unpleasant for Black, but after the exchange of rooks 31 ... ♖c3 32 ♖xc3 ♗xc3 33 ♘c6 a5 34 ♔f4 ♔e8 White's victory is far away.

31   ...   h6
32   h4   ♔e8
33   ♘f3   ♖c2

It is now evident that a counterattack on White's queenside pawns is Black's only hope. The battle is lost for him on the rest of the board.

34   a4   ♖b2
35   ♘d4   ♗e7
36   h5

I spent a lot of time on this move. It goes without saying that 36 g5 hg+ 37 hg with the threat of a break on the f-file also gives winning chances, but I had an intuitive feeling that it would be more useful to settle on the sealing up of Black's kingside pawns. I am not exaggerating when stating that at this moment I had already calculated a fine combination, ten moves deep. But despite this, I won't deny the fact that I had misgivings about the possibility of a pawn break.

36   ...   a6
37   ♔f3   ♗c5
38   ♘e2   d4
39   ♘f4

It's not possible to win the d4 pawn, despite its obvious weakness. The king is somewhat constrained to the defence of the knight. But there is no need for this anyway.

39 ... ♔d7
40 e6+ ♔e8

It's impossible to take on e6 now or later due to the loss of the g7 pawn.

41 ♔e4 a5*(101)*

Preventing b3–b4 in the event of the rook moving away from the b-file.

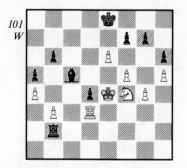

The game was adjourned in this position. Analysis showed that the win is achieved by way of a study.

42 ♖f3!

The sealed move, which seems to be the strongest. The rook lies in wait with the paradoxical, at first glance, aim of attacking the black king!

42 ... ♖b1

Preparing to meet 43 ♔d5 with 43 ... ♖g1 44 ♘d3 ♖xg4 45 ♘xc5 bc 46 ♔xc5 fe 47 fe ♔e7 in which case Black holds the position. However, the white knight moves in quite a different direction.

On other Black replies the victory is achieved more simply. Here are two important variations: 42 ... ♗d6 (the white rook quickly invades the seventh rank after 42 ... fe 43 fe) 43 ♘d5 fe 44 fe ♖e2+ 45 ♔xd4 ♖xe6 46 ♘xb6 ♗e5+ 47 ♔c5 ♗d4+ 48 ♔xd4 ♖xb6 49 ♔c3 ♖b4 50 ♖f5 with a won rook ending; 42 ... ♖c2 43 ♘d5 ♖e2+ 44 ♔d3 ♖e1 45 f6! gf 46 ef+! ♔xf7 47 ♖xf6+ ♔e8 48 ♖xh6 ♖g1 49 ♖g6 ♖g3+ 50 ♔e2 d3+ 51 ♔d2 ♔f7 52 ♖f6+, and the rest is easy.

43 ♘d5! ♖g1

After 43 ... ♖e1+ 44 ♔d3 fe 45 fe the e6 pawn is invulnerable because of ♘c7+, and the white rook finds its way to the seventh rank: 45 ... ♔d8 46 ♖f7 ♖xe6 47 ♖xg7 (threatening 48 ♖g6) and not 47 ... ♖e1 48 g5 hg 49 h6.

The move 43 ... ♔f8 gave the most trouble in analysis. I started by looking at 44 ♘c7, but it all came to a halt when it was found that after 44 ... ♖e1+ 45 ♔d3 (45 ♔d5 ♖e3 46 ♖f1 d3 47 ♖d1 ♔e7 48 ♘c4 fe 49 ♘xe6 ♖e4+ 50 ♔d5 ♖xg4 leads to equality) 45 ... ♖e5! Black holds the position. It was only on the next morning that the correct path was discovered—44 e7+! (instead of 44 ♘c7) 44 ... ♗xe7 45 ♔xd4 ♖g1 46 ♔c4 ♖xg4+ 47 ♔b5 ♗d8 48 ♖c3! h4 49 ♔c6! ♖xh5 50 ♔d7 ♖xf5*(102)*.

And here the last point was made by Zaitsev—51 ♘xb6! Now 51 ... ♗xb6 ends in a quite amusing mate: 52 ♖c8+ ♗d8 53 ♖xd8 mate, so the exchange must

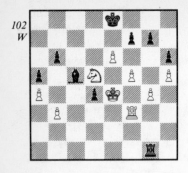

be given up by 51 ... ☖f3, and after 52 ☖xf3 ♗xb6 the inevitable break b3–b4 decides. A unique event, when one of the kings is the main conductor and executor of an attack on the opposing king!

44 ♔d3!   ☖xg4
45 f6! *(103)*

The quintessence of White's plan.

Threatening 46 ♘c7+ and 47 e7+, and neither of the pawns can be taken: 45 ... fe 46 f7+ ♔f8 47 ♘c7 and 48 ♘xe6+, and a whole rook is lost after 45 ... gf 46 ♘xf6+. 45 ... ☖g5 46 ♘c7+ ♔d8 47 e7+ ♗xe7 48 fe+ ♔xe7 with hope for the kingside pawns.

Sokolov didn't think for long in

this position, and it became clear to me that White's study plan was a complete surprise to him.

45 ...   ♗d6
46 ♘xb6   ☖g5

Again 46 ... fe doesn't work— 47 f7+ ♔f8 48 ♘d7+. 46 ... gf doesn't help either: 47 ☖xf6! fe 48 ☖xe6+ ♗e7 49 ♘d5 transposing to a won pawn ending.

47 fg   ☖xg7

The last hope to save the game lies in 47 ... fe 48 ♘c4 ♔e7 (and on 48 ... ♗b4 then 49 ♘xa5! decides) 49 ♘xa5 ☖xg7 50 ♘c6+ ♔d7 51 ♘xd4, although I suggest that I would be able to cope with these difficulties.

48 ♘c4   ♗b4
49 ef+   ☖xf7

If 49 ... ♔f8 then 50 ♘e5 and 51 ♘d7+ (♘g6+).

50 ☖xf7   ♔xf7

The combinational storm has blown itself out, and the game enters a technical phase. The impression is that the worst is behind for Black, but the study continues.

51 ♘e5+!   ♔f6
52 ♘c6   ♗e1

53 ♘xb4 was threatened, and after 52 ... ♗c5 53 ♘xa5 ♔g5 54 ♘c6 ♔xh5 55 b4 the a-pawn promotes to a queen.

53 ♘xd4   ♗b4

53 ... ♗f2 doesn't save Black: (53 ... ♔g5 54 ♘f3+) 54 ♘c6 ♔g5 (54 ... ♗b6 55 ♔c4 ♔g5 56 ♔b5 etc.) 55 ♘xa5 ♔xh5 56 ♔e2!, followed by 57 ♔f3 and, if necessary 58 ♔g2, and the queenside pawns advance easily. Sur-

prisingly, the knight appears stronger than the bishop despite play on both flanks.

54	♘c6	♗e1
55	♔e2	♗c3
56	♔d3	♗e1
57	♔c4	♔g5
58	♘xa5!	

Both the most spectacular and the most effective way. Black cannot decline the piece capture: 58 ... ♔xh5 59 ♘c6 ♔g4 60 b4 h5 61 a5 h4 62 a6 ♗f2 63 a7 h2 64 a8 (♕) and 65 ♘e5+. On 59 ... ♔g5 60 b4 h5 a decisive tempo is gained by way of 61 ♘d4 with the threat 62 ♘f3+.

58	...	♗xa5
59	b4	♗d8
60	a5	♔xh5
61	♔b5	♗g5
62	a6	♗e3
63	♔c6	

Black resigned

The score stands at +3 in my favour, and the result of the Super-Final is decided.

Karpov–Gurevich
Moscow 1988

1	d4	♘f6
2	c4	e6
3	♘f3	b6
4	g3	♗a6

The variation of the Queen's Indian Defence with the 'lateral' move ... ♗c8–a6 was met quite often in my first match with Kasparov in 1984, and its popularity has grown in recent years. The 55th USSR Championship made a valuable contribution to the development of this variation. The text game, and also a number of others included in the notes, are taken from this strong competition.

In recent years the bishop move to a6 has been considered to be strongest, with a fascinating struggle revolving around the point c4. However, the fianchetto is also frequently used. A few interesting games were played in this very USSR Championship (Moscow 1988). After 4 ... ♗b7 5 ♗g2 ♗e7 White gains nothing in the variation 6 0-0 0-0 7 ♘c3 (the game Kasparov–Karpov m(2) Moscow 1984/5 is devoted to the continuation 7 d5) 7 ... ♘e4 8 ♘xe4 ♗xe4 9 ♘e1 ♗xg2 10 ♘xg2 d5 (Salov–Ivanchuk).

Play is also clearly equal for Black after 6 ♘c3, going by the game Karpov–Salov: 6 ... ♘e4 7 ♗d2 ♗f6 8 ♕c2.

I will digress here and mention three examples of my own: 8 0-0 (instead of 8 ♕c2) 8 ... 0-0 9 ♖c1 ♘xd2 (more accurate than 9 ... c5 10 d5 ed 11 cd ♘xd2 12 ♘xd2 d6 13 ♘c4 ♗a6 14 ♕b3 ♗xc4 15 ♕xc4 a6 16 a4 ♘d7 17 e3 ♘e5 18 ♕e2 c4 19 ♗e4 ♖e8 20 ♘c2 ♖c8 21 ♘e4, and I gradually succeeded in outplaying Portisch; Tilburg 1988) 10 ♕xd2 d6 11 d5 e5 12 b4 ♘d7 13 ♘e1 a5 14 a3 ab 15 ab ♗a6 with unclear play (Torre–Karpov, Brussels 1987); 9 ... d6 10 d5 ♘xd2 11 ♘xd2 ♔h8 12 ♘de4, and White is scarcely better (Ftacnik–Karpov, Dubai

1986). The game Eingorn–Khalif-man, from the same USSR Championship, developed interestingly: 8 0-0 c5 9 d5 ♘xc3?! 10 ♗xc3 ♗xc3 11 bc 0-0 12 e4 ♗a6 13 ♖e1 ♗xc4?! 14 ♘e5 ♗a6*(104)*.

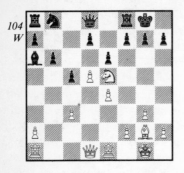

104
W

15 ♘xf7!! ♔xf7 (15 ... ♖xf7 16 de and 17 ♕d5; 15 ... ♕f6 16 de etc.) 16 e5!! with terrible threats. White obtained an overwhelming advantage after 16 ... ♔g8 17 de ♘c6 18 ♕b3 ♔h8 19 ♖ad1 ♘a5 20 ♕a4 ♖b8 21 ♕g4 ♕e8 22 ed ♕e7 23 ♕h4! g5 24 ♕h6 ♗b7 25 ♕d6!, although he subsequently contrived to let it slip.

We shall now continue with the game Karpov–Salov. 8 ... ♘xd2 9 ♕xd2 d6 10 0-0 0-0. All of 15 years ago, I myself equalized easily as Black against Korchnoi: 11 ♖ad1 ♘d7 12 ♘e1 ♗xg2 13 ♘xg2 ♕e7 14 ♘e1 c5 15 ♘c2 ♖ac8 16 b3 ♖fd8 17 e4 ♘b8 18 ♖fe1 cd 19 ♘xd4 (Moscow 1974). Against Salov I now played 11 d5, but after 11 ... e5 12 e4 ♘d7 13 b4 g6 14 ♗h3 ♕e7 15 a3 ♖fb8 16 ♕c2 h5 17 ♖fd1 a5 White again has nothing to boast about.

After 4 ... ♗b7 5 ♗g2 the move 5 ... c5 also underwent new tests—6 0-0 cd 7 ♕xd4 ♗e7 8 ♘c3 0-0 9 ♖d1 d6 10 ♗g5 ♘c6 11 ♕f4 ♕b8 12 ♖d2 ♘e5 13 ♘xe5 de 14 ♕h4 ♗xg2 15 ♔xg2 (Karpov–Smirin) and I was subsequently able to outplay the young Master.

Apparently, 6 d5 is an even stronger reply to 5 ... c5. Here is how the game Karpov–Gavrikov continued: 6 ... ed 7 ♘h4 b5 8 0-0!*(105)*.

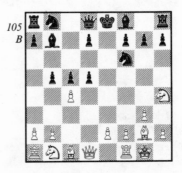

105
B

A substantial improvement (8 cd and 8 ♘c3 had previously been played): White doesn't respond to Black's queenside operation. 8 ... bc 9 ♘c3 ♗e7 10 ♘f5 0-0 11 ♘xe7+ ♕xe7 12 ♗g5. An unusual position. Black has two extra pawns, but it is not apparent how he can give them up in return, if only to preserve the balance. 12 ... h6 13 ♗xf6 ♕xf6 14 ♘xd5 ♗xd5 15 ♕xd5 ♘c6 16 ♕xc4 ♕xb2 17 e3 ♖ab8 18 ♕xc5 ♖b6 19 ♖ad1 ♘b8 20 ♗d5. White has an overwhelming positional advantage. I think that this game dealt a serious blow to the system with the move 5 . . . c5.

    5   b3   ♗b4+
    6   ♗d2   ♗e7

In the game Karpov–Short (Amsterdam 1988) after 6 . . . ♗xd2+ 7 ♕xd2 0-0 8 ♗g2 c6 9 0-0 d5 10 ♕b4 ♘e4 11 ♖c1 ♘d7 12 ♕a3 ♗b7 13 cd ed 14 ♘c3 f5 15 e3 the dark-squared strategy brought White success after 15 . . . ♕f6 16 ♖c2 a5 17 ♖d1 ♖ac8 18 ♘e2 g5 19 ♘c1 g4 20 ♘h4.

    7   ♗g2

The move order 7 ♘c3 0-0 8 e4 is discussed in detail in the notes to the game Karpov–Sokolov.

    7 ...   c6*(106)*

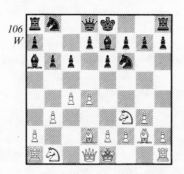

This preparation of the move . . . d7–d5 has recently taken over from the immediate influence on the centre by way of 7 . . . d5 or 7 . . . ♗b7 8 ♘c3 d5 (8 0-0 d5). Such an order of moves was met in my first match with Kasparov. I will avail myself of the opportunity to recall them.

Kasparov–Karpov, m(4) Moscow 1984/5: 7 . . . ♗b7 8 ♘c3 d5 9 cd ed 10 0-0 0-0 11 ♗f4 ♘a6 12

♕c2 c5 13 ♖fd1 ♕c8 14 ♗e5. This manoeuvre, which was brought into practice by Yusupov, allows White to exert serious pressure. 14 . . . ♖fd8 15 ♖ac1 ♘e4 16 ♕b2 ♕e6 17 ♘b5 (17 dc bc 18 ♘xe4 de 19 ♖d2 is not bad either) 17 . . . ♗f8 18 ♗f4 ♕e8 19 a4 ♗c6 20 dc bc 21 ♘e5 ♗xb5 22 ab ♘b4 23 ♕b1! ♘f6 24 ♘c6 ♘xc6 25 bc ♕xc6 26 ♗g5 a5 27 ♗xf6 ♕xf6 28 ♗xd5 ♖a7. White has an obvious endgame advantage on account of his active light-squared bishop, and now he could have increased it with 29 ♖d3! After 29 ♖c4 was played I succeeded, albeit not without difficulty, in achieving a draw.

Kasparov–Karpov, m(6) Moscow 1984/5: 7 . . . 0-0 8 0-0 d5 9 cd ♘xd5 10 ♘c3 ♘d7 11 ♘xd5 ed 12 ♖c1 c5 13 dc bc 14 ♘e1 ♘b6 15 a4 ♖c8 16 a5 Draw agreed (after 16 . . . ♘a8 the instability of the pawn pair c5 and d5 is counterbalanced by the weakness of White's queenside pawns).

The impression might be formed that Black easily equalizes in this variation of the Queen's Indian Defence. However, this is far from so. Simply Kasparov was stricken by the drawing virus, and didn't strive for the initiative in this part of the marathon. In other circumstance he would have played, for example, 13 ♗e3 (instead of 13 dc) or 15 ♘d3 (instead of 15 a4) 15 . . . ♖c8 16 ♗h3 ♖c7 17 ♗f4 ♗d6 18 ♕d2 with quite unpleasant pressure on Black's position. So it's not surprising that in the next game of the match I chose the variation as White.

Karpov–Kasparov, m(15) Moscow 1984/5: 12 ... ♖e8 (instead of 12 ... c5 *(107)*.

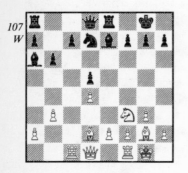

107
W

13 ♖c2! This plan to regroup forces for pressure on the c- and d-files was new at the time. 13 ... c5 14 ♖e1. Maybe 14 ♗e3 ♗b7 15 ♕c1 ♖c8 16 ♖d1 is more accurate, saving an important tempo. Black would already be without his plan of counterplay, adopted in the game, after 14 ... ♘f6 15 ♖e1, and after 15 ... ♘e4 16 dc bc 17 ♘d2 White has the better prospects (Gavrikov–Sokolov, USSR Championship 1985).

14 ... ♗b7 15 ♗e3 a5! 16 ♕c1 a4 17 ♖d1 ab 18 ab ♗f6 with a sharp and roughly equal game. It's true that I subsequently succeeded in obtaining the better endgame and even won a pawn, but Kasparov constructed an impregnable fortress and on the 93rd move I submitted to a draw.

8   ♗c3   d5
9   ♘e5

In the game **Kasparov–Karpov, m(18) Moscow 1984/5**, in the per-

iod when my opponent didn't particularly try for active play, there followed **9 ♘bd2 ♘bd7** (more accurate than 9 ... ♗b7 10 ♘e5, as was played in game 16 which is given below) **10 0-0 0-0 11 ♖e1 c5 12 e4 de 13 ♘xe4 ♗b7!** (the most clear-cut path to equality) **14 ♘fg5 cd 15 ♗xd4 ♕c7 16 ♘xf6+ ♗xf6 17 ♗xb7 ♕xb7 18 ♘e4 ♗xd4 19 ♕xd4 ♖ad8 20 ♖ad1 ♕a8 21 ♕c3 ♘b8 22 ♘f6+ Draw agreed**.

9   ...   ♘fd7

In the fourth game of the match Yusupov–Sokolov (Riga 1986) after 9 ... ♗b7 10 ♘d2 Black played 10 ... ♘bd7 and thereupon abstained from castling for quite a while. And although the encounter ended in a draw, in the opening stages there was a White initiative: 11 0-0 c5 12 ♘xd7! ♕xd7 13 dc bc 14 cd ed 15 ♗xf6! ♗xf6 16 ♖c1 ♖c8 17 e4! etc.

After the games Kasparov–Karpov, m(16) Moscow 1984/5 and Torre–Sokolov (USSR v Rest of the World, London 1984) the variation lost its lustre: 9 ... ♗b7 10 ♘d2 0-0 11 e4 ♘a6 12 0-0 c5 13 ed ed 14 ♖e1 cd 15 ♗xd4 ♘c5 16 ♘g4! dc 17 ♘xc4 ♗xg2 18 ♔xg2. Black doesn't manage to achieve full equality in the case of 18 ... ♘xg4 or 18 ... ♘e6.

The new move 9 ... ♘e4 was played in the 10th game of the match Yusupov–Sokolov (Riga 1986). After 10 0-0 ♘xc3 11 ♘xc3 0-0 12 ♖e1 ♗b7 13 cd cd White made the programmed advance 14 e4, although the subsequent moves of the game show that Black has solved all of his opening problems: 14 ... ♗b4! 15 ♖c1 ♗xc3 16 ♖xc3 de 17 ♗xe4 ♗xe4 18 ♖xe4 ♘d7!

10	♘xd7	♘xd7
11	♘d2	0-0
12	0-0	♖c8
13	e4*(108)*	

13 ... b5

White has the initiative after 13 ... de 14 ♗xe4 b5 15 ♕c2 h6 16 ♖fd1 bc 17 bc (Ftacnik–Adorjan, Szirak 1986). Apparently 13 ... c5 is also insufficient — 14 ed ed 15 dc dc 16 c6! cb 17 ♖e1 b2 18 ♗xb2 ♘c5 19 ♗a3!, with a clear advantage to White (Georghiu–Cherna, West Berlin 1986).

14 ♖e1 bc

It would be worth mentioning here one of my first games with Kasparov, where in this position I took on c6 with the other pawn.

Kasparov–Karpov, m(6) Moscow 1984/5: 14 ... dc 15 bc ♘b6. A controversial move; 15 ... bc would lead to the text game Karpov–Gurevich.

16 cb (16 c5! is stronger) 16 ... cb 17 ♖c1 ♗a3 18 ♖c2 ♘a4 19 ♗a1 ♖xc2 20 ♕xc2 ♕a5. A colourful position (although 20 ... ♕e7 is more accurate). A rare event, in that my opponent's pieces are so tightly congested on an outside file of the chessboard. The situation subsequently changes like a kaleidoscope. Having played 21 ♕d1!, White obtains a strong passed d-pawn, which should have brought home the point quicker than anything. However, Kasparov let the victory slip in time trouble, and thereupon also a forced draw. A rook ending eventually arose with an equal amount of pawns, which I succeeded in winning, study-like, on the 70th move.

14 ... de is an interesting try: 15 ♗xe4 c5! 16 d5 ed 17 ♗xd5 ♗f6, and Black has equalized (Chernin–Timman, Amsterdam 1987).

15 bc dc

15 ... ♗xc4 16 ♘xc4 dc 17 a4 ♕b6 18 ♗f1 ♕a6 19 a5 c5 20 d5 ♖fd8 21 e5 with more than adequate compensation for the pawn (Dolmatov–Ehlvest, Minsk 1987).

16 ♕a4!?

The game so far is a repeat of my meeting with Kasparov (game 21, third match). Then I continued 16 ♕c2 and after 16 ... ♕c7 17 ♘f1 e5 18 ♘e3 ed 19 ♗xd4 ♗c5 chances were level, although White's resources are not yet exhausted in this variation.

16	...	♗b5
17	♕c2	♗a3!
18	♘b1	

White could retain a minimal advantage after 18 ♘xc4 ♗xc4 19 ♕a4 c5 20 ♕xa3 cd 21 ♗xd4.

18	...	♗d6
19	a4	♗a6
20	♘d2	e5?!(*109*)

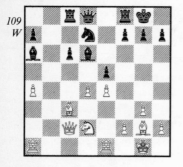

20 ... c5! 21 d5 ♘e5 is more accurate, with double-edged play.

21	♖ad1	♕e7
22	♗f1	♕e6
23	de	♗xe5

23 ... ♘xe5 24 ♗xe5 ♗xe5 25 ♗xc4 is no better.

24	f4	♗c7
25	e5	♘b6

There would be all to play for after 25 ... ♗b6+ 26 ♔h1 ♘c5. Now it is White who obtains a serious advantage.

26	f5!	♕h6
27	♘e4!	♘d5
28	♗d2	♗b6+
29	♔h1	♕h5
30	♗e2	♕h3
31	♘g5	♕h6
32	♗xc4	

In time trouble, I miss the opportunity of dealing the strong blow 32 ♘xf7! ♕h3 33 ♘d6 etc.

32	...	♗xc4
33	♕xc4	♕h5

34	♕e4	♗f2
35	g4	♕h4
36	♘f3	♕d8
37	♖f1	♗b6
38	♖de1	♖e8
39	♖e2	♕c7
40	♖c1	♕b7
41	♕c4	c5
42	♔g2	♘b4(*110*)

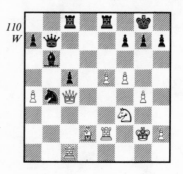

| 43 | e6! | |

White accomplishes the decisive break.

43	...	fe
44	♖xe6	♔h8
45	♖ce1	♕d7
46	a5!	♗xa5

46 ... ♗c7 also loses—47 ♗xb4 cb 48 ♕xc7!

47	♕xc5!	♘d3
48	♕xa5	♘xe1+
49	♖xe1	♖ed8
50	♔g3!	♕b7
51	♕a3	♖d7
52	♗f4	♕b5
53	♖e5	♕c6
54	♕e3	♖b7
55	♖e6	♕a4
56	♖e4	♕b5
57	♗e5	♕c6
58	♗d4	♕d6+
59	♔h3	♖f8?!

A time-trouble oversight in a difficult position.

60 ♗c5
Black resigned

Yusupov–Sokolov
Tilburg 1987

1	d4	♘f6
2	c4	e6
3	♘f3	b6
4	g3	♗a6

All of the Queen's Indian Defences encountered in my contests with Kasparov are mentioned in this volume. One game remains, which has some standing in modern theoretical research. We give it here to complete the picture.

Kasparov–Karpov, m(24) Leningrad 1986: 4 ... ♗b7 5 ♗g2 ♗b4+ 6 ♗d2 a5 7 0-0 0-0 8 ♗g5 ♗e7 9 ♕c2 h6 10 ♗xf6 ♗xf6 11 ♘c3 g6 12 ♖ad1 d6 13 h4 h5 14 e4 ♘d7 15 e5. The start of an operation which leads to a devastated board. 15 ♖fe1 is stronger, with which I continued, soon after the return match, against Korchnoi (Tilburg 1986). After 15 ... ♗g7 16 ♘b5 ♕b8 17 d5 e5 18 b3 ♕d8 19 a3 ♗h6 20 b4 White has a noticeable superiority.

15 ... ♗g7 16 d5 ♘xe5! 17 ♘xe5 ♗xe5 18 de ♗xg2 19 ef+ ♔xf7 20 ♔xg2 ♗xc3 21 ♕xc3 ♕f6 22 ♕xf6+ ♔xf6. A rook ending arises which is favourble to Black. However, I didn't succeed in my attempt to win and

level the score in the match, and the game concluded in a draw.

5 ♘bd2
A fair amount has already been said about the move 5 b3, and therefore, for variety, we will examine another way of defending the c-pawn.

Incidentally, in the Candidates final (Riga 1986) Yusupov placed his choice, a few times, on 5 b3, but he gained nothing by it and therefore he now prefers a less well-trodden path. (I will point out in passing that I invariably played exactly 5 b3 against Sokolov in the Super Final, and, as you know, it wasn't to my opponent's taste.)

5 ... ♗b7
It may be surprising to the inexperienced reader that, when the black bishop goes to a6 it sooner or later retreats to b7: why this loss of a tempo? The very point of the manoeuvre ... ♗c8–a6–b7 is to achieve a certain aim, for example, a slight weakening of the queenside (b2–b3) or the appearance of the white knight on d2 (its normal place is c3). On the other hand, besides 5 ... ♗b7, the immediate 5 ... d5 or 5 ... c5 are often encountered.

6 ♗g2 ♗e7
It's also possible to play 6 ... d5 at once. After 7 cd ♗xd5 (7 ... ed 8 0-0 ♗e7 9 ♘e5) 8 0-0 ♘bd7 9 ♘e1 ♗e7 10 e4 ♗b7 11 e5! ♘d5 12 ♘e4 0-0 13 ♗g5 White has the advantage (Korchnoi–Polugayevsky, Tilburg 1985).

The move 6 ... c5!? is hardly

good—7 e4 cd 8 e5 ♘g4 9 0-0 ♕c7 10 ♖e1 f6 (10 ... ♗c5 11 ♘e4!, Adorjan–Kudrin, New York 1987; the older continuations 10 ... ♘c6 and 10 ... h5 also offer Black little prospects) 11 ♘e4! (the hesitant 11 h3 gives Black equal play; Timman–Agdestein, Reykjavik 1987) 11 ... ♘xe5 (11 ... f5 12 ♘xd4) 12 ♘xe5 fe 13 ♗g5 with advantage to White.

7   0-0

In the Candidates tournament (Montpellier 1985) Timman offered Sokolov a pawn—7 e4—and after ... ♘xe4 8 ♘e5 ♗b4 the new move 9 ♕e2!? was played (instead of 9 ♕g4), with the further 9 ... d5 10 cd ♕xd5 11 ♘d3 ♗xd2+ 12 ♗xd2. Here 12 ... ♘a6! would give Black fully equal chances, but the actual 12 ... ♘d7 13 ♖c1 0-0-0 14 ♗f4 e5 15 de g5 16 ♗xg5 f6 17 ♗f4 fe 18 ♗g5 ♖de8 led to a sharp game, which Black, in the end, managed to hold.

7   ...   0-0
8   ♕c2   d5 *(111)*

Spraggett chose 8 ... ♘a6 against Yusupov in their recent Candidates match. White led the game along subtle lines and achieved a tangible positional advantage, whereupon Yusupov lost his way in time trouble, and his opponent succeeded in equalizing. I will provide you with the full score of the game without notes.

Yusupov–Spraggett (Quebec 1989): 8 ... ♘a6 9 a3 c5 10 b3 d5 11 ♗b2 dc 12 ♕xc4 ♕c8 13 ♕d3 ♖d8 14 ♖fc1 ♕b8 15 ♕c2 h6 16 dc ♘xc5 17 ♗e5 ♗d6 18 ♗xf6 gf 19 b4 ♘d7 20 ♘d4 ♘e5 21 e3 ♖c8 22 ♕b3 ♗xg2 23 ♔xg2 ♕b7+ 24 e4 ♗f8 25 ♕e3 ♖d8 26 ♘2f3 ♘xf3 27 ♘xf3 Draw agreed.

9   cd   ed
10   ♘e5   c5
11   dc

In the game Korchnoi–Sokolov from the same Candidates tournament (Montpellier 1985) White preferred 11 ♘df3 and now the new move 11 ... ♘a6 (instead of the previous 11 ... ♘bd7) and the further 12 ♗h3 ♘e4 13 ♗e3 ♗d6 14 a3 ♕e7 15 ♖fd1 c4! led to an excellent game for Black, and Sokolov came out on top after a sharp struggle.

11   ...   bc *(112)*

Sokolov twice took on c5 with the bishop in this Tilburg tournament. The game with **Nikolic** quickly ended in peace: **11 ... ♗xc5 12 ♘df3 ♖e8 13 ♗f4 ♘bd7 14 ♘d3 Draw agreed. Timman** played the immediate **12 ♘d3** and created a miniature after a few mistakes by his opponent: **12 ... ♗e7 13 ♘f3 ♘bd7 14 ♗f4 ♖c8**

15 ♕a4 a5 16 ♖ac1 ♘c5 17 ♘xc5 bc 18 ♖fd1 ♕b6 19 e3 d4? (19 ... ♗c6 20 ♕c2 ♗d7 is correct) **20 ed cd 21 ♘xd4 ♗xg2 22 ♔xg2 ♕xb2 23 ♘c6 ♕a3?** (the decisive blunder; it would follow to retreat the queen to b7) **24 ♖c4! ♕e8 25 ♕c2 Black resigned.**

In any event, the pawn capture on c5 is more principled.

112
W

12 ♘dc4!?

An idea of **Vaganian**, which he used in his game against **Timman** (Amsterdam 1986), which went **12 ... ♕c8 13 ♘a5! ♗a6 14 ♗f4 ♕e6 15 ♖fd1 h6 16 e4 d4 17 ♕b3! ♕xb3 18 ab.** White has the advantage. As the game is quite short, we can bring it to its conclusion: **18 ... ♗d6 19 ♘ac4 ♗xe5 20 ♗xe5 ♗xc4 21 bc ♘fd7 22 ♗xd4 cd 23 e5 ♘c6 24 ♗xc6 ♖ad8 25 f4 ♘b6 26 b3 d3 27 ♔f2 ♖d4 28 ♔e3 ♖fd8 29 ♖xa7 d2 30 ♗e4 Black resigned.**

12 ... ♕c7 would be more accurate than 12 ... ♕c8: 12 ... ♕c7 13 ♗f4 g5 (13 ... dc 14 ♘g6!) 14 ♗xg5 dc 15 ♕f5 ♗xg2 16 ♗xf6 ♗xf6 17 ♕xf6 ♗e4 18 ♘g4 ♖e8 19 ♕g5+ or 15 ...

♘e8 with unclear play. Black generally prefers to delay moving his queen for one move, and this novelty doesn't turn out too well.

12 ... ♖e8
13 ♗f4

Not falling into the trap—13 ♖d1? ♕c7 14 ♗f4 dc (the bishop at e7 is defended).

13 ... ♕c8

Sokolov goes along Timman's path and also runs into difficulties. 13 ... ♘bd7 was more logical: 14 ♖fd1 ♗f8 15 ♘xd7 ♕xd7 with a minimal advantage to White, but not 15 ♕b3 ♘xe5! 16 ♗xe5 ♗a6 17 ♗xf6 ♕xf6 18 ♗xd5 ♖xe2.

14 ♘a5

14 ♕b3 is insufficient: 14 ... ♘c6 15 ♘xc6 ♖xc6 16 ♘a5 ♗d7! 17 ♗xd5 ♘xd5 18 ♕xd5 ♗b5, and Black has abundant counterplay for the pawn.

14 ... ♗a6
15 ♖fd1 ♘bd7 *(113)*

113
W

A position from the stem-game Vaganian–Timman is reached after 15 ... ♕e6 16 e4 d4 17 ♕b3. I will point out that the text game was annotated in detail by

Yusupov's regular trainer, International Master Mark Dvoretsky, and we will avail ourselves of his notes to illuminate the second half of the game.

16 &h3!

Restricting the possibilities of his opponent's pieces to the utmost. It wouldn't do to take the d5 pawn, as Sokolov would obtain serious counter chances after 16 &xd5?! &xd5 17 ♖xd5 &f6 18 ♖d2 ♕h3.

16 ...   ♕c7

17 &ec4   ♕c8

17 ... ♕d8 18 &c6 ♕c8 is hardly better, in view of 19 &4e5! &f8 (19 ... &d6 20 &xd7 ♕xc6 21 &xf6+) 20 ♕a4! with advantage to White.

18 &e3!

Yusupov is not quite so convinced by the variations 18 e4 &xc4 19 &xc4 dc 20 e5 ♕a6 or 18 ♕a4 dc 19 ♖xd7 &xd7 20 &xd7 ♕d8 21 ♖d1 c3.

18 ...   d4

19 &ec4   &xc4

It's a pity to have to play such a move, but there doesn't seem to be another defence to the threat 20 &g2. Besides this, one has to consider the undermining b2–b4 or e2–e3.

20 &xc4   ♕a6

21 e3!   &b6

22 &xb6   ♕xb6

23 ed   cd

24 &c7!?

Forcibly winning a pawn. 24 &e5 &c5 25 &xf6 gf 26 ♖ac1 is also very strong.

24 ...   ♕c5

25 ♕xc5   &xc5

26 ♖ac1   &e4?(114)

26 ... &b6 is sounder: 27 &xb6 ab 28 ♖xd4 ♖xa2 29 ♖b4 h5 30 ♖xb6 &g4 31 &f1 &e5, intending 32 ... ♖d8. White would have been left with certain difficulties in realizing his extra pawn. The text move allows Yusupov to force victory elegantly.

114
W

27 &f5!   &b6

28 &d7!

The simple 28 &xb6 ab 29 ♖xd4 is also sufficient for the win.

28 ...   ♖e7

29 &c6   ♖f8

30 &xb6   ab

31 ♖e1!   f5

32 f3   d3

33 ♖cd1   d2

34 &d5+   &h8

35 ♖xd2!

But not 35 ♖e2? or 35 ♖e3? in view of 35 ... &c3!

35 ...   &xd2

36 ♖xe7

White takes his rightful pawn and also locks up the hostile knight in his own camp.

36 ...   g6

37 ♖e2   &b1

38 ♖e1   ♖d8

39 ♖d1!

Black resigned.

Index of Complete Games

Page numbers in *italics* refer to complete games quoted in the notes to the main games.

Index of Openings

As this book is not a study of the whole of any particular opening, only the major variations dealt with are listed in this index. Transpositions are dealt with in the text, and the reader is recommended to study all of the games in each section, rather than considering each game in isolation.